STUCK ON COMMUNISM

A volume in the NIU Series in
SLAVIC, EAST EUROPEAN, AND EURASIAN STUDIES
Edited by Christine D. Worobec

For a list of books in the series,
visit our website at cornellpress.cornell.edu.

STUCK ON COMMUNISM

Memoir of a Russian Historian

Lewis H. Siegelbaum

Northern Illinois University Press
an imprint of
Cornell University Press
Ithaca and London

First published 2019 by Cornell University Press

ISBN 978-1-5017-4737-3 (pbk)
ISBN 978-1-5017-4739-7 (pdf)
ISBN 978-1-5017-4738-0 (epub/mobi)

Cover design by Yuni Dorr
Composition by BookComp, Inc.

Librarians: A CIP record is available with the Library of Congress.

CONTENTS

I'm always thinking Russia,
I can't keep her out of my head,
I don't give a damn for uncle Sham,
I am a left-wing radical Red.
—H. H. Lewis, "Thinking of Russia," 1932

One test might be whether, as the years pass,
you come out better from your own story, or worse.
—Julian Barnes, *The Only Story*

PREFACE AND ACKNOWLEDGMENTS

When is it time to write one's memoirs? Maybe never, unless one is so moved. More precisely, it might be when you still think you have something to say and hope that others will be sufficiently curious to learn what it is. I decided to give it a go when, about to retire, I couldn't face being retired. I backed into it. Prompted by the suggestion of a friend who shall remain anonymous to put together a collection of my articles published in the heyday of labor history, I started out writing an accompanying introduction. Proof of this origin story is that the title I gave the Microsoft Word document folder containing the memoir is still "Labor History (my)." In the midst of writing that introduction, things sort of got away from me. Before I knew it, I was back in graduate school, then college, then an even more callow youth. Ah, you might think, such is the way with historians—always explaining something by its antecedents. Not this historian. I don't ever recall intending to write about a subject and getting pushed back inexorably to an earlier time. Until now.

I have read a sufficient number of memoirs to know that the ones that work best are not merely reflective or, in current lingo, self-reflexive, but reflective about their self-reflexivity. They ask themselves not only "why did I do or think this," but "how did my doing or thinking this affect me?" I don't know if this memoir will work, but piecing together my life as a historian of Russian and Soviet history has been a fascinating experience for its author, both satisfying and humbling. I discovered much I didn't know about Lewis Siegelbaum. But enough about me.

Here, I want to acknowledge the encouragement and assistance I received along the way. One of the tasks assumed by those of us in the academy is to serve as an anonymous reader for publishers seeking experts' input about whether a manuscript is worthy of publication and how it can be improved. I have done this many times, mainly because it seemed a good way of learning about new work. I also have benefited from others' reading of my submitted work. But it was not until I received the readers' reports on this manuscript that I realized we have been engaging in a genuinely communist—that is, reciprocally beneficial—practice that involves neither monetary gain (other than the nominal emolument paid by the publisher either in currency or books) nor ego enhancement. We do it conscientiously because we want our manuscripts read with the same degree of conscientiousness. We do it because we want to maintain or better still raise the quality of works in our field. We do it, in Marxian terms, so that as producers of a material object, we can expect to get a full return for our labor.

Because of their generosity of spirit as much as their specific recommendations for improvement I am happy to express communist greetings to the anonymous readers whom the press persuaded to spend time with my manuscript. Other readers I had to persuade. Early in the process, Steve Stowe, a historian of the American antebellum South as well as a former journal editor, agreed to read a draft as a "rank outsider," and produced six single-spaced pages of comments to which I returned again and again. I imposed an early draft on Charles Keith, my current tennis partner and a much younger historian of Vietnam. Ron Suny and Diane Koenker, two individuals whose names crop up fairly often in the memoir, read drafts for different purposes, but both gave me honest, critical feedback. I did not subject others among my immediate circle of friends to the task, but they nonetheless provided observations and encouragement that helped more than they know. They include Sean Forner, Karrin Hanshew, and Mickey Stamm in East Lansing, Geoff Eley, Kali Israel, and Alan Wald (who supplied the first epigraph) from the Marxist Study Group in Ann Arbor, and Mark Harrison in England. At Northern Illinois, Amy Farranto was as enthusiastic and efficient an editor as one could wish for, Marlyn Miller's copyediting vastly improved upon my prose, and Nathan Holmes, the managing editor, provided assurances when they were most needed. I also wish to acknowledge with thanks Steve Siegelbaum, Liao Zhang, and Julie K. Taylor, the MSU Library's Espresso Book Machine Coordinator extraordinaire. Finally, Leslie Page Moch, with whom I have shared my life these past twenty years, gave close readings to three iterations of the manuscript. Her contribution is inestimable, and it is to her I dedicate this memoir.

INTRODUCTION

The last time I taught Soviet history, in the spring 2017 semester, I had a curious encounter with a student. We had just finished discussing the Great Terror, Stalin's decimation of the party and leading state institutions during the late 1930s. What I am about to describe happened just after the end of class on February 21. The student, a young woman who hitherto had said very little in class, approached the front of the room where I was switching off the console connecting my computer to the overhead projector and gathering my things before heading off for lunch. "Yes," I said, acknowledging her presence, "what can I do for you?" "I'm just wondering," she uttered in a low voice that made me strain to catch her words, "what I can do about this despair I am feeling."

At first, I thought she must be referring to the unprecedented bloodletting we had talked about and that maybe I had overdone the tragedy it represented. But no, she made it clear that she had in mind the state of contemporary politics in the United States. Donald Trump had taken office just a month before. The ban on entry into the country of Muslims, Trump's statements about the dangers that Mexicans ("rapists," "bad hombres") posed, and the lamentable cabinet appointments he made had demonstrated that his awfulness had met or even exceeded our worst fears about his election. Her cri de coeur provoked both gratitude that she had come to me with something that evidently mattered deeply to her, and fear that I would fail to respond adequately. But maybe because I shared the student's feeling that something terrible had happened and had given some thought about how to cope, I proceeded to tell her three things: first, as a historian I could assure her that people had suffered worse times and had managed to survive; second, that joining a movement, a discussion group, or any association that put her in contact with like-minded people working to change circumstances, political or otherwise, might overcome her sense of helplessness; and third, that in the meantime, doing history provided a good escape, or to put it another way, one could lose oneself in history.

I am not describing this brief conversation to demonstrate my persuasive powers. No thunderclap of enlightenment rent the air after I made my three points. The student merely thanked me and walked out, the look of doubt never leaving her face. It recently occurred to me, though, that my response encapsulated a lifetime's commitment to practicing history and, implicitly, my abiding fascination with the alterity of Soviet communism. Why and how history and communism combined to animate my career and shape my life is the subject of this memoir. It spans three continents and roughly half a century of contending with the ideologies at the heart of the Cold War and their legacies—from the 1960s when the full weight of McCarthyism's victimization of my father hit me, up through the implosion of the Soviet Union and beyond. The memoir plunges the reader into the tumult of student rebellion at Columbia University during the Vietnam War, describes graduate study at Oxford and a year in Moscow as an exchange student at the height of détente, and reconstructs research projects—abortive and fulfilled, individual and collective—pursued first as a neophyte historian in Melbourne and then as a mid-career and senior professor in Michigan. It recreates journeys of discovery and self-discovery to Soviet archives, the coalfields of eastern Ukraine, and newly independent Uzbekistan.

Sometimes I have regarded the twin commitments to history and communism as a blessing, and sometimes as a curse. They at first seemed inextricable. Growing up the child of a Red in the 1950s, I learned that history was not "bunk" as Henry Ford had claimed, but the opposite. History contained the truth. That truth told of ordinary but heroic working people fighting for their emancipation from slavery and the rule of capital, of the FBI's hounding of Paul Robeson and persecution of Julius and Ethel Rosenberg, of the martyrdom of Rosa Luxemburg and other Communists, and of the crimes of imperialism, especially American imperialism. However, none of these truths were taught in school. For reasons never clear to me, my secondary school did not offer history; we had "social studies," known in an earlier generation as "civics." Exposing the suppressed truths of history became a mission. But in later years as the mission developed into the pursuit of a profession, and that pursuit required professional training, I learned that there were many, sometimes conflicting truths, that history was more than the suppressed politics of the past, that it was contradictory and complicated. I also learned I had to disguise my own political disposition if I were to pass through one hoop after another.

My ambivalence about both communism and history—but really about my own identity—is represented in the dualities that announce and structure most of the chapters in this memoir. "Tennis and Communism," the opening chapter, brings together my youthful passion for an elite sport and my encounters with family friends who dedicated themselves to the ideology of working-class emancipation. A boy's camp in the Berkshires of western Massachusetts is the setting where the two coexisted. Chapter 2, "Revolutionary or Scholar?" corresponds to my undergraduate years at Columbia University. It draws inter alia on letters to a friend from high school that reflect late adolescent anxieties about scholarly endeavors, campus political activism, and which to pursue more seriously. It also reconstructs some of the courses I took based on syllabi and lecture and reading notes, and recalls professors—fondly and otherwise. The history of the Russian Revolution emerges as a way that my political commitment could become compatible with a career in academia.

"Oxford and Moscow," the third chapter, depicts my experiences between 1970 and 1975 of these places steeped in British upper-class and Cold War legend. It is structured by successive phases of the DPhil thesis, replete with research trips to Paris and Helsinki, and contacts with advisors, informal mentors, lifelong friends, and the woman who would become my first wife. The chapter also contains observations about academic practices and cultures, and assessments of how events of global proportions impinged on students in both Oxford and Moscow universities. The chapter concludes with the successful, albeit traumatic, defense of the doctoral thesis.

The first part of "Melbourne and Labor History" recounts moving Down Under to take up a position in the History Department at La Trobe University, then still quite a new institution located in Melbourne's northeastern suburbs. Acclimating to Aussie rules proved challenging, but both colleagues and students provided much intellectual stimulation and friendship. Amid teaching and parenting responsibilities, I found the wherewithal to launch and complete several discrete projects and eventually convert the Oxford thesis into a book. The second part of the chapter describes another kind of conversion—to social, and in particular, labor history—pays homage to E. P. Thompson who inspired a whole generation of social historians throughout the English-speaking world, and offers a retrospective survey of labor and Soviet history at the end of the 1970s and early 1980s.

"Labor History and Social History via the Cultural Turn" encompasses the first two decades of my career after arriving at Michigan State University as an assistant professor in August 1983. It situates me among historians determined to expand inquiry into the Soviet past to the factory floor and other worksites to elucidate struggles associated with "building socialism." Ironically, much of this labor history, including my book on the Stakhanovite movement, appeared just as industrial work in both advanced capitalist countries and the Soviet Union itself was fast disappearing. I explain my partial and ambivalent application of the "cultural turn" in disparate projects as a reaction to the loss of labor history's contemporary resonance.

Before 1989, my research in the Soviet Union had brought me only to Moscow and Leningrad. Even during my year as an exchange student, when others took excursions to far-flung parts of the country, I never ventured beyond day trips to nearby towns. "Centers and Peripheries" refers to my encounters with these two cities but also with other places in the Soviet Union as it imploded, and then among its successor states during the 1990s. Whether collaborative or solo, the projects that inspired this travel put me in touch with an amazing variety of people contending with sometimes heart-wrenching changes to their lives and expectations, all in the midst of political instability, cultural effervescence, and economic catastrophe.

Seventeen Moments in Soviet History, an online sourcebook for teaching the subject, and *Cars for Comrades*, the award-winning book on the Soviet automobile, frame the penultimate chapter, "Online and on the Road." The ups and downs in the development and maintenance of the website and the emotional highs and lows of pioneering research on a Soviet object so richly symbolic of capitalism alternate with accounts of editing books, observations on graduate education, and recollections of the death of my father. A final chapter narrates my conversion to "The Migration Church" and happiness in coauthoring a book with a church elder on "repertoires and regimes of migration in Russia's twentieth century."

Stuck on Communism instructs on many levels. It provides an account of an academic self, shaped by family background, the political tenor of changing times, and multiple mentors. It offers a guide for budding academic humanists through the maze of conflicting pressures, recounting the path one scholar took to integrate his political and academic commitments. It demonstrates the difficulties but also rewards of academic collaboration, shifting of concentrations, and modes of dissemination. Finally, it reveals how attractive communism could be as an object of study decades after its disappearance from the landscape of its origin.

As countless other memoirists have discovered—but not always acknowledged—I found it humbling to reassemble my professional life in prose. I often winced as I pored over correspondence, reading notes, and successive drafts of articles and books. If only I had written differently that complaining letter to a publisher, the turgid passages in an article, and the flippant comment in an e-mail message. At the same time, as I put the pieces of my past together, they began to speak to each other. My father as a beacon illuminating why the past mattered, my youthful efforts to find my own narrative voice, my discovery that history could be both a way of engaging with the politics of the present and an escape from their awfulness, my enduring love of the discipline of history and ambivalence about the academic profession emerge here as themes because they helped shape who I became professionally and otherwise.

Writing the memoir thus proved a not entirely unfamiliar exercise. As with most historical writing, I found the material engaging in a dialectical dance with the themes/arguments, each determining and delimiting the appropriateness of the other. Issues of sequentiality, causality, and consequentiality—so central to the historical enterprise—cropped up early in preparing the text. The notion that no matter what historians take as their subject they are always writing about themselves suddenly took on a retrospective validity I could not have imagined earlier.

Stuck on Communism suggests not only fascination but affection. In what sense if any, though, does communism deserve affection? Terrible things were done in its name, and the excuse that those who did those things do not deserve to be called real Communists does not impress me. My love for communism is from afar. It comes from being an American—an often exasperated, appalled, and alienated American—who recognizes that communism was identified and cast itself as the antithesis of American hegemony and the myths concocted to perpetuate it. The communism I am stuck on is people, working people, coming together to fight for social justice and against the barbarism of capitalism. It is radically egalitarian, anti-racist, and anti-sexist. It promotes a husbanding of natural resources that are finite and without which life cannot exist. That successive Soviet governments strayed badly from these positions—that in competing with the capitalist West they adopted some of the worst features of their declared enemy—is undeniable. But, though rarely acknowledged or reciprocated, my initial identification with—and even love for—the people of that country as they strove to realize the promise of communism, endured. Stuck on Communism therefore can be read as a romance.

CHAPTER 1

TENNIS AND COMMUNISM

"Stevie," I asked, gazing out of the car window at the houses separated from the road by broad, manicured lawns, "will people still be living here when communism comes?" We were driving through Forest Hills, an upper middle-class neighborhood in the borough of Queens where the houses and some of the apartments are Tudor style, as in Merrie Olde England. I must have been twelve years old and my brother eighteen or nineteen. I can't remember what had drawn us there. We didn't go to the West Side Tennis Club, which hosted the US Open, because my only visit to that fabled ground happened about ten years later—in 1971 when I saw the Czech Jan Kodes upset the number one men's seed John Newcombe in the opening round. Perhaps our trip had something to do with my brother having become a freshman at nearby Queens College, though why I accompanied him as a passenger is a mystery never to be solved.

"Sure," he replied after some hesitation. "There will just be more people living in those houses." My question must have arisen from my dim awareness of a certain tension between the aesthetic appeal of looking at these dwellings and the realization that their owners embodied the class communism would dispossess. My brother therefore gave the perfect answer: these wealthy people would not be thrown out of their houses; they simply would have to share them with other people. My brother seems to have intuited what in fact constituted the initial practice of Communists in power, the Bolsheviks after 1917.[1] Or is this something my parents had discussed with him out of my earshot?

"Communist king," Lester ("Lettie") Fogarsky would shout at me tauntingly. Maybe he shouted the same thing at other kids in the neighborhood, but those words seemed to have special meaning for me, the son of a Communist. Lettie's father owned a drug store from which my friends and I would occasionally steal packets of Topps baseball cards and other precious items—not because we were motivated by communism but from the lack of money. Lettie had a couple of years on me and therefore a couple fewer than my brother. I don't recall playing with him often—maybe only football games in the park. When I was growing up in the 1950s and early sixties, a Communist meant someone who owed his or her loyalty primarily to the Soviet Union, or "Russia," as most Americans reductively referred to it. At the very least, it signified a tendency to take the Soviet bloc's side in its myriad disputes with the "Free World." "Communist king" may have been childish gibberish, but it did encapsulate two political regimes anathema to all red-blooded Americans.

Yet, I was undeniably both red-blooded and American—born in the Bronx in 1949, raised on Long Island in a two-story brick colonial house, an avid fan of the Yankees who idolized Mickey Mantle. I absorbed enough episodes of *Davy Crockett*, *Maverick*, and *Gunsmoke* to turn the bushes and trees surrounding my house into the wilderness of Kentucky or alternatively a western landscape where my friends and I played cowboys and Indians. Thanks to Stevie, I knew and could croon lots of rock 'n' roll hits from Frankie Lymon and the Teenagers' "Why Do Fools Fall in Love" to Martha and the Vandellas' "Dancing in the Street." Nevertheless, Lettie's taunt got to me. He knew I didn't quite fit in, and I knew it too. Yet, we all played at being a normal suburban family, snapping photos of each other, as in the one from 1964 in which Grandma Sadie poses proudly in front of our house with her three grandchildren—Steve standing tall at twenty-one, me the awkward fifteen-year-old middle child, and my nine-year-old sister Ellen tightly clutching her Barbie doll.

"He didn't fit in the world in which he lived. He was always trying to save the Soviet Union, which was the country that had saved him." Thus did Ronald Suny, the University of Michigan's Charles Tilly Collegiate Professor of Social and Political History, eulogize Moshe ("Misha") Lewin in 2011.[2] A short but powerfully built man of Eastern European Jewish origin, Misha stood as a giant among historians of the Soviet Union. As I reflect upon Ron's gently mocking yet profoundly respectful characterization, I am struck by its resonance. Did I fit into the world I lived in, did the Soviet Union save me, and did I try to save it, even retroactively? These questions are surprisingly difficult to answer. How did the Soviet Union save Lewin? Leslie Page Moch and I summarized the story of his escape from the Nazi onslaught in 1941 as follows:

> Misha, a Jewish boy of nineteen, asked if he could hitch a ride with a truck full of Soviet soldiers retreating from Vilna, but the officer in charge turned him down. Fortunately for him, the peasant conscripts were more accommodating. With a wink, they helped him clamber aboard. Never again seeing his parents, Misha made it to the Urals, joined the Red Army, and as an officer witnessed the Victory Day parade on Moscow's Red Square.[3]

FIGURE 1.1 "Grandma Sadie poses proudly in front of our house with her three grandchildren—Steve standing tall at twenty-one, me the awkward fifteen-year-old middle child, and my nine-year-old sister Ellen tightly clutching her Barbie doll."

I had heard from Misha himself a little bit about this, but when I read Ron Suny's published eulogy, all the pieces fell into place. Of course, I knew the Soviet Union had saved all of us—the entire world—from the triumph of Nazism. I emphasized the point year after year in my classes on Soviet history, noting as well, the increased domestic legitimacy the Soviet state and Stalin had earned, but also the heavy price the Soviet population had paid. But when I had attained the same age as the self-evacuated Misha, I felt it was my own country that needed saving, not the Soviet Union. I had reached nineteen in 1968, the spinal year in the Vietnam War and a tumultuous one in domestic politics. At Columbia University, rebellion engulfed the campus. Students occupied five buildings in protest against the administration's complicity in the prosecution of the war in Vietnam as well as its landlordism against residents in Harlem. I participated in the protests from start to finish, receiving a whack on the head from a billy club wielded by one of New York's finest for my troubles.[4]

Of course, by opposing the American prosecution of the war in Vietnam, I and millions of other Americans thought we were trying to save the Vietnamese. But our motivation to rescue America from being on the wrong side of history, from leadership that had gone astray, from violence perpetrated in our names also animated our protests. I may not have fit in, but that didn't necessarily make me less American. "I'm obsessed with Vietnam and therefore everything else seems vague," so I wrote to a high school friend in November 1967. I understood the United States' involvement in Vietnam as an outgrowth of its by then decades-long hostility to communism. And from this, I believed, my country needed to be rescued. So, I became a foot soldier in the anti-war movement but also a student of communism. I shared with many students throughout the country my fascination with those defined by our elders as enemies. We filled courses on revolutions, peasant societies, and guerrilla movements. We read Frantz Fanon, Régis Debray, and Mao Zedong, debated the finer points of revolutionary strategy, and ardently believed that our grasp of the theory would lead to better practice—or maybe the reverse, that practicing revolution would improve the theory.

It has become fashionable to ridicule the revolutionary ardor of students in the late '60s, so I will not indulge. I shared that ardor but differed a little from my closest comrades in that while peasant revolution and guerrilla armies fascinated them, I wanted to learn as much as I could about where the revolution had started and why. That is, I wanted to know more about Russia and its revolution.

Whence this interest in Russia? The answer to that question has changed over the years. I used to think it had to do with family origins: my grandfathers hailed from Odessa and Riga and my step-grandfather grew up in Skvira, a town in Kiev province where Jews made up roughly half the residents according to the census of 1897. Of the three, I only knew my mother's stepfather, Morris Sosnow (abbreviated from Sosnovsky), my "real" grandfathers having died before I entered the world. My maternal grandmother, born Sadie Rubel, came from Kolomea (Kolomyia, in Ukrainian), a town in Galicia still under Habsburg rule when she left it around the turn of the century. She had divorced my mother's father, Saul Nevins, sometime in the early 1940s. Soon afterward she met and married Morris, a milliner. We always called him "Morris," never Grandpa Morris, whereas my siblings and I spoke of "Grandpa Saul" and "Grandpa Louis." Did I, when I decided to pursue Russian history, subconsciously try to learn something about these long-deceased ancestors beyond the little my parents told me? Perhaps, but then why have I never bothered to visit either of their native towns or, with one slight exception, pursued in a scholarly way anything that had to do with their lives? I am persuaded that the impulse to study Russia lay more in communism than in Russia's Yiddish-speaking borderland Jewish minorities, and therefore my father rather than his or my mother's antecedents.

Born in New York City in 1915 as the youngest of Ida and Louis's four children, Morton (Morty) Siegelbaum graduated from DeWitt Clinton High School in

1933 and entered City College in the teeth of the Depression, the only one among his siblings to advance beyond high school. Graduating in 1937, he became a social studies teacher in the New York City public school system. He "flirted" (his word) with Trotskyism in college, but joined the Communist Party in 1939, the same year the Soviet Union and Nazi Germany signed their non-aggression pact. I always had trouble understanding how he could have done such a thing, especially as he always professed support for the Popular Front against fascism. Many American Communists were withdrawing their membership at the very time he joined the party. He did so, he explained, because those whom he most admired among his fellow teachers already belonged.[5] He admired them because, as members of the New York Teachers Union (TU), they had fought for better conditions not only for fellow teachers but especially for children, and among the latter, those in Harlem. A recent history of the TU—the subject of a great deal of calumny disguised as scholarship—tends to endorse this view:

> In the case of the TU, the evidence is clear that many in leadership were in the Communist Party and used the union to push Party policies. However, it is also true that many members of the TU, including Party members, saw the union as a crucial vehicle to improve the lives of teachers, children, and communities.[6]

A few years ago, my brother alerted me to a photograph in a book about the Teachers Union. The photo originally appeared in the November 3, 1945, issue of the *New York Teacher News*. It showed a group of about thirty teachers demonstrating in support of extending benefits to substitute teachers. A woman stands in the front row holding a sign demanding "FULL APPOINTMENTS" for them. And there in the fourth row, wearing wire-rimmed glasses and smiling, stood someone with a strong resemblance to my father—not yet my father.[7]

What connection did my father have to communism as an ideology and the Soviet Union as its fountainhead? Had he, for example, read the classics of Marxism-Leninism? I don't remember seeing any on the bookshelves that lined his office (a.k.a. the "sun parlor") off the living room of our house. Maybe he kept them elsewhere. Maybe by the time I started prowling, he had hidden them. Instead of Marx and Lenin, I consumed Howard Fast's novels that stood like soldiers on his shelves—novels about Spartacus, citizen Tom Paine, John Altgeld (the Illinois governor who had pardoned the three surviving prisoners convicted for the Haymarket bombing in 1886), the fictionalized ex-slave Gideon Jackson, and the fictional Adam Cooper who fought at the Battle of Lexington. These and a book—lost to memory—about Vercingetorix, Skanderbeg, and other rebels against imperial power fired my historical imagination.

One book in that room, *The Death House Letters of Ethel and Julius Rosenberg*, clouded my youth.[8] Set between blue soft covers, the letters themselves spoke of little more than their anxieties, concern about their two sons, and the tenderness each felt for the other. But if not from this book then from my parents, I must have known of the execution of this loving couple on that dark day in 1953. Why did "J. Edgar Hoover" have them killed? Because they were Communists and Jews, I gathered. But so was my father. My parents regarded the official charges that Julius spied for the Soviet Union and Ethel aided and abetted him as trumped up. The fact that the judge who presided over their trial, Irving Kaufman, was Jewish suggested that the government sought to tamp down the anti-Semitic sentiment that it had stoked in the first place. Conversations along these lines, whispered among comrades, friends, and relatives, somehow reached my ears. But above and beyond the substance of the case and the fevered interpretations to which I was exposed, the very title of the book is what gave me nightmares. Where was this death house? Did others exist closer to home that I didn't know about? And if the Rosenbergs could be killed for something they did not do, why couldn't the Siegelbaums—including me?

Although to his dying day Dad remained unapologetic about his member-ship in the party, he had reason to be discreet about his political affiliation. People throw around the term McCarthyism with such abandon that it has lost its histori-cal specificity. Outside of its anti-communist animus, the term means nothing. The Board of Education purged my father along with hundreds of other teachers from the New York City school system either because they refused to answer its infa-mous question about whether they "are now or have ever been" Communists, or because they refused to "name names." Banning these dedicated teachers from the profession they loved, the righteous purveyors of American patriotism continued to hound them. Neighbors told me years later that FBI agents knocked on their doors to ask if they had noticed suspicious gatherings at our house. Dad's teaching career cut short, he sold insurance for a few years during which he went back to college (in his forties) to prepare himself for the brave new world of computer electronics. Digitronics, Redactron, Burroughs—these corporations employed my father as a sales manager.[9] He hated every minute of it, but thereby provided the middle-class upbringing that my older brother, younger sister, and I sometimes took for granted.

We did so thanks in large part to my mother, who, like so many middle-class white women of her generation, performed the myriad tasks of homemaker. At

FIGURE 1.2 "He assumed all grandmothers were as wonderful as his grandma." Mom and Sami, ca. 1987.

the memorial service in her honor in June 2017, Sami, my thirty-six-year-old son, remarked that as a youngster he assumed that all grandmothers were as wonderful as his grandma—endlessly patient, fascinated by whatever he said or did, showering him with affection. Only then did it occur to me that my mom had performed the same trick on me. Though subordinated within the family as the stay-at-home wife of the male breadwinner, she never expressed the desire—at least within my hearing or recollection—to return to her premarital job of dental technician, or any other form of paid employment, for that matter. When she was twelve years old, her parents divorced, something that she experienced as shameful. I know how much it hurt her because in her last declining years, she repeatedly returned to the subject, describing how "kids in the neighborhood" would taunt her by asking "where is your father," to which she responded, "he is away on business." The cocoon of security she spun for her three children thus stemmed in part from her own deprivation.

I experienced that domestic warmth throughout my early years, including summers when I visited "the bungalow" near South Fallsburg in the Catskills, otherwise known as the Borsht Belt. This was the only remnant of "Rubel's Mansions," a colony of such structures founded by my maternal great grandmother,

Baba Dreizha and her husband, Josef. I have vivid memories of the building set back from the road a fair distance, with its stucco walls and central corridor dividing a series of bedrooms scarcely large enough to accommodate a bed and dresser. The large kitchen in the rear where my grandma and her younger sisters Adele, Rose, Betty, and Hilda would prepare meals, play cards, and kibbitz in their particular mixture of Yiddish and English, served as the social center. To the right as one faced the bungalow lay a blueberry patch with bushes considerably taller than I, laden with berries in such profusion as I never have witnessed again; to the left, a field separating the bungalow from Gilbert's, the hotel built on land previously occupied by Rubel's Mansions.

There must have been some arrangement with Gilbert for visitors to the bungalow to enjoy the hotel's facilities gratis, for I remember swimming in its outdoor pool and traipsing through the lobby. In my recollections, the bungalow represented my mother's family—large, boisterous, speaking in thick East European accents ("Sout Fallsboig"), formerly well-to-do but still bourgeois. Eventually, with the exception of my grandma, they all migrated to Florida. My father's family, far less flamboyant and matriarchal, gathered less frequently. Of my paternal Grandma Ida I remember little other than her admonishing me not to go "boorvis" (barefoot) in the house and her very high-pitched giggle that might be likened to the cackle of a witch. Of my dad's older siblings, two brothers and a sister, only Uncle Irving, a salesman and an actor in amateur theater, showed any affection toward me. None shared my father's political outlook; they were too busy trying to make ends meet.

So how, then, did my father influence me? If not for his deeply Marxist understanding of the world and his erstwhile communist politics, I probably would not have learned how to read *The New York Times* critically; become acquainted with the independent Left weekly, the *National Guardian*; or identified with workers on strike, civil rights activists in jail, Nicola Sacco and Bartolomeo Vanzetti, and the Rosenbergs. From age ten or eleven I helped him distribute leaflets, going door-to-door on behalf of Neighbors Unlimited, a civic group determined to combat white flight from our increasingly black community of Lakeview. At night, from the upstairs bedroom I shared with my brother, I would strain to hear what Dad and other members of the organization were saying in our living room, though his booming voice did not require much strain to hear. In short, if not for my father, I would have fit more snugly into the professional middle class, much as my white friends at Malverne High School did. Dad made me quite unlike them.

Dad never had a bad thing to say about communism. This made for my slightly schizoid upbringing whereby in school and among my childhood friends

FIGURE 1.3 Baba Dreizha (18??–1955), my maternal great-grandmother.

like Lettie communists represented the subversive enemy, while at home they signified fighters for world peace and social justice. As for the USSR, which my father lauded as a bulwark against American imperialism, I will never forget Misha Lewin's quip when one evening I told him about Dad's erstwhile Communist Party of the United States of America (CPUSA) affiliation: "they knew what they didn't like; so, they liked what they didn't know"—the "they" referring to Western Communists in general. This is a little unfair, because my father did try to inform himself via voracious reading. Later in life, in 1985—his seventieth year—he finally got to visit the Soviet Union. He, my mother, and friends of theirs went on a two-week guided tour of Moscow, Leningrad, Tbilisi, Erevan, and Krasnodar.[10] Mom described the little schoolchildren they met in Krasnodar as "adorable," and the food as so-so. Dad expressed cautious optimism about perestroika, did not care for the friend of a friend I arranged for them to meet, but otherwise said little. I think this must have been because he did not find the Soviet Union he was looking for, the one that he liked before he visited. Maybe what that Soviet Union represented to him was hope. Maybe Misha was right.

As I think back on my childhood home and its décor, I realize that my father's taste in both art and politics enveloped me, as in a cocoon. A reproduction of Honoré Daumier's *Third-Class Carriage* that the Met's website describes as depicting "the hardship and quiet fortitude of third-class railway travelers," had a prominent position near the front door.[11] A Pablo Picasso, I think from his Blue Period, adorned a bedroom wall. When did I know that Picasso was a Communist? Possibly when I knew that Rockwell Kent, the American painter and illustrator whose Mexican subjects adorn a pitcher, plates, and other objects we use to this day, suffered for his prominence among friends of the Soviet Union. David Siqueiros, one of Mexico's trio of great muralists, counted among that country's Communists. In 1965, my parents met him in his home while on a *Guardian*-sponsored tour and snapped photos that made an impression on me. Years later, I learned that he had been among those who attempted but failed to assassinate Leon Trotsky, three months before Ramón Mercader finally got the job done.

I attribute to my father rather than to my mother the fact that unlike my Jewish friends I did not go to Hebrew school and did not have a bar mitzvah. Instead, I attended Yiddish school, albeit briefly. My mother, who knew what lay in store for her when she married my father in 1940, acquiesced in these decisions. The disaster of my older brother's bar mitzvah, held in an un-air-conditioned Orthodox shul somewhere in the Bronx on what must have been one of the hottest July days of the twentieth century, probably helped persuade her to limit to one the number of phony bar mitzvahs the family had to endure. So that I wouldn't feel deprived, when I turned thirteen, Dad drove three friends and me to Hunter Mountain in the Catskills to go skiing. The car skidding off the winding Taconic Parkway at night and coming to a rest facing oncoming traffic is my most vivid memory of that trip.

In high school, I was unexceptionally exceptional. I took honors courses and received grades high enough to be salutatorian of my class, played saxophone in the band and second base on the baseball team, and edited the school newspaper until I resigned over the faculty advisor's refusal to print an editorial I wrote. The editorial protested against the withdrawal of an invitation to Pete Seeger to perform at another Long Island high school because of his alleged communist past; the advisor deemed the matter irrelevant to our high school. I had a leading role in a school play that inventively combined the cartoon characters Archy (a cockroach) and Mehitabel (an alley cat) with Shakespeare's *Midsummer Night's Dream*. None of this endeared me to any of the girls for whom I pined. Mr. Besse, my favorite teacher, taught social studies as American history. A retiring man with a broad but rarely seen grin, he lived alone in the upstairs apartment of a two-story house in Malverne. I know this because near the end of my senior year, he invited several of his students to tea. At graduation, he presented me with a deluxe edition of Tom Paine's *Common Sense*.

I spent several summers of my teenaged years at To-Ho-Ne (pronounced Tohoknee), a boys' camp on Lake Buel in western Massachusetts. Founded in 1920, To-Ho-Ne appealed to mostly Jewish parents from the New York metropolitan area who willingly parted with their sons and a considerable amount of money for eight weeks.[12] Dad had been a counselor there beginning in late 1930s and after marrying Mom in August 1940, brought her along with him. The years they put into the camp meant that they paid only a fraction of the regular tuition when Steve and I were old enough to be campers.[13] One of my earliest memories from the camp is a musical performance of *Tommy Pitcher*, listed in the sources I have consulted as an opera intended for a juvenile audience, that George Kleinsinger (1914–1982) composed.[14] Kleinsinger was a prolific composer whose most famous work was "Tubby the Tuba," also for children. I listened to the record at home countless times. The memory of *Tommy Pitcher* is of a fragment from one of the songs that went "Tom Pitcher was sitting along the riverside / Tom Pitcher was fishing, his eyes were open wide." I mischievously "rewrote" these lines as "Tom Pitcher was pissing along the riverside / Tom Pitcher was pissing, his fly was open wide." Kleinsinger, who also wrote the music for the Broadway show *Archy and Mehitabel* that premiered in 1954, probably would not have appreciated my improvement to the libretto.[15]

FIGURE 1.4 "After marrying Mom in August 1940, [he] brought her along with him." Morton and Blanche Siegelbaum, Camp To-Ho-Ne, summer 1941.

What connection, if any, did Kleinsinger have to To-Ho-Ne? Several tantalizing clues exist. One is that according to his entry in Wikipedia, *Tommy Pitcher* was first performed in 1952 at the Indian Hills Music Workshop in Stockbridge, Massachusetts, a town located some ten miles from the camp. Another is my brother remembering that "we shared a house with the Kleinsingers before you were born," and that "Tom Pitcher" was "a theater piece he wrote for the camp with Alan Arkin in the title role."[16] Finally, the titles of some of Kleinsinger's wartime and postwar works—"Overture on American Folk Themes"; "Ode to Democracy"; and "I Hear America Singing," the latter, recorded along with "Ballad for Americans" by Paul Robeson—reflect the kind of communist popular front culture one encountered at the camp, about which more in a moment.

At sixteen, I worked at the camp as a waiter, then in successive years as counselor-in-training, counselor, and eventually, group leader. To-Ho-Ne resembled many other summer camps in the area. Its name—"here we will camp" in Algonquin—represented an appropriation of Native American culture characteristic of at least boys camps at the time. It had a waterfront with a fleet of diminutive sailboats and at some point in the '60s, waterskiing; it had a picturesque lodge overlooking the lake where we played basketball, watched plays, and on July 21, 1969, the moonwalk on a TV set up especially for the occasion; it had a baseball field, archery and rifle ranges, and tennis courts. Its counselors came from all over. I remember the "Springfield" and "Lock Haven boys" (from Springfield College in Massachusetts and Lock Haven State College in Pennsylvania, both teacher's colleges), but also Kenny Moss and Jeff Ross, both from Long Island, a few Englishmen, a pair of Austrian brothers (Edgar and Ernie Sudek, the former a soccer player who introduced the sport to the camp, the latter a genuine Olympian shot-putter), and Tom Waddell, an extraordinary athlete and individual who placed sixth among thirty-three competitors in the decathlon at the 1968 Olympic Games in Mexico City. About four years earlier, Tom had organized an Olympics at To Ho Ne in which every camper competed. I entered the decathlon for the team coached by my brother, then, like Tom, a counselor. Waddell went on to become a physician, set up a practice in the Castro district in San Francisco, found the Gay Olympics (now, the Gay Games), and die of AIDS in 1987 at the age of forty-nine.[17]

For all I know, though, Camp Half Moon at the other end of the lake also had exceptional staff members. But whereas Half Moon became a refuge for children whose parents had fled (Cuban) communism, To Ho Ne had been a haven for Communists.[18] Did Pete Menaker, the camp's owner, actually belong to the party? My dad regarded him as a comrade, and in my youthful assessment, he behaved like one, which is to say gruff, mercurial, and oblivious to anything related to popular culture. He almost inherited his communism. His parents, Jewish immigrants from Odessa, named each of their sons after revolutionaries. Aside from Pete (named after Kropotkin, or could it have been Lavrov?), I knew Enge (Friedrich Engels) best.[19] Enge ran the guest camp next to To-Ho-Ne where parents stayed when visiting their sons. He also owned the farmhouse up on Lake Buel Road, where I later would spend a romantic weekend with a Barnard student.

Those neo-McCarthyite historians Harvey Klehr and John Earl Haynes describe Enge as "an openly Communist journalist," who "ran a League of American Writers home for anti-Nazi refugees in France" and later cooked for "some exiles in the home of the Arenal family in Mexico City."[20] Klehr and Haynes cite Daniel Menaker's memoir, published in 1987 and disguised as a collection of stories, as the source for their information. In the memoir, Enge is Uncle Sol, an old Communist in his eighties who still reads the *Daily World* and is censorious of his nephew's profligate ways. So much did Daniel Menaker make of Uncle Sol's communism, in fact, that he titled the stories *The Old Left*.[21] I dimly perceived Enge's politics; just as I did his sexual orientation. Although Sophie, a woman roughly his age, lived in the farmhouse, Enge preferred men. Years later, I somehow became aware that not long after Tom Waddell came to To-Ho-Ne in 1959, he and Enge became lovers.

But among the Menakers, as I already have indicated, Pete seemed the real Communist. How then did he justify running a summer camp for well-off kids? As Pete himself once explained to me, he regarded them as deprived. They lacked the experience of cooperation, of working on projects for the intrinsic value of creating something with their own hands, of having contact with nature unmediated by their parents. This struck me then and still seems now disingenuous and self-serving. But how else could Pete get the money to build and maintain that waterfront, hire those great counselors and feed us all? Like the capitalism he abhorred, Pete embodied contradictions: he drove his motorcycle around the camp's grounds at breakneck speed, beat and in other ways humiliated his wife Sarah, but also showered affection on campers indiscriminately and resembled some biblical prophet. He taught me that Communists were not necessarily more moral, well-behaved, or consistent than anyone else.

In those years, these issues did not overly concern me. I wanted to see more of those breasts like the ones the camp nurse provocatively exposed to me one evening down by the waterfront; I wanted to meet a pretty girl at Camp Fokine or another of the girls' camps where we had socials, and "make out" with her. Most of all, I wanted to become the best tennis player at camp if not the world. Tennis?! Why tennis? Could this "most isolating of games" have attracted me because, as someone put it recently, it "draws the obsessive and the brooding"?[22] There might be something to this. Tennis is all-consuming; it is impossible to think of anything else while playing. Each point, indeed each shot, is a challenge. So, in some sense, tennis represented a suspension of everyday concerns. All I needed to care about occurred within the lines on the court.

The other thing is that I played pretty well. By the time I got to high school, I could beat my brother who bested me in everything else. I had learned to play tennis at the Hempstead Lake State Park, a short walk from my house. My friends and I used to sneak onto the clay courts and play after the clubhouse had closed simply by climbing over a six-foot-high chain-link fence. My father had played, though I don't recall him teaching me the game. Nor do I think I ever inquired where this New York City born and bred son of Louis Siegelbaum, a plumber, had learned to play. He had friends who played too: Marvin Luftig, founder in 1950 of Luftig Associates insurance company (today, Tennis Club Insurance Associates of Great Neck, Long Island), for which Dad worked briefly after his teaching career ended so abruptly; and Irving Siegel, erstwhile fellow teacher. After moving with his family further out on the Island, Marvin would occasionally return to play tennis at Hempstead Lake State Park, using our house to change and shower. Irv and his wife Doris were exceptional among my parents' friends in resisting suburban fever. They remained along with their daughter Vivian in Stuyvesant Town/Peter Cooper Village. Once, during my student years at Columbia, I played tennis with Irv. He drove me out to some courts in Queens and, much to my dismay, beat me handily.

At To-Ho-Ne I became a tennis counselor. This meant endlessly tossing balls to campers, sweeping, watering, rolling, and otherwise maintaining the courts, and on good days, hitting with Alexander (Sandy) Meiklejohn. A few years older than I and a much better tennis player, Sandy had a dry, avuncular manner except when he found something funny in which case, a high-pitched giggle emanated from his lips. I idolized him. Sandy's grandfather, after whom he was named, was a philosopher and keen advocate of free speech. In 1949, the year of my birth, he had crossed swords with Sidney Hook, an erstwhile Trotskyist, in a "literary duel" published in *The New York Times Magazine*. Alexander Meiklejohn defended the right of Communists to teach in the public schools.[23]

CHAPTER 2

"REVOLUTIONARY OR SCHOLAR?"

I went to Columbia because I didn't get into Amherst College. Why Amherst? Because Sandy's grandfather had served as President decades earlier; because Henry Steele Commager, a respected American historian, taught there, and I had heard of him; but also because it had a high reputation among small liberal arts colleges. I wanted to go there so much that I persuaded my father to take me on a campus visit, a practice then not as common as now. He, quite fond of Emily Dickinson's poetry, loved her house, and I found the school much as I had pictured it. The quota system might have done me in, though—too many New York suburban kids applying.

Why Columbia? One evening at a family circle meeting at Grandma Sadie's apartment in the Bronx, my cousin Marilyn's husband, Mel Schwartz, asked me about the colleges I had applied to. The Rubels held such meetings every six months or so to discuss issues in common. I remember the upkeep of Baba Dreizha's grave in Queens as the most frequently discussed. Usually, I would wander in and out of the living room where everyone gathered before conking out—from boredom—in the bedroom. On this particular evening—it must have been early in the application season—I mentioned Amherst and one or two other schools. "What about Columbia?" asked Mel, who happened to be in the Physics Department. Well, what about it, I thought.

The institution of the family circle meeting served as one of the investments first- and second-generation immigrant Jews from eastern Europe made to maximize their social capital. Who knows how many cheap or no-interest loans, free advice, and agreements to pool resources members of the extended family entered into? Mel, who went on to share the Nobel Prize for Physics in 1988, may not have been in a position to help me get into Columbia, but just putting it into my head that I should apply started me on that path. So, fortune smiled on me in a way that had evaded my brother. Stevie started college at Queens, flunked out because he spent his freshman year at jazz clubs in the City, then got into a small college in southeastern Ohio from which he nearly got expelled when the dean of students learned that his then-girlfriend and future wife had spent a night in his dorm room—or at least that is what family lore reports.

How my father could afford to send me to Columbia is a mystery. To be sure, tuition costs have outpaced inflation over the decades. But still, the $1,900 charged by Columbia in 1966 would amount to $14,729 in 2018.[1] Even though Dad made me understand that I had to earn money in the summer and assume complete responsibility for funding my education beyond college, his commitment to covering the cost of the four years humbles me. In 1999 my older son Sami got into New York University—then just about the most expensive university in the country—and told me he wanted to go there instead of the far less costly but still excellent University of Michigan. When I replied that I didn't see how I could afford it, this normally reserved young man burst into tears, at which point my resistance evaporated. I suppose I managed to do it the way Dad did.

I arrived at Columbia in the fall of 1966 eager to demonstrate I belonged there, or in other words, that I had smarts. The problem was so did most other freshmen. Nothing clarified more the distinction between high school and college than the "C" grade I received from Professor Michael Rosenthal for an essay I wrote in his English composition class on something like "the meaning of courage." I devoted most of the essay to *Man of La Mancha*, the 1965 Broadway musical adaptation of Miguel de Cervantes's *Don Quixote* that I had seen as a high-school senior. Rosenthal's haughty dismissiveness of the Broadway musical's value stung me. Only one student received an "A," which of course guaranteed that the rest of us would detest him.

That year, I played tennis on Columbia's freshman team. I wasn't very good, and in that respect fit into our mediocre team. We mostly played against prep schools whose jeunesse dorée usually beat us. Aside from tennis, I acted in repertory alongside my classmate Gerrit Graham, who the following year would appear with Robert De Niro in Brian De Palma's *Greetings*; I took the bus once a week to Harlem where I tutored a fourth-grade kid; and I devoted every spare minute to sitting in Furnald Hall's study room reading and taking notes for my Contemporary Civilization (CC), Art Humanities, Music Humanities, Geography-Geology, French, and damned Rosenthal's English classes. In June after the end of freshman year and before I headed off to teach tennis at To-Ho-Ne, I visited my brother and sister-in-law in Chevy Chase, Maryland. They were living in the house owned by the dentist for whom Bobbi worked, while Steve (no longer Stevie) completed his MA degree in African Studies at American University. While there, I watched the UN debates over the Six-Day War on television, becoming fascinated by the Soviet ambassador's remarks—not so much their content as the sound of the Russian language: "Sovetskaia delegatsiia," "Israelskaia agressiia." Nikolai Federenko's voice still resonates in my mind.

What prompted Steve to focus on Africa, I cannot recall, but it did not extend to learning an African language. By the following year, he had become a father and a secondary school teacher in New York City, thereby following in the footsteps of our own father. He would carve his own unique career in the public-school system, founding two middle schools of his own devising that he called The Computer School. In the meantime, I had enrolled in first-year Russian. I already had a good command of French, thanks to a pioneering program to expose elementary school kids to the rudiments of the language and an excellent high-school teacher. I enjoyed my freshman French class, but French did not seem to satisfy my budding interest in communism. In the summer of '68 after my tumultuous sophomore year, I did second-year Russian at Hofstra University. To earn some money, I also worked behind the deli counter at a supermarket near my parents' house in Huntington Station, Long Island. From the "revolutionary" barricades at Columbia to slicing lox—what a comedown.

Anticipating that sophomore year, I had written a letter the day before classes began in September 1967 to Virginia ("Ginna") Sybert, a friend from high school with whom I maintained a somewhat tortured correspondence throughout my college years. "It's going to be one hell of a year. It will take patience, discipline, commitment . . ." It is hard to tell whether this referred to the qualities I would need for my studies or for fulfilling the expectations of my comrades in Students for a Democratic Society (SDS), which I had just joined. As it turned out, I still put in long hours in the study hall and managed to maintain excellent grades, at least in the fall semester. This did not preclude attending the March on Washington in October 1967 along with 100,000 other anti-Vietnam War protesters. But even as late as March 11, 1968, when I again wrote Ginna, scholarly pursuits still had the upper hand:

> I've kept busy. Looking for a work-study job on campus for the summer, figuring out where I'm going to live, speaking at SDS rallies (!), "flicking out," and of course working. . . . You know, I just can't help working. Some people get hooked on liquor, cigarettes, and worse. With me it's books. And you know what's worse? I like it. I can see myself thirty years from now, LEWIS SIEGEL-BAUM, PROFESSOR OF _____.

Even if I had yet to determine my specialization, I seem to have come down on the side of the scholar. The events of only a few weeks later radically altered my orientation. Others have chronicled the protests at Columbia in systematic and detailed ways.[2] My own involvement, like that of many, stemmed from: Columbia's involvement in the American prosecution of the Vietnam War via its connections to the secretive Institute for Defense Analysis (IDA), a weapons research think tank working for the Defense Department; the university administration's determination to impose disciplinary action against SDS's chairman Mark Rudd and the other "IDA Six" for their organization of the protest inside Low Library; and Columbia's encroachment on Morningside Heights to build a new gymnasium with a separate ("segregated") entrance for Harlem's residents. I had marched to President Kirk's office in Low Library on March 25; attended the university's memorial service for Martin Luther King on April 10 before joining more than forty other students in walking out; and helped to tear down the chain-link fence surrounding the construction site for the new gym on April 23.[3]

Occurring in close succession, the events of those weeks exhilarated me. I clearly remember tasting the sweetness of transgression as we marched out of St. Paul's Chapel with fists raised and assembled on the Sundial at the center of the campus to hear speeches by Rudd and others. Initially, the occupation of Hamilton Hall following the mayhem at the gym site evoked the same feeling. Those classrooms where lofty professors normally presided now belonged to us. Imprisoning Columbia College dean Henry Coleman in his office enhanced our sense of empowerment. But within a few hours, the Students' Afro-American Society (SAAS), wary of being sidetracked or upstaged by SDS and its motley supporters, asked us white students to leave. We hardly could refuse the request, which SAAS members voiced without equivocation, and upon emerging from the building fanned out to occupy others. It is possible that I went back to my dorm room in Furnald Hall to wash up and change clothes, but within hours my friend Chuck Bethell and I found ourselves in Fayerweather, among a mostly graduate student crowd.

From this moment on, I no longer interspersed protest with attending classes and trying to keep up with reading. Now, "the revolution" took over. For nearly a week, we lived as a commune ("Fayerweather Commune") in all its chaotic wonderfulness. We formed committees to prepare food brought in from outside, keep the premises reasonably clean, communicate with occupiers in other buildings, and even organize makeshift classes. Faculty, fearing attacks against us from counter-demonstrators organized by the Majority Coalition (dubbed by us "the jocks"), formed a buffer outside, wearing arm bands to identify themselves. At one point, a red-haired professor clambered to the front of the big room where we were all sitting on the floor to harangue us about abandoning our "revolutionary dreams" because as an expert on the Russian revolutionary movement he knew only too well how little we resembled real revolutionaries. For his pains, Leopold Haimson received a chorus of boos, and seriously suffered from the rebuff for years thereafter. I also remember Barnard students voicing complaints about second-class treatment from male students, possibly the first time I had heard this feminist complaint articulated.

And then in the wee hours of April 30, the cops showed up—in force—to arrest us. Before they stormed the building, we received instructions about how to behave: we could either lock arms and offer passive resistance, or simply walk to the paddy wagons. I unheroically chose the latter. Charged with "criminal trespass," we were driven down to "the Tombs" (the Manhattan House of Detention) on Centre Street in Lower Manhattan.[4] I spent about four or five hours sitting uncomfortably in a large holding pen with maybe forty or fifty other protesters before being released on bail. Doris Siegel, my parents' friend who lived nearby, had posted bail and met me as I emerged, shaken, from the Tombs.

As I returned to campus, the sight that greeted me at the top of the stairs of the 116th Street and Broadway subway station more than compensated for the negativity of my short-lived incarceration. Leaflets called for a meeting at Wollman Auditorium to organize a general strike of students. Banners festooned the campus already announcing it. The meeting, which I attended, approved six "non-negotiable" demands including the removal of all police from campus, the resignation of the detested president Grayson Kirk and vice-president David Truman, and the fundamental restructuring of the university. The administration in its turn cancelled all classes for the week, imposing a lockout, in labor-management terms. Instead of formal classes, sympathetic faculty organized teach-ins.[5] The campus turned into a festival, a magnet for radicals, and a bit of a tourist attraction. H. Rap Brown and Stokely Carmichael had already come to lend their support to the black students in SAAS. Now, the Grateful Dead performed outside Ferris Booth Hall. Tom Hayden, then living in Newark, stopped by as did other veterans of the anti-war movement. Meanwhile, the Rolling Stones' new release, "Street Fighting Man," competed with "Let's Spend the Night Together" as the best expression of our desires.

One night, as a bunch of us were sitting around in the strike committee's headquarters, Rudd asked if anyone knew what Norman Mailer looked like. I had never met Mailer, although I had attended a party at his amazing, multileveled Brooklyn Heights apartment hosted by his daughter, Susie, a Barnard student. But I had seen him in newspaper photographs and on television and thus volunteered to go to the West End Bar on Broadway and 114th Street to escort him onto campus. A notorious egomaniac, Mailer liked to "make the scene" in the sixties sense of that phrase, and thanks to its radical students, the Columbia campus definitely had achieved that status. "Mark Rudd, this is Norman Mailer; Mr. Mailer, Mark Rudd." Such was my brush with a literary lion.

The festival atmosphere lasted until another occupation of Hamilton Hall, and a second bust on May 22.[6] Anticipating the invasion of campus by the police, we built barricades out of police sawhorses at the 116th Street entrances to the campus at Amsterdam Avenue and Broadway. As darkness fell, the police began dismantling the barricades and slowly advanced on the crowd tightly packed on the walk. How I got to be in the very front of the crowd facing Amsterdam Avenue I don't know, but I found myself facing some really menacing looking dudes from the city's Tactical Patrol Force (TPF). Making matters worse, my comrades farther back in the crowd had launched various projectiles (bricks? paving stones?) at the cops. "I wish they wouldn't do that," I said to myself and maybe out loud as well. And then in a flash, the police raised their truncheons and brought them down on protesters' backs and heads. The crowd stumbled in retreat. I made it nearly all the way back to the Broadway side of campus, but upon seeing a cop waling away on a defenseless protester on College Walk, I shouted "hey, you can't do that!" or some other ridiculous imprecation. At which point a weighted club came down on my head from behind. I crumpled to the ground and woke up in St. Luke's Hospital with a gash that required twenty-three stitches to close.

Throughout the upheavals, I tried to keep my parents informed. Mom betrayed her anxiety with such phrases as, "Well, Lewis, I just hope you know what you're doing." Dad, who could be critical of what he described as the New Left's lack of discipline, nevertheless threw himself into the parents support group. There, he found a soul mate, Leo Hurwitz, a documentary filmmaker whose commitment to combating racism and fascism in the 1930s and '40s earned him a place on the notorious blacklists of the 1950s and early '60s. The parents, among other things, raised money for the legal defense of students charged with everything from willfully damaging university property to causing riots. I don't want to minimize the tensions between new and old leftists, a prominent theme in the 1960s. Yet, as suggested by this small example, common ground could be found. That Dad had bestirred himself not just for my sake but the cause I was part of made me proud. I think he was proud of me too.

The somewhat somber commemoration of the fiftieth anniversary of the protests at Columbia included observations about their racial component, specifically, how the media tended to minimize the role of SAAS and inflate that of the predominantly white SDS. Several white former protesters confessed to having "complicated feelings" about their ejection from Hamilton Hall by their erstwhile black comrades.[7] Having cut my teeth on residential integration struggles characterized by interracial collaboration, I too might have bristled. Today, I see it quite differently. Thanks to their connections—real or alleged, it doesn't matter—with the Harlem community, SAAS held the upper hand. Hence, the Columbia administration and the police treated black students more cautiously.[8] We white students had no such constituency, only our white skin privilege, which broke down in these circumstances. Indeed, like the hard hats who fell upon anti-war protesting students on Wall Street in May 1970, it is possible that the cops laid into us with unrestrained vigor out of a certain class animus precisely because of our whiteness.[9]

My reflections on Columbia '68 thus stem from both an active memory periodically revived and my commitment as a professional historian to reconstruct and analyze the past. I would like to pause here for a moment to consider the larger global context. We student protesters knew back then that we belonged to a worldwide movement against imperialism, militarism, and bureaucratic authoritarianism. We felt solidarity not only with Vietnamese peasants fighting against American aggressors, but also the Black Panthers (some of whose rhetoric we adapted), young people in Prague seeking "socialism with a human face," the German SDSers (Sozialistische Deutsche Studentenbund or Socialist German Student Union) who formed the leading element in the "extra-parliamentary opposition" to the grand coalition then ruling West Germany, student and worker protesters in France, and even in some cases the Cultural Revolutionaries in China waving their Little Red Books.[10] All of us in one way or another were engaged in actions we thought revolutionary and despite differences of ideology and emphasis considered ourselves part of the same revolution that soon would succeed.

It did not take more than a few years to demonstrate the illusoriness of this expectation. Yet, I would argue that illusions are essential to any revolutionary upheaval, indeed the very stuff of revolutions, and why "heady days of revolution" and "revolutionary intoxication" are such common phrases. One can look back with some embarrassment at the excesses of youthful optimism, yet still be proud of having associated oneself with that moment and its transnational solidarities. More than once in recent years I have come across a *soixante-huitard* or "'68er," and felt an immediate kinship. And when, as happened only a few months ago, a former student of mine now teaching in a private school in suburban Detroit arranged for me to speak to her class about the student rebellions of the sixties, I felt fortunate to be able to relate my own experiences and convey these feelings.

But to return to the immediate aftermath, as the fall semester approached—after a summer of slicing lox at the supermarket deli counter and studying Russian at Hofstra—I felt nothing if not conflicted. To Ginna I wrote on September 3, as far as Columbia is concerned, nothing has been resolved . . . Basically, it is a personal conflict between scholar and revolutionary. I hate revolution-aries—at least the ones at Columbia. Everything from their vacuous rhetoric to their snobbishness really turns me off. On the other hand, I regard scholars as the biggest cop-outs, the most aimless people in creation.

"Which," I concluded with somewhat less than full ardor, "means I'll probably side with the revolutionaries—boycott classes, continue the strike, and who knows what else?"

It is hard to say how accurately this letter represented the real state of my mind at the time. One is often prey to the disposition of one's interlocutors, and Ginna's lack of sympathy for the street fighting man may have caused me to distance myself from the "revolutionaries." I may have envied some who seemed more courageous or devil-may-care than I, but I certainly did not "hate" them. Some would abandon political activism for good, but for many among the SDS leadership, the events at Columbia served as training for the life of a professional revolutionary. Josephine ("Josie") Duke, who arrived on campus as a society girl, "withdrew" from Bar-nard to agitate full-time among army inductees at Fort Dix, New Jersey.[11] Expelled from Columbia, both Mark Rudd and John Jacobs ("J. J.," as we called him) figured among the eleven signatories of the "Weatherman Manifesto" that they presented to the national convention of SDS in Chicago in June 1969.[12] Their breakaway group, later known as the Weather Underground, launched what they called a National Action in October (the "Days of Rage"). By 1970, they, along with several others expelled from the university, had become fugitives. Ted Gold, an amiable and stu-dious individual whom I knew fairly well, did not make it out of 1970 because he died along with two other Weathermen on March 6 of that year in the accidental explosion of bombs they were making in a Greenwich Village townhouse.

This, in the popular dialect of the time, was some heavy shit. By the time it happened, I was in the last semester of my undergraduate program. It crystal-ized for me how far removed I had become from "the struggle." Let me try to reconstruct how and why I had resolved the dilemma between revolutionary and scholar, between street fighting and studying. On September 29, 1968, I wrote to Assistant Dean for Student Affairs Robert Laudicina. Full of hurt and anger, the letter insisted that

It is *you* who continually suppressed legitimate and widespread dissent. I sub-mit, therefore, that it is you who must take the responsibility of nearly a thou-sand students violating your rules. For, short of capitulation, we had no other course of action. Finally, it is you who called in the police and are therefore responsible for the violence which followed.

Such righteous indignation! "Dean Laudicinia [*sic*]," it went on, "where is your admission of guilt? . . . Does your vindictiveness (for I know not what else to call it) know no bounds?" The only problem with interpreting this angry denunciation as an example of youthful defiance is that unlike many of my comrades in SDS who ignored the threat of expulsion, I admitted that I had violated Section 356 of the University's *Statutes* and requested the dropping of charges as well as my reinstatement as a student in good standing. Why? Hadn't I told Ginna I would join the boycott of classes and continue the strike? Whom did I try to con—her or myself? "I value a Columbia education in spite of the Columbia administration," I miserably confessed to the dean. "It is ironic," I added, "that the very institution which taught me to act out of conviction and not expediency has now forced me to do just the opposite in order that I may remain a student."

I did not feel good about writing this and reading the letter half a century later makes me squirm. What would have happened to me had I taken the more courageous position of refusing to play by the rules? Might I have joined the Weathermen, gone "underground," and become a fugitive? Did I really "value a Columbia education" so much, or fear expulsion and exposure to the draft and military service in Vietnam?[13] I did actually get called up in my senior year and went to Fort Greene in Brooklyn for my physical. That led to another compromise—a session with a psychiatrist sympathetic to the anti-war movement who documented a(n actual) case of eczema on my hands but blew it way out of proportion to claim a nervous condition that warranted monitoring and treatment. At Oxford, I located a similarly sympathetic doctor who went along with the ruse and sent periodic reports back to my draft board.

Maybe I wrote but did not send the letter. For if I did send it, why do I have it in my possession? It could not be a photocopy, for access to that technology still lay in the future, and it does not look like a carbon copy. Is it possible that the administration decided to grant me amnesty after all, thus obviating the need for requesting reinstatement?[14] Most of the students involved in the protests did receive amnesty, a decision one can interpret either as a concession or as a clever maneuver to decapitate the movement.[15] New leaders emerged to take the place of Rudd & Co. Stu Gedal, with whom I had addressed a group of anxious parents in Great Neck during the summer of '68, and Robbie Roth remained on campus to lead hundreds of students in new building occupations and strikes. But these were far smaller, if no less militant, actions, and the fact that I can't remember

whether I participated in them speaks volumes about my progressive disengage-
ment. Of course, I continued to attend SDS meetings and the odd demonstration
at the Sundial. I reduced but did not renounce my participation, reverting to my
scholarly persona. I also indulged in some psychotropic drugs (mainly "speed"),
pursued some Barnard girls, and deepened my interest in classical music. I even
played some tennis on the green clay court improbably located in front of John Jay
Hall in the middle of the campus. My opponent, Manuel (whose surname I have
forgotten) took no part in the events of '68.

Because, au fond, I considered myself a political person, I majored in political
science (then called government at Columbia). Some of my government courses
highly engaged me, none more so than the CC 1203–1204 sequence that Stephen F. Cohen taught in my sophomore year. Then not quite thirty and in the
last year of his PhD program at Columbia, Cohen assigned an eclectic group of
readings for 1203. My notes emphasize Karl Marx's youthful humanism (e.g., *Economic and Philosophic Manuscripts of 1844*), his "sociology of bourgeois society"
and late interest in Russia; Eduard Bernstein's revisionism ("practiced long before
it was theorized"), Russian autocracy and nineteenth-century radicalism from
Mikhail Bakunin and Nikolai Chernyshevskii to the Populists and Georgii Plekha-
nov; Vladimir Lenin's "re-radicalization" of Marxism up through the 1917 Revolution, the succession struggle, Stalin's "revolution," Georges Sorel's opposition
to the de-radicalization of Marxism in Western Europe, and then in somewhat
random fashion, Friedrich Nietzsche, Max Weber, and Robert Michels. My last
notes for the course are dated January 16, 1968, and they include the following
observations: "Weber & Michels explain bureau. of Russia, explain Stalin's rise to
power, cannot explain Stalin's actions once he attained power which were essentially irrational & dynamic, not rational & conservative." So, it seems, Cohen tried
to employ major European social theorists of the nineteenth and early twentieth
centuries to analyze the Stalinist outcome of the Bolshevik Revolution. How fascinating! And only a few comments (at least in my notebook) on Nikolai Bukharin,
the subject of what would be Cohen's first and best-known book.[16]

The spring course (CC 1204) contained four sections: mass politics in industrial society; communism, fascism, and the totalitarianism debate; revolution and
modernization; and America in the post-industrial age. Compared to reading lists
these days, Cohen assigned a lot. For just revolution and modernization, we read
Barrington Moore's *Social Origins of Democracy and Dictatorship*, Che Guevara's
Guerilla Warfare, Fanon's *Wretched of the Earth*, Lin Piao's *Long Live the Victory of
the People's War*, and, I suppose to represent the other side, an article by Samuel
Huntington from a 1965 issue of *World Politics*. For America in the post-industrial

age, John Galbraith's *New Industrial State*, Ralf Dahrendorf's *Class and Class Conflict in Industrial Society*, and one of the following: William Styron's *Confessions of Nat Turner*, Malcolm X's autobiography, James Baldwin's *Nobody Knows My Name*, or Claude Brown's *Manchild in the Promised Land*.

Three months into the course, the campus erupted in student protest. Ironically in view of what partly animated those protests, only books by or about African Americans went unread. Among the others, Moore's *Social Origins* made the strongest impression. Highly structuralist in its broad-ranging analysis of "lord and peasant in the making of the modern world," it would appear on several syllabi during my undergraduate years. Galbraith's *New Industrial State* would lie dormant on my shelf for decades until, while drafting an article about ten years ago on the principles governing Soviet architecture and town planning in the 1960s, I consulted it anew and found its case for system convergence quite persuasive.[17]

Unlike many on the Columbia faculty, Cohen supported the student strike. I may not have heard of the term "role model" yet, but he served as one, partly, I suppose, because of his youthfulness but mainly because the way he practiced political history appealed to me. I don't think his Jewish identity counted for much, but to the extent that ethnicity, race, or gender enable minorities and women to identify more easily with inspiring teachers, diversifying the faculty along these lines is definitely warranted. Although I would abandon political science—indeed, flee from it—after leaving Columbia, Cohen's kind of political history remained appealing, and I continued to regard him as a mentor. His moment of glory came in the late 1980s when Mikhail Gorbachev read the Bukharin biography and acknowledged that it had fundamentally altered his understanding of the Soviet past and possibilities for economic reform. During the 1990s, Cohen became something of a media star, appearing frequently on the nightly news and the op-ed pages of leading newspapers to help Americans interpret post-Soviet Russian developments. More recently, his full-throated opposition to the get-tough posturing of Barack Obama's administration toward Vladimir Putin's Russia made him a maverick among commentators. He seemed to enjoy his role as bad boy or victim of the mainstream's intolerance of dissenting views, and this made me wince a few times, but I still fundamentally respect the man, and continue to be in contact with him.

Next to Cohen's, Joseph Rothschild's course on eastern Europe (Government G6435: Political and Institutional Developments in East Central Europe) meant the most to me. Rothschild had a knack for making the successive subjection of Czechoslovakia, Poland, and Hungary to authoritarian dictatorship, fascism, and communism both distinct yet interrelated.[18] The recipient of a Kellett Fellowship that sent him to Oxford, he nominated me for the award. I am sorry I did not keep in touch with this genial man who died in 2000 at the age of seventy.

I also have a strange affection for the course that Roger Hilsman taught on international relations. Hilsman came to Columbia after serving as assistant secretary of state for Far Eastern affairs in John F. Kennedy's administration, where he had played an important—if controversial—role in shaping its policy toward Vietnam. He left for Columbia not long after Kennedy's assassination, because, so he claimed, he opposed the escalation of the war by President Lyndon Johnson. The only assigned reading I can recall, *To Move a Nation*, was Hilsman's own account of "the politics of foreign policy in the administration of John F. Kennedy."[19] I remember only two other things about that class. One is Hilsman regaling us with tales of his derring-do as a member of Merrill's Marauders during the war against Japan. The other is that he invited everyone to his apartment for dinner, a unique experience in my four years at Columbia.

Michel Oksenberg's "Political Systems of Revolutionary and Post-Revolutionary Societies," which I took in the fall of 1968, occupies a unique position in my education. Coming hard on the heels of our own attempt at revolution, the course attracted a large number of students, as would any course with the word "revolutionary" in its title. How disappointing that Oksenberg cared far more for Weber, Émile Durkheim, and Talcott Parsons than he did for Marx or Mao, and that just as the Cultural Revolution in China reached its crescendo, he touted Crane Brinton's jaundiced view of the possibilities for permanent revolution.[20] The graduate students in the class occasionally interrupted Oksenberg's lectures with shouts of "bullshit" (Mark Rudd's by then famous epithet) and otherwise displayed their displeasure. Looking now at the syllabus and my class notes, the course seems less objectionable than it did at the time. Is this because the times have changed or because I have? Perhaps both, although both periods have witnessed challenges—to be sure, very different sorts of challenges—to the hegemony of the global liberal order.

Oksenberg would leave Columbia a few years later for the greener pastures of Stanford and then Jimmy Carter's National Security Council, where he served as National Security Advisor Zbigniew Brzezinski's "right hand" man for relations with China.[21] This revolving door between academia and the "real world" experience of government typified the careers of many professors who stood before me in the classroom. Warner Schilling, who notoriously had opposed the student occupation of buildings in '68; Brzezinski, who refused to make alternative arrangements for me to complete his course on "The Dynamics of Soviet Politics" in spring 1970 when we once again went on strike; Alex Dallin, who taught a course on Soviet foreign policy; and the expert on China, A. Doak Barnett, who had been Oksenberg's doctoral advisor, all had government service behind or ahead of them. The government courses I took thus seemed to be preparing students for careers in . . . government or to serve as policy advisors, following in the footsteps of our professors. Perhaps at some other time, say, ten years earlier or later, I would have reveled in the privilege of being so close to the levers of power. But in the late sixties and particularly after the events of '68, they appeared compromised, and my proximity to them seemed to incriminate me.

Exposed to many of the same professors, my classmate Dov Zakheim, like me, would proceed to St. Antony's College in the fall of 1970 on a Kellett Fellowship. Even though the college had no more than sixty or seventy students in residence, our paths rarely crossed there. An Orthodox Jew, Zakheim pursued the study of how to make war more successful and profitable. After earning his DPhil, he taught at Yeshiva University and the National War College, worked in the Defense Department during Ronald Reagan's administration, and, like so many others with whom he served, threw in his lot with George Bush in the 2000 campaign. From 2001 to 2004 he occupied the position of the Defense Department's comptroller. He sat on the boards of various right-wing think tanks and journals and in 2010 retired as a senior vice president of Booz Allen Hamilton, Inc., a major government contractor.

Dov Zakheim also helped me to define myself: I was not Dov Zakheim. Unlike his version of Judaism, mine did not reside in religious observance but in awareness of heritage. Jews who transcended their own ethnic or religious particularities to contest all social injustice inspired me. When exactly I came across Isaac Deutscher's formulation of the "non-Jewish Jew," I don't recall. It might have accompanied me, as an amulet, in the summer of 1970 when I visited Israel with Melaine, my girlfriend from college who would be studying there. But whenever I read it, the book resonated.[22] I would be Jewish the way that Heinrich Heine, Rosa Luxemburg, Leon Trotsky, Sigmund Freud, and Isaac Deutscher were Jewish— rootless cosmopolitans all! Second, whereas the training Zakheim received from the Government Department at Columbia proved to be the stepping-stone for his career in government, it made me increasingly schizophrenic. I would have one vocabulary for communicating with friends, family, and fellow students and another to talk the talk of political science. Physicists, chemists, and other natural scientists may be able to tolerate this sort of radical disjuncture, but I didn't want to turn people into the objects of science. I wanted to deepen my understanding of Marxism and what made it such a powerful revolutionary force. Maybe this held the key to resolving the revolutionary/scholar bifurcation. Maybe I could be both.

The opportunity came to do just that in the fall semester of my senior year at Columbia when the French philosopher Lucien Goldmann arrived to teach a graduate course in sociology. The course, G4068x, contained a formidable reading list still in my possession. It started with Marx ("Theses on Feuerbach," volume one of *Capital*, and the preface to the *Critique of Political Economy*), then Marx and Engels' *German Ideology* and *Communist Manifesto*; Engels' *Anti-Dühring*; Bernstein's *Evolutionary Socialism*, which I already had read in Cohen's course; *What Is to Be Done?* and *The State and Revolution* by "Lénine" (I quote from the list); Luxemburg's *Reform or Revolution* and *The Russian Revolution*; "Lessons for October" and *The New Course* by "Trotski"; and works by Georg Lukács, Karl Korsch, Antonio Gramsci, Louis Althusser, Goldmann, Serge Mallet, and Raymond Aron. Check marks indicate the ones I read, and they appear next to every item except for Lukács and Korsch because Goldmann assigned the German editions. Whether I actually did read Goldmann's *Recherches dialectiques* and Mallet's *La nouvelle classe ouvrière* is doubtful, although I should add that within a year I had read Lukács's *History and Class Consciousness*.

Those dank, sunless Wednesday afternoons, with the portent of winter hanging in the air, are still memorable. I along with nearly a hundred other students would trudge off to Havemeyer Hall eager to soak in the wisdom offered by this genial man who, sadly, would live scarcely another year. I dutifully wrote down what I barely understood: "Mechanical materialism assumes that Man is a machine. If such is the case, we must ask what made the machine bad and how can it be changed?"; "The difference between sensuous activity and thought activity is human activity, which is an objective process (activity)"; "The maximum possible consciousness which a group possesses can be defined as that beyond which the group changes its nature." And, immediately following that opacity, another: "Peasants for instance cannot adhere to cooperative idea at once. Thus Lenin supported movement for seizure of land."

Goldmann delivered these aphorisms in heavily accented English, liberally sprinkled with French and Gallicisms. A couple of graduate students stood next to the podium to take questions and translate them into French for the master to understand and then, as often as not, translate into English his long-winded French replies. I wrote a term paper on "The Collective Subject and the Fetishism of Commodities in Marxist Thought," relying on several of Marx's works, supplemented by George Lichtheim, and Aron's *Main Currents in Sociological Thought*.[23] I received a "B" for the course, and that may have been generous. For at least Goldmann's version of sociology spoke a language—one moreover with a Cartesian inflection—that I had trouble identifying with and assimilating.[24] History, I surmised, would allow me to speak in my own voice even as I entered into a dialogue with voices from the past.

FIGURE 2.1 Columbia counter-commencement photo from *Newsweek*, June 15, 1970. My face is on the right side of the photo. Photo by Bernard Gotfryd.

It is worth clarifying what I mean by "my own voice." I mean precisely seeking connections with "voices from the past." Transcending the limits of one's own experience in the present space one occupies seems—and for as long as I can remember has seemed—the best way of coping with mortality. Connecting with people who came before us—their artifacts, their cultures, their words—radically expands our sense of who we are, and what we are capable of. The discipline of history, I began to believe already as an undergraduate, does that better than any other. Now I would add that anthropology and great fiction have that capacity too.

As I gained my own voice, my own self gradually and painfully matured. By the summer of '69 I could nearly fill an entire letter to Ginna with news about the repression of the Panthers and internal squabbling within SDS. ("They're up shit creek and this is only the beginning.") "Many of my friends at Columbia are in jail now serving 30-day sentences," I added, probably referring to Stu Gedal and therefore exaggerating a bit. But I also mentioned the "fuckin' B" that Seweryn Bialer gave me in his course on communist politics, "that course with the oral exam, . . . the bastard!" So, I still cared about my grades.

On June 1, 1970, Columbia University honored a few scholars and one appointee of President Richard Nixon, Arthur Burns, chairman of the Federal Reserve. Several hundred of the graduating seniors walked out of their commencement and staged an alternative because President Andrew Cordier had refused a request to include among the commencement speakers the Boston University historian and anti-war activist Howard Zinn (Columbia PhD, 1958).[25] A photographer from *Newsweek* caught my participation in the counter-commencement.[26]

CHAPTER 3

OXFORD AND MOSCOW

During the summer of 1970, I toured Western Europe with Melaine, my girlfriend from Barnard whom I had met in Joseph Rothschild's class. We spent six glorious weeks with another couple from college, Rich and Bobbie Polton, motoring in their squareback VW through France, Italy, Switzerland, and Spain, sleeping in youth hostels, and delighting in every destination's aesthetic and culinary pleasures.[1] I then accompanied Melaine to Israel where she would be enrolling at Hebrew University, and after a few awkward weeks in a country I neither understood nor liked, flew to London to spend a few days acclimating before taking a British Rail train to Oxford.

While we had been discovering Europe, George Szell, conductor of the Cleveland Orchestra and one of the giants of classical music performance, passed away. As my musical tastes had gravitated from rock 'n' roll to classical, I came to revere Szell's recordings of Mozart's symphonies and piano concerti. When, in my senior year at Columbia, I traveled to Cleveland to meet Melaine's parents, I attended a performance of the orchestra at Severance Hall. I thus came to associate the orchestra and its conductor with what had been at least for me a distressingly chaste college romance. Szell's death should have been a portent. Some three months after I started at Oxford, Melaine arrived for a visit during which she seemed distant. A series of aerograms exchanged after her return to Israel confirmed that she had met someone in her Hebrew class and our relationship—serious enough to inspire thoughts of marriage—ended.

My arrival in London coincided with the passing of another musical giant. On September 18, 1970, Jimi Hendrix died of an overdose in a Notting Hill flat just two miles north of where I bedded in Earl's Court. Hendrix's demise seemed an echo of the American life I left behind. It and a lecture on the evils of communism by the exiled Polish philosopher Leszek Kolakowski (1927–2009) constitute the only memories remaining from those first days at St. Antony's College, the premier area studies graduate college at Oxford. In pursuing a higher degree in Russian studies, I joined a heterogeneous group of young scholars from Israel,

India, Australia, and England. They included Gaby Gorodetsky, Mark Harrison, and Madhavan Palat, all of whom would remain friends long after we carved out our respective careers in history and economics in widely scattered parts of the world. Mark and Madhavan had had prior exposure to the Oxbridge approach to higher education—the tutorial at which one defended a paper written in advance before the tutor who had set the subject. Neither Gaby nor I had such training. I did attend some lectures to undergraduate students, but purely on a voluntary basis, and found them rarely worth the bother. The core of graduate training at Oxford, it turned out, consisted of lecture series or seminars organized by different centers and given by both the local talent and guests, often from abroad.

I lived during my first year at 5 Winchester Road, a street lined with three-story houses. Those on the west side of the street backed onto the college grounds. My one-room ("bedsitter") apartment shared the ground floor with those occupied by George Bergstrom and Joanna De Groot. George had a bonhomie characteristic of Americans abroad that I found appealing, and this outweighed our vast political differences or rather, what seemed political indifference in his case. Joanna, who would become one of Britain's leading experts in Iranian history and also an activist in the University and College Union, shared my political outlook as did her younger sister, Lucy, then an undergraduate at another Oxford college. Mrs. Allardice, a no-nonsense Scottish woman, served as the "scout" of our building, which meant among other things that she made our beds and kept our rooms (and ourselves) in order.

My breakup with Melaine interrupted this charming and certainly privileged existence. In a fit of rage and self-loathing, I squeezed a bottle so hard that I unintentionally inflicted a deep wound in the palm of my left hand. Inconsolable, I flew back to the United States at the end of the first term to spend a month with my parents. They had moved temporarily to Westborough, Massachusetts, where my father had been posted by the company that paid his salary. I must have had to vacate the Winchester Road flat because upon my return for the spring ("Trinity") term, I took up residence on St. Bernard's Road, a narrow, winding street extending from the other side of the college toward the working-class district of Jericho. Here, I resided one floor below Gaby, who, having arrived from Israel a few years earlier, had set himself up nicely. Nobody else I knew owned both a television and a car. We spent evenings watching *Monty Python's Flying Circus*; more rarely, we took drives in his mid-sixties VW to Great Tew and other cuter than cute villages in the Cotswolds. Our mutual discomfort among the college's senior fellows plus shared interests in Russian history and classical music—in Gaby's case, leavened by his expertise on the clarinet—created strong bonds.

What makes friendships endure? Mine with Gaby did for many years after we went our separate ways. But then it didn't. Did evolving differences (in political orientation and cultural tastes) overwhelm earlier bonds? Or, is it simply happenstance—I never ventured to Israel after my visit in 1970, and when I encountered Gaby during his infrequent trips to the United States, including one to East Lansing that I helped to arrange, we did not manage to overcome the awkwardness that had crept into our relationship in the intervening period. By contrast, my friendship with Yves Charbit, who came from Paris to write his DPhil thesis on the history of French demographic theory, has deepened with the years. It doesn't hurt that Yves is a consummate networker, a skill, he once explained, that he developed after arriving in France from Tunisia as a Jewish boy of sixteen without any connections. Many Siegelbaums have benefited from his and his wife Véronique's hospitality, and I have hosted peripatetic Yves in East Lansing on several occasions.

With Maria (Mena) Filomena Mónica, a Portuguese woman who wrote a thesis in sociology and then returned to her native country to take up a position at the University of Lisbon, friendship came much later. This stunningly attractive woman, four years older than I but so much more experienced in the ways of the world, dazzled me. When I met her, she had a(n estranged) husband and two children cared for by her well-to-do pious Catholic family in Lisbon. Although she never reciprocated my attentions, she at least tolerated them, meanwhile developing a warmer, albeit platonic relationship with Gaby. As discussed in her own memoir, she also had quite a few lovers, each of whom exceeded the other (and, of course, me!) in suavity.[2] I lost touch with Mena after leaving Oxford only to reconnect some thirty-five years later when I made my first trip to Lisbon. Thereafter, we started a correspondence that I treasure for its mutual frankness and affection.

The privileged, indeed precious existence I led at Oxford included playing sports—both unfamiliar and familiar. Soccer, a game whose rules I hardly knew, would never have occupied my time if it were not for the deceitfulness of Roger Brew, an Englishman who studied Latin America. Here is a reconstruction of our conversation one evening in the Junior Common Room:

ROGER: Lewis, do you play basketball?
LEWIS: Why, yes, I do.
ROGER: We are forming a team and we need someone who can jump and is good with his hands.
LEWIS: I'm in.
ROGER: Great! You are the goalkeeper of our football club.
LEWIS: Huh?

I don't recall playing more than a game or two. I think we lost but did not humiliate ourselves.[3]

The familiar was tennis but for the first time in my life on grass courts in the nearby University Parks—for free, any time I wanted to and could persuade someone to play with me. I found a willing partner in Dick Menaker, another nephew of Pete and Enge who had preceded me by a year at Columbia and then Oxford. Dick had played varsity singles at Columbia wearing an attachment on his stump of a right arm to toss the ball when he served. He played fiercely and more than competently, and the day I managed to defeat him on those beautiful University Parks courts just may have been the high point of my tennis career. When it came to politics, Dick did not take after his uncles. He evinced a liberalism I instinctively rejected as both too complacent about social injustice and too alarmist about communism. Liberals were in power not only in Washington but also in academia, in the courts, and in corporate America. Dick, a student of law at Oxford, seemed to be only too eager to join C. Wright Mills's "power elite." On reflection, I am grateful to Dick and his ilk because they helped me to better understand myself. They made me realize that I could not be on the inside.

So, why then did I choose Oxford, the ultimate gateway to the establishment? Aside from the Kellett Fellowship, I went to Oxford to escape from political science and the United States. When it turned out I could convert my masters' program into the pursuit of a more elongated PhD (DPhil in British parlance) degree, I decided to stay beyond the fellowship's two years, seeking additional funding from Oxford. I received an annually renewable loan that covered tuition and a bit more. I always assumed I would return to the United States after getting my degree, but sometimes wonder how different my graduate education, self-cultivation (what the Germans call *Bildung*), and subsequent career would have been had I gone to Berkeley, Princeton, or wherever else I had applied.

This might be the most appropriate place to mention Sheila Fitzpatrick's memoir of her "postgraduate" years and how her itinerary and mine resembled each other but moved in opposite directions.[4] Sheila started out in Melbourne, then went to St. Antony's after which she took up a position at Columbia; I started at Columbia, got my DPhil at St. Antony's and then took up a lectureship in Melbourne, all seven years or so after she did. Although of vastly different backgrounds and temperaments, we both felt awkward around the dons at the college. They included Max Hayward, Sheila's dissertation supervisor and my "moral tutor" after I initially had been assigned Theodore Zeldin. A French historian, Zeldin cultivated an air of eccentricity extreme even for Oxford. Hayward replaced Zeldin not long after I arrived because I needed additional Russian language instruction.

He had translated *Doctor Zhivago* (with Manya Harari), works by Vladimir Maya-kovsky, Anna Akhmatova, and many other great poets. A bachelor, he reminded me of Richard Burton and not only because of his reputed fondness for the bottle. He seemed shy and for a moral tutor supremely uninterested in either my morals or morale.[5] We met in his spacious quarters above the Russian Centre on Church Walk. He would ask me to read something out loud in Russian—a paragraph or two—and then I would translate the passage. Although he did not have the text, he invariably knew whenever I stumbled or made a mistake what the word or phrase had been, as if he had committed it to memory. I regarded him with awe.

The sense I had of being an outsider has never left me and bears some exam-ination. Most obviously, it has to do with class and my ambivalence about joining those with class privilege. Even if my father exuded pride in my accomplishments, I wondered whether I had betrayed his commitment to social equality and justice by becoming part of the academic elite. But it went beyond that. Even as Gaby and I ridiculed much of English upper-class culture, I secretly admired the seeming ease with which "those twits" comported themselves. This must be why I managed to smooth the rough edges of my New York–inflected accent, something I noticed on returning home when talking with members of my family.[6] I wanted it both ways—to belong and not to belong. Eventually, I came to recognize these com-plicated feelings as the source of my determination to succeed, to best or at least equal those for whom it all came so naturally.

Tennis. Just as I had converted the sense of inferiority toward my taller, more athletic, and in every other way more accomplished brother into the creative energy to beat him at the game—after which it became *my* sport—so at Oxford and beyond I overcame social awkwardness and intellectual self-doubt through sheer self-discipline and hard work. It occurs to me that I psychologically reenacted a syndrome familiar to Jews in Europe, but also racial minorities breaking into pre-viously all-white schools in the United States, women breaching formal and infor-mal gender barriers, and other interlopers. Show you can beat them at their own game. Show that you do belong, even if you disdain their company and they aren't particularly longing for yours. The analogies are imperfect but suggestive.

Sheila's ambivalence toward Oxford stemmed in part from her status as a colo-nial; mine had to do with being a New York Jew. Jews had long since stormed the bastions of Oxford by the time I arrived at St. Antony's. Sir Isaiah Berlin, whose occasional lectures I dutifully attended, directed the neighboring college, Wolfson. The Isaiah Berlins and Lewis Namiers paved the way for others—Theodore Zeldin and Harry Shukman, for example. Shukman's father, a tailor, had emigrated from Russia before 1917. But by the time I made his acquaintance as the supervisor of my

DPhil thesis, Harry seemed perfectly suited to the life of an Oxford don. His publications tended toward popularizations, such as *Lenin and the Russian Revolution* (1967) and *The Russian Revolution* (1998). But in 2006, Valentine Mitchell, which describes itself as "a publisher of books in the fields of Jewish, Middle Eastern and Holocaust studies," brought out his most original book. This focused on what happened to Russian Jewish men in Britain after His Majesty's government introduced conscription in 1916 and then after the overthrow of the tsar. Harry's interest in this subject originated with his father's experience of returning to Russia in 1917 to defend the revolution only to reverse course during the ensuing civil war.[7]

The point is that, wherever they had been born—tsarist Poland in the case of Namier, tsarist Russia in Berlin's case, British Palestine (Zeldin), or working-class Nottingham (Shukman)—these Jews had succeeded in totally Anglicizing themselves. I could never do that. My rebellious, antiestablishment self would have considered the transformation a betrayal, even if I could have pulled it off. Joshua Sherman, a transplanted New York Jew who had graduated from Columbia in 1954, helped me to chart the distance I would have had to travel. A sometime banker with a Harvard law degree, Joshua entered St. Antony's in 1967. After completing his doctorate in 1970, he stayed on as a research fellow. Kind to me and a sweet man in general, he nevertheless exhibited a contentment and an Anglophilia antithetical to my own self-image. Straight from the barricades of Morningside Heights, sporting one of those cast-off army jackets so popular among anti-war activists and with hair too long to be ruly, I enjoyed antagonizing the fusty dons at the Russian Centre. Not for nothing did Mena remember me in her memoir as a "hardline Marxist" ("marxista puro e duro") and Ronald Hingley, a translator who masqueraded as a historian, refer to me as "the bête noire of the College."[8]

Shukman treated me with more tolerance, though I might have benefited from more instruction. When in October 1972 I wrote to him requesting a letter of recommendation in support of my application to the American exchange program in Moscow, I noted that "despite our infrequent contact over the past two years, I am confident that you have sufficient knowledge of my work to give a judicious evaluation of it." But the truth is that my work consisted of nothing more than a paper I had written for another don ("in which you found much to criticize") and "our informal chats and reading sessions during my first two terms at Oxford." Not much to go on. I blame myself as much as Harry, but the Oxbridge approach to "postgraduate" education was the real culprit. I have before me a version of a curriculum vitae I wrote in 1974 when I started applying for academic positions in the United States. It contains a list of seven "relevant courses" in which, as the explanatory note below the list indicates, "No grades are given, and attendance is optional." In such a

FIGURE 3.1 St. Antony's College, October 1971. "Sporting one of those cast-off army jackets so popular among anti-war activists and with hair too long to be ruly," I am in the sixth row, second from the right. Gaby Gorodetsky is in front of me, Madhavan Palat is third from the left in the sixth row, and bespectacled Mark Harrison is fourth from the left in the third row. Harry Shukman (second from right), Ronald Hingley (sixth from right), and Theodore Zeldin (seventh from right) sit in the front row; Joshua Sherman stands behind Hingley and Zeldin.

manner did I pathetically attempt to compensate for the lack of a transcript, then as now an essential piece of documentation for aspiring academics.

The list includes a course described as a "social history seminar" conducted by T. Mason, and one on Marxism taught by R. Harrison and L. Siegelbaum. Tim Mason, a working-class lad, identified himself as a Marxist. Along with the German historians Lutz Niethammer and Detlev Peukert, he would revolutionize the study of Nazism by approaching it "from below," which, in his case, meant the working class.[9] My interest in his seminar, held in Trinity Term (mid-April to mid-June) 1972, must have stemmed from a dim awareness that social history might be worth looking into. How could I previously have been so oblivious to the appeal of this approach to history? When did I become aware of it? *The Journal of Social History* had published its first issue in 1967. It did not ignore Russia, as attested by early issues containing articles by Dan Brower, Peter Czap, Robert H. McNeal, and Reginald Zelnik, all Russianists. But these articles—and indeed most others that appeared in the journal—concerned peasants, women, and workers, subalterns all. As a self-identified Marxist, I should have been interested in them and indeed reading about them did appeal to me. But I had no training whatsoever in how to study them, never having been exposed to a real-live social historian until I met Tim at meals in the dining hall at St. Antony's, and then attended his seminar.

By this time, I had committed myself to a dissertation on Russia's "commercial-industrial class." My need to concentrate on this more elevated social category meant I had only the faintest awareness of an alternative movement within the discipline dedicated to giving voice to workers, women, and socialists all, which took shape just down the road from my living quarters. The History Workshop met at Ruskin College on Walton Street in Oxford's Jericho district under the benevolent guidance of Raphael Samuel (1934–1996). Born in London, a Jew, and an erstwhile Communist, Samuel might have served as my role model if I had gotten to know him any better. Once, after returning from my year in Moscow, I hosted in my Winchester Road flat several visitors attending the Workshop's annual meetings/festivals. These drew as many as a thousand devotees, but not me.[10]

As for the other "course," it never existed, at least not in a formal sense. It represented the ambition of my friend Mark (whose lawful given name was Roger Marcus) Harrison and me to steep ourselves in Marxism by meeting periodically with other St. Antony students (a.k.a. Junior Common Room members) at one or another's flat to discuss readings we had assigned ourselves. For a while, we constituted ourselves as a *Capital* reading group, then read some dependency theory (I think Andre Gunder Frank and Samir Amin). I learned the most from Ernesto Laclau (1935–2014) and Gavin Kitching, fellow graduate students who probably should have been identified as the instructors. Laclau would become one of the leading post-Marxists of the 1980s and, although not at St. Antony's, resided with his Argentine family and a maid or two on the same street where I lived. Kitching started out as an Africanist, then in the early 1990s turned successively to post-Soviet Russian agriculture, Ludwig Wittgenstein, and most recently, critiques of post-modernist thought, while also cranking out plays and crime fiction.[11]

My CV also contained a list of "papers presented." I still have in my possession a thirty-seven-page paper on "Class Consciousness in the Russian Nobility and Obligatory State Service (1689–1762)," the one in which Shukman "found much to criticize." It argued that Georg Lukács's definition of class consciousness could be applied to the Russian nobility of the eighteenth century. That, strictly speaking, the nobility did not constitute a class at all, but rather a social estate (*soslovie*), did not phase me. "Consciousness," the paper proclaimed at the outset as a kind of manifesto, "does not develop automatically; it emerges from the nexus of productive relations not as a predetermined product but as a phenomenon which influences, and is in turn influenced by, those relations." Harry Willets, for whom I wrote the paper, must have looked askance at this attempt to apply a Marxian lens to a precapitalist formation. Nevertheless, Harry recommended the paper for the biannual British Universities' Conference on Eighteenth-Century History. As for other papers, "The Russian Bourgeoisie in the First World War," which I presented at a conference on War and Society at the London School of Economics in March 1972, served as the fruit of a few months of reading and thinking about my future dissertation topic. "Strikes in Russia, 1914–17" came forth a month later and also adumbrated a thesis chapter.

I regularly attended seminars in the basement-level room of the college's old building. My notes indicate that scarcely a month into my first term, I heard a lecture by St. Antony's own Michael Kaser on "The Economics of Totalitarian Control." Kaser brought the breadth of his learning to the subject, observing, for example, that Diocletian's Rome and John Calvin's Geneva constituted "examples of pre-industrial attempts to centrally direct economies (in Europe)." He defined totalitarianism (idiosyncratically pronounced with the accent on the first syllable, just as he invariably put the accent on the second syllable when referring to "cap*it*alism") as "the attempt to reorient society to achieve a specific goal." Stalin had chosen the goal of industrialization, which he "accorded priority . . . not because of [any] inherent qualities but because some supreme priority had to be chosen," and because it served as "justification for Party dominance." Such an interpretation is just the sort of quirky thinking that thrived at St. Antony's. Another of Kaser's lectures on "Economic Development of Communist Countries" ranged historically from the Crimean War to Leonid Kantorovich's linear programming prescriptions.

In addition to Kaser's, I also heard a lecture on "Totalitarian Control of the State and Legal Institutions," but skipped another on "Totalitarian Control of Culture." Fortunately, the seminars didn't just focus on the damned "T word." Iring Fetscher, a guest from Goethe University Frankfurt, talked about "Three Historical Conceptions of Hegel and Marx." Oxford's own Bernard Rudden informed us about "Family Law in the Soviet Union," and Alec Nove came down from Glasgow to lecture on "The Changing Soviet Peasantry." Finally, one Moshe Lewin, recently appointed to a faculty position at the University of Birmingham, read a paper on "NEP, the 1930s, and the Politics of Economic Reform," the subject at the heart of the book he published several years later. At the time, I knew little about this combative individual with a twinkle in his eye. That soon would change.

Generally, I had no context in which to place these people or fully appreciate what they had to offer. Take the lecture on the radical pacifist Willi Münzenberg who had befriended Lenin in Zurich during World War I, joined the Spartacists in Germany after the war, founded International Workers Aid and led other Comintern-sponsored undertakings of the 1920s and early '30s, only to break with Moscow in the late 1930s and die in France while fleeing the Nazis in 1940. We learned about him from Babette Gross who delivered her lecture in heavily accented German. But did I know that Gross had been Münzenberg's common-law wife?[12] Did it dawn on me that I had not seen any other woman addressing the seminar in the entire two years I attended them? Unlikely. I don't mean to beat myself up about this, but instead to underscore how things that would become important in years to come and that today are so terribly obvious barely impinged on one's consciousness at the time.

When it came to choosing a thesis topic, my deliberations had little to do with these seminars or, for that matter, my advisor Harry Shukman. I initially came up with the idea of a political biography of Grigory Zinov'ev, one of Lenin's close comrades who led the Communist International and the Leningrad party organization during the 1920s before running afoul of Stalin. It is quite likely that the inspiration came from Stephen Cohen's project on Bukharin, Zinov'ev's comrade and sometime antagonist. However, the idea did not survive a conversation I had one evening after dinner in the Junior Common Room with Chimen Abramsky (1916–2010). Abramsky, who shared the same eastern European Jewish background as Moshe Lewin, did not have an official post at St. Antony's or any other Oxford college, but I often saw him engaged in serious conversation with both dons and students.[13] On this one occasion he must have asked me what I intended to write about, and so I told him. "Not worth the effort," he told me. "A scurrilous fellow." "Besides," he added, "you won't be able to get any archival material on him in Moscow." I don't remember what else he said but that sufficed. I needed to find another topic.

Fortunately, not long before this conversation, I had read George Katkov's *Russia, 1917: The February Revolution* (1967). Katkov (1903–1985) had taught at St. Antony's but retired a few years before I arrived. He epitomized the conservative historian who blamed the Freemasons, liberals, and Alexander Kerensky in particular for bringing down the old regime and paving the way for the hated Bolsheviks. His book contained a sufficient number of references to pique my interest in a civic organization created during the First World War by liberals to increase supplies to the army and not incidentally profits to industrialists. That organization, the war-industries committees (WICs), became my dissertation topic. Several things attracted me to it. First, nobody had bothered to write much about it, except for a few Soviet historians whose perspectives had to fit the predetermined Marxist-Leninist mold.[14] Second, archival material existed in abundance and because the topic did not extend beyond 1917, it could be accessible to foreign scholars. Third, studying an organization created by Russia's bourgeoisie—or commercial-industrial class, as I referred to them—to support the war effort appeared to have contemporary resonance. I can almost recite from memory the dissertation's opening paragraph:

> War is a terrible thing, but it is also a terribly profitable thing. It can bind a nation together by riveting attention on a foreign enemy; it can eliminate that enemy as a competitor for economic wealth; it can stimulate industries and new productive processes; and for all these reasons it can be an avenue of political power for those willing to serve it.

Finally, to promote cross-class collaboration, the WICs sponsored workers' groups, surely a doomed undertaking in the circumstances of growing class antagonisms and one worth exposing, I thought.

I therefore imagined indicting supporters of the war in Vietnam by demonstrating how an earlier pro-war effort backfired. As for the Menshevik-inclined workers' groups, I delighted in the prospect of demonstrating how they discredited themselves by associating with bourgeois politicians and industrialists, much as George Meany and other anti-communist labor union leaders were doing in the United States in the 1960s and '70s. Thus inspired, I set off on a research trip in December 1971 to Paris—Paris because its Bibliothèque de Documentation Internationale Contemporaine (BDIC) contained runs of newspapers from Russia for the years of the First World War, otherwise difficult to consult in those years before digitization, and because, well, it was Paris. I remember the trip fondly. My comprehension of French had reached its peak and so I felt perfectly comfortable interacting with people. I loved taking the train out to Nanterre, hotbed of student radicalism in May '68, and spending the whole day poring over the old, brittle pages of *Birzhevye vedemosti* (Stock exchange news), *Utro Rossii* (The morning of Russia), and other newspapers from World War I. The apartment where I stayed (courtesy of a fellow Antonian) so reeked with atmosphere, I imagined running into F. Scott Fitzgerald or Ernest Hemingway in the corridor.

I did fortuitously run into Moshe Lewin one day in the metro returning from Nanterre. I recognized him from his lecture at St. Antony's, introduced myself right there in the subway car, and earned an invitation to dinner in his apartment off the Place Pigalle. As I would discover later when visiting him in Philadelphia, Misha loved playing the gracious host, and he certainly charmed me. St. Antony's insularity—a vestige of the paramountcy of Oxbridge among English universities—had militated against me venturing to Birmingham where not only Lewin but also the economic historian R. W. Davies taught. Or maybe I simply felt that they would not be of much assistance because my topic concerned pre-Soviet Russia and they wrote about the 1920s and '30s (and even more contemporary history in the case of Lewin's soon-to-be published book).[15]

Six months later, on Midsummer Night's eve 1972, I arrived in Helsinki. The University of Helsinki's Slavonic Library (now part of the National Library of Finland) stood alone as the only such institution outside the Soviet Union that before 1917 had the right to receive every publication within the Russian Empire. Located in a gracious early nineteenth-century building just off the Senate Square, it contained riches I could not have imagined. These riches attracted quite a few American PhD students and young faculty. I joined them at lunch in the cavernous basement cafeteria or the one next door at Porthania, a sixties modern building serving Helsinki University's student population. There I met Leena Törmä, my future wife, and her friend Kaarina Timonen, both introduced to me by Stuart Grover. Then a junior faculty member in Ohio, Stuart also gave me the benefit of his experience on the IREX (International Research and Exchanges Board) program with the Soviet Union, the next step on my research agenda.

I spent the summer beavering away in the library, returning to Oxford (via an overnight cruise to Copenhagen and thence a flight to London) sometime in late August or early September. After a brief trip home to see my parents, I came back to Helsinki in late October by which time winter had set in. I want to pause here for a moment to comment on research travel. An essential part of most historical projects, it usually requires a lot of logistical planning and money. My failure

FIGURE 3.2 "I relied on my International Student Identity Card to obtain the lowest fare." This one I obtained in 1974, after leaving the Soviet Union.

throughout much of this memoir to mention sources of support is not because I didn't need and receive funding, but because my memory of the details is hazy, and documentation is lacking. Funding, though, rarely covered more than basics, guaranteeing a spartan regimen. In the case of this research travel, I relied on my International Student Identity Card to obtain the lowest fare, shared a room in a student dormitory with a young Israeli woman who came to Helsinki to study Finnish fabric design, ate a lot of *makkara* (Finnish sausage), and scrimped in every other way possible. That included walking out of downscale department store Anttila with a winter hat I didn't pay for. Over Christmas, Kaarina visited her parents in central Finland giving me the opportunity to move into the apartment on Alppikatu (Alps Street) that she shared with Leena, and that is how Leena and I became lovers.

In the meantime, I had applied to IREX. The application form, which I overdramatically described to Shukman as having been "devised by sadistic bureaucrats," required an "Autobiographical Sketch." My opening sentence confidently proclaimed that the origin of my interest in modern Russian history "quite simply is the belief . . . that the Russian Revolution constituted the most significant political event of the twentieth century." After identifying the war-industries committees as among the "quite outspoken opponents to the monarchy within the Russian bourgeoisie," I referred to my desire to "arrive at an understanding of their interrelationships with other elements in the supply network, with the military, with the government, and, of course, with labor." "Too often," I added sententiously, historians relied on "theories of spontaneity which . . . mask an unwillingness to hypothesize and test their hypotheses through meticulous research." Ye gods, did Katkov's conspiratorialism infect me? More likely, I strove to make the case "after almost two years of research in the United States and Western Europe" for doing archival research in Moscow.

While in Helsinki, I had an interview for IREX with a distinguished Russian historian from Stanford, in the lobby of a fancy hotel on Mannerheimintie, the city's main north-south thoroughfare. In the meantime, I began taking Russian conversational lessons from Maria Eskola, an elegant elderly woman who had emigrated to Finland during the Russian civil war, married a Finnish cavalry officer, and, after his death, settled into a comfortable apartment. Contrary to the stereotypical "White Russian" émigré, Madam Eskola's politics ran to progressive, and we got on very well. Several years later, I received a nice, chatty letter from her in which she mentioned her English literature class, the detective stories by a Swiss novelist she had devoured, and her impending visit to Rome, a first for her. "Lewis," she added, exhibiting maternal concern, "are you writing a book in order to become a professor and further your education? I hope that you and Leena will not forget your Russian." How could twenty-seven-year-olds ever truly appreciate the affection showered on them by their elders? I know I didn't.

Once we learned that IREX had accepted my application, Leena and I started making preparations for the momentous year in Moscow. First, we had to get married, a precondition for Leena to accompany me as per the straight-laced official US government policy of those days. As children of the sixties, we thought so little of the formality that a few days after she arrived in Oxford from Helsinki, Leena and I walked to the magistrate's office and, with Gaby and his new wife Sue as witnesses, raised our right hands as we swore the obligatory oath. The four of us then dined at a local restaurant. That summer, we lived with my parents. Leena started studying Russian with some assistance from me. These I remember as happy times.

In August, we flew to Moscow where, along with other American exchange students (*stazhery*), I received several weeks of excellent Russian-language instruction from the Preparatory Faculty/Department at Moscow State University (MGU). The IREX experience in those years fostered long-lasting friendships among fellow exchange students. In my case, Diane Koenker and Dan Orlovsky have proven lifelong friends. Marriages, by contrast, suffered—mine included. Thrown together in a tiny seven- by twelve-and-a-half-foot dorm room in the iconic MGU tower, and cut off from family except for the occasional letter and even more occasional phone call, couples often had a hard time adjusting and maintaining their equilibrium. To its credit, the Handbook of Information for American Participants (in the) Graduate Student/Young Faculty Exchange with the Soviet Union distributed to us before our departure contained useful advice about how to minimize the difficulties. But it also bore the marks of its time. Of its eight sections, the one on "spouses and families" seems the most antediluvian. Its advice to "accompanying spouses" addresses them in entirely gender-neutral terms. But the section on "wives and families remaining in the United States or relocating overseas" is all about "wives not accompanying their husbands" and "wives" who "should inform their husbands of the date on which they submitted their visa applications." Apparently, a wife could not be a *stazher* unaccompanied by her husband.

The second striking thing about the Handbook from the vantage point of 2019 is how varied were the items it deemed essential: electric frying pan and coffee pot, corkscrew, potholder, dishtowel, good serrated knife, paring knife, vegetable peeler, sponge, spatula—and that only covered the kitchen items. For clothing—an iron, spot remover, clothesline, et cetera. Inevitably, some of the advice proved useful and some did not. For instance, I never pursued the opportunity to use the bookbinding store "two blocks down the street from the big Pravda printing plant." Nor did I seek to mail out pre-'45 books, though I did try to take some with me on the train to Helsinki at the end of the ten months, only to get caught and have them confiscated. But we did frequent the foreign currency-only Beriozka store on Kutuzovskii Prospekt. We also shopped occasionally at the US Embassy's commissary, and when we did so, ate in the snack bar where I can still hear the waitress shouting to the cook behind the counter "*Alfredo, odin gamburger, pozhaluista*" (Alfredo, one hamburger, please).

Making the acquaintance of Soviet students on our floor—the sixth in Zone V—did not present much difficulty, although getting beyond superficialities in the face of mutual suspicions proved more challenging. Lara Putsella, a vivacious young woman with a devil-may-care attitude and a fondness for speaking rapid-fire, colloquial English, managed to overcome the obstacles and served as an entrée into life not only at the university but beyond. Thanks to her, we got tickets to see Iurii Liubimov's production of Fedor Dostoevsky's *The Gambler* at the avant-garde Taganka Theater. We listened to the gravel-voiced Vladimir Vysotskii's albums in her room, returning the favor by supplying her with American cigarettes. I also got to know Vadim Cherkassky, a mathematician who already had graduated and lived with his wife Irina in Maryna Roshcha, then a gritty neighborhood in the northern part of the city. The previous year, Vadim had befriended another American at Oxford, Dennis O'Flaherty, who supplied me with his telephone number. Vadim remains a good friend.

My experiences in Moscow differed significantly from those Sheila Fitzpatrick describes in her memoir. My Russian friends, more my age than of an older generation, neither revolved in high places nor associated with liberals or dissidents. I never felt myself nor was suspected of being a "spy in the archives" or anywhere else in the Soviet Union.[16] And I certainly did not attract the attention of the Central Committee of the Communist Party. The closest encounter I had with the kind of paranoia induced by the purges of the 1930s to which Sheila makes frequent reference happened when I delivered a few sketches by Oleg Prokofiev to his mother, Lina, the Spanish-born widow of Oleg's father, the composer Sergei. My Oxford friend Dennis, who knew Oleg, asked me to carry the sketches to Moscow and give them to Oleg's mother. Although in her mid-seventies, Lina struck me as a woman of great beauty. Before we sat down to chat, she turned the dial of the phone sitting on a stand by her sofa so that she could insert a toothpick into it thereby thwarting, so she thought, the efforts of the KGB to listen to our conversation. I thought this cautiousness excessive but did not know then that she had spent several years in the Gulag—evidently for trying to send money to her mother in Spain during or just after the war.

Rarely did I feel observed or the object of curiosity; most of the time when not scribbling in the library or the archives, I was the one doing the observing. Within a few days of the September 11 coup in Chile, Leena and I attended a performance at the university by Inti-Illimani, a very talented group of Chilean folk musicians. I noticed quite a few students weeping *before* as well as during and after the spirited performance. I could only assume they had invested considerable hope in the Chilean version of socialism and felt distraught at its brutal suppression. The event belied claims I would encounter later among Sovietologists that the younger generation in the Soviet Union had become cynical about socialism and politics in general. I also attended film showings at the university, a couple of which made strong impressions on me not so much because of the films themselves as the audience's reactions. Mikhail Romm's documentary *Ordinary Fascism* (1965) had a special screening at the university. The students I observed clearly did not miss the parallels Romm suggested through parody and irony between Nazism and Stalinism. The other movie, *Here the Horizons Are Quiet* (1972), about female border guards in Karelia during the Great Patriotic War, evoked open sobbing—even wailing—among many audience members both student-aged and older. The heavy ideological lifting the film had performed to bind wartime and postwar generations had succeeded, at least at this showing.

Had I noticed, though, that the Soviet Union had entered its period of "stagnation," the now common way of referring to the 1970s? The answer is no, but. The shortcomings I observed—many of which thrust themselves on me every day—I tended to attribute to Russia's historical "backwardness," the destructiveness of World War II, and/or the sacrifices necessitated by the Cold War. At the same time, the lack of evidence of ideological fervor among some Russian friends and acquaintances, their indifference to anything beyond their immediate circumstances, boded ill, I thought. As I wrote to Yves Charbit in May 1974 shortly before leaving the country, "Most of those things we know about the Soviet Union in the West—the configuration of the Politburo, the repression of intellectuals, space shots, clever diplomacy, excellent ballet—it's all quite irrelevant to people here for whom life is hard and only getting slightly better." "I must admit to considerable disillusionment," I added. No wonder John Bushnell's "The New Soviet Man Turns Pessimist," an article that drew on observations he made while working as a translator for Progress Publishers in Moscow that same year, resonated with me when I read it in the early 1980s. It still seems one of the best assessments of the period of late socialism in the USSR.[17]

Like other historians who went on the exchange program, I intended to do archival research, and in those days, that meant working on the Imperial period. To my knowledge, Sheila Fitzpatrick's experience of using archival material for a dissertation on the Soviet period had no parallel because, as she explains in her memoir, she had connections, determination, and a strong "sense of righteousness."[18] Indeed, even more senior scholars could not gain access. E. H. Carr's magisterial *History of Soviet Russia*, published in fourteen volumes between 1950 and 1977, did without Soviet archives. Because archives represented—and remain—the coin of the realm for historians, one typically pursued Soviet studies in the United States in a social science as opposed to a history department. Soviet history practically did not *exist* in the American academy when I went to graduate school. Looked at another way, the Soviet Union as a living historical subject—as opposed to a branch of political science—lasted less than two decades, from the mid-1970s until the USSR became "former." This brief span defined the generation of historians to which I belonged.[19]

By choosing a dissertation topic that culminated in the revolution, I did bump up against the limits of what Soviet authorities permitted in the way of archival access. In a letter generously responding to my request for advice about gaining permission to use archives, Alex Rabinowitch, then writing a book about the Bolsheviks coming to power in 1917, admitted that "because of the sensitive nature of my own research, I have never made a serious attempt to use Soviet archival materials." Permission to read material in the archives came suddenly and mysteriously from on high, as did its withdrawal. One submitted a research plan to the Foreign Section (Inotdel), worked out in advance with one's research supervisor. In my IREX application I had requested Vladimir Iakovlevich Laverychev as my supervisor, largely on the basis of a book he had published in 1967 on "the struggle of the Moscow bourgeoisie with the revolution."[20] Instead, I got Valerii Ivanovich Bovykin (1927–1998), whom I had indicated as my second choice.

Bovykin, a specialist on the history of foreign investment in tsarist Russia and Russian banks, suited me just fine. He had done research in Paris and struck me as both worldly and kind. My internship in Moscow coincided with his appointment as scientific secretary of the Institute of History.[21] Yet, he still taught at MGU and invited me to attend a seminar. There, one day, I found the students engaged in a discussion of a recently published monograph by an American economic historian on foreign entrepreneurship in Imperial Russia. But for the fact that they spoke Russian, we might have been at Indiana University or the University of Illinois instead of Moscow State.[22] When I returned to Moscow in 1981 to do more research, Bovykin had me over for dinner. Diane Koenker, who ran into him at a conference the next year in Paris, reported that he told her I had "been a great hit with his mother-in-law." Later, during the turbulent years of perestroika, younger Soviet historians, who pushed for a clean break with past compromises, identified Bovykin as a conservative. This may be. Yet, he remained well liked by his former students, many of whom populated academic institutes in the post-Soviet decades. In 2007 I discovered to my delight a group of them meeting as a seminar at MGU. I liken the encounter to coming across a tribe one had belonged to, but with which one had lost contact long ago by force of circumstances.

After I presented him with the research plan I had painstakingly typed up in Russian, Bovykin emended it with a very un-Soviet pink marker. He must have intended at least some of the changes to make the plan conform to standard bureaucratic language. Instead of "description of the dissertation," he wrote "plan of the dissertation," plan being an almost sacred word in the Soviet lexicon. Instead of my politically incorrect phrase about the "inadequacy of the state's mobilization and the founding of the war-industries committees," he inserted "the political crisis in Russia in 1915 and the organization of the war-industries committees"; instead of "large military-industrial concerns," he wrote "military industrial monopolies." Although, as I wrote in the final report to IREX, "I do not know how or why . . . permission was delayed for several weeks and then given," it is to Bovykin that I surely owe what archival access I did receive. Other *stazhery* waited longer and received less access due to the irresponsibility of their supervisors, gender bias, or some other factor.

When I fronted up to the building on Bol'shaia Pirogovskaia that housed the Central State Archive of the October Revolution (TsGAOR), I had little foreknowledge of what awaited me other than the horror stories of previous exchange students. Once in the archive, one did not get to consult any finding aid or inventory list (*opis'*) but had to rely on citations from Soviet publications and the good graces of the archive's staff. Soviet and Western researchers read materials brought to them in separate reading rooms. The woman who presided over foreigners rarely extended herself to assist us, spending an inordinate amount of time, as I crankily wrote in my final report, "on the telephone with her ailing mother." These and other peculiarities of archival research in the Soviet Union surrounded it with a mystique that inspired many tall tales even while it militated against questioning how the tsarist state's determination of what it deemed worth collecting shaped our research questions.

Soviet historiography also affected the questions we asked. Either we abjured their Marxist-derived categories (for example, employing "middle class" instead of "bourgeoisie," or "civil" in place of "bourgeois" society), or, as in my case, used them selectively in constructing our own narrative. But either way, we positioned our version of their country's past always conscious of the presence of their version. The teleology of the revolution proved more difficult to avoid. Everything before 1917 seemed to contribute in one way or another to the revolution; and if it didn't, well, then it didn't matter. Class occluded other forms of oppression. Despite its temporal proximity to the downfall of tsarism, the great Turkestan revolt of 1916 did not attract serious scholarship in the West until the 1990s. It still would be another decade before gender became "a useful category of historical analysis."[23]

The issues my dissertation addressed include some of little interest to anyone else then and of no interest now, but others that have since preoccupied scholars— and not only scholars. Among the former, the question of whether the war-industries committees significantly contributed to improving the supply of munitions and other materials to the army or merely got in the way did not even interest me, although of course I had to wade into, analyze, and make semi-coherent the details of contracts, their distribution, and fulfillment.[24] Whether if not for the war, the revolution (particularly, in its Bolshevik form) would have happened divided Soviet from most Western historians, but the heat generated by this issue started to dissipate even before the Soviet Union's end. Indeed, why the revolution happened at all ceased to be of any great interest after 1991 if not before. Until its centenary revived attention to the event, interest in the revolution persisted in a coterie of historians committed to parsing its details, which they spun out at annual meetings in England and in two or three panels at conventions of AAASS (American Association for the Advancement of Slavic Studies, the major organization of Slavicists in the United States, whose name changed to ASEEES, Association of Slavic, East European and Eurasian Studies, in 2010).

The centenary of the revolution occasioned an outpouring of commemorative activity. In Russia itself, the government did its best to ignore the event, but intellectual curiosity and the desire to reconnect with the country's past in an honest way proved irrepressible. To cite but one example, an enterprising journalist Mikhail Zygar assembled a tech-savvy team to launch the website "Project 1917." From November 2016 until January 18, 2018, the website provided daily updates from diary entries kept by those who witnessed and participated in the events exactly one hundred years earlier.[25] This real-time access to the revolution proved a boon to teaching about it, which I did for the last time in the spring of 2017. Elsewhere, the output ranged from intellectually stimulating to tendentious. "The Red Century" series published in *The New York Times* provided insight into the revolution's long-term global effects. Remarkably, at least some cast them in a positive light. Contrast that with the preponderance of publications that represented the Bolsheviks as nothing more than a criminal enterprise, the revolution as at best a "tragedy," and its long-term effects as nothing but dolorous. A new biography of Lenin slapped together for the occasion typifies this perspective.[26]

At the same time, some historians rose to the occasion. Tsuyoshi Hasegawa's *Crime and Punishment in the Russian Revolution: Mob Justice and Police in Petrograd* (Belknap Press, 2017) shed new light on a phenomenon previously given only cursory treatment. Many years earlier, I had visited Tsuyoshi ("Toshi") at his home in Santa Barbara, renewing our relationship that went back to the year we both spent at MGU. "Toshi, where is the struggle," I recall asking him as we sat in his sun-drenched living room with an orange tree outside, close enough to be picked from the window. It is good to see that Toshi did not need struggle to produce a high-quality work of history. Andy Willimott, a young British historian, refreshingly has interpreted the revolution as liberating for many urban-based youths who took advantage of its opportunities to refashion their lives in very practical ways.[27] And Diane Koenker, whose dissertation and first book concerned Moscow workers during the revolution, provided a brilliant restatement of what had animated her and others' projects long ago.[28]

For the past two decades, the dominant interpretation of the revolution viewed it as part of a "continuum of crisis" that began if not with the 1905 revolution then at least with 1914 and associated that crisis with "modernity."[29] Of what this modernity consisted remained in dispute. Some historians emphasized cultural angst provoked by the weakening of estate ties, industrialization, and even sexual emancipation; others stressed practices traced back as far as the Great Reforms of the 1860s such as increased reliance on technical expertise, the application of population statistics to governance, and attempts to apply universal scientific laws. The relationship between the war and revolution thus became less causal than fraternal, part of the same nexus of transformational modernity, which, so historians argued, extended into the early Soviet era.[30]

I had tried to establish a nexus between war and revolution, but of a different kind. Hard as it might be to imagine, when I wrote my dissertation, very few English-language works on Russia had waded into the war to analyze socioeconomic processes. Mine broke new ground in taking on as its subjects the commercial-industrial class, the core element in what Marxists refer to as the bourgeoisie. In a chapter devoted to the regulation of the war economy, I argued inter alia that "in Russia, where on the eve of the war, the state owned and controlled a larger share of the economic resources within its borders than other states within theirs," it adopted regulatory measures during the war in the least systematic fashion and to a lesser extent than elsewhere. I also argued that "the hidden hand of market forces was choking Russia to death," and "the war strengthened tendencies toward a command economy but had not produced a commander."[31]

Animated by a desire to indict the WICs as an organization of patriotic poseurs, my dissertation research ironically increased my respect for their leading lights: the brothers Pavel, Sergei, Nikolai, and Mikhail Riabushinskii—bankers, industrialists, Progressive Party politicians, and patrons of the arts; Aleksandr Konovalov, the Duma deputy who would become the Provisional Government's minister of trade and industry, and in exile, an accomplished pianist; and Aleksandr Guchkov, leader of the Octobrist Party, chairman of the central WIC and minister of war in the Provisional Government. I now find myself at least as curious about those elected to serve in the workers' groups, brainchild of Konovalov. Kuz'ma Gvozdev, president of the metalworkers' union who became chairman of the Petrograd workers' group and later served as the Provisional Government's last minister of labor, comes to mind.

Although I quoted extensively from their correspondence (internal memoranda, letters to various ministers) and stenographic reports of their speeches, my assessment of the dissertation in reading it over for the first time in decades is that it erred on the side of structural explanations, emphasizing determinism at the expense of acknowledging choice or human agency. In other words, I wrote like those "Soviet historians whose perspectives had to fit the predetermined Marxist-Leninist mold." Workers had attitudes or responded to situations en bloc based on their class positions vis-à-vis their employers. The commercial-industrial class, divided between a Moscow-based "domestic" faction and a more finance-capital oriented, internationally connected, St. Petersburg-based group, played its assigned role as the drama of war and revolution unfolded. And, "unfold" it did—like the opening up of a napkin to its full and predetermined size. I didn't do a bad job explaining why various "well-intentioned" objectives of the workers' groups—a network of urban and rural labor exchanges, a factory elder system, conciliation boards, et cetera—had failed.[32] But I never dreamed of asking myself how I knew what the intentions were, or why they mattered.

I also corrected to excess the record established by other historians. In lengthy footnotes, some nearly covering the entire page, I took on George Katkov's version of the story, describing it now as "puzzling" and "inaccurate," now as "mistaken" or "not the case," because "he has not seen the archives cited here."[33] This criticism emanated from genuine disagreement but also from trying to achieve what neophyte historians typically do: create legitimacy for themselves by demonstrating their faithfulness to the facts as well as their research and interpretive skills. Challenging statements by historians whose work I otherwise revered—such as Valentin Diakin (1930–1994) or Leopold Haimson (1927–2010)—now seem pedantic. I actually considered Diakin's book on the Russian bourgeoisie and tsarism in the war the best produced by a Soviet historian.[34] Haimson, the very same professor who had tried to persuade us would-be revolutionaries occupying Fayerweather Hall to stop our childish games, had written a groundbreaking article on growing workers' support for the Bolsheviks during the First World War.[35] He spent the winter ("Hilary") term of 1972 as a guest of St. Antony's College. Sitting at breakfast in the dining hall smoking his cigar, he cut an uncouth figure among the dons who shuffled in and out giving him unfriendly stares. We bonded as fellow New Yorkers, and, along with Shukman, he wrote in support of my IREX application.

Embarrassment at one's youthful follies comes easily with age. What cannot be gainsaid is the hard work I did to track down obscure publications and leads in archives located not only in Moscow and Leningrad, but also New York, London, and Helsinki. In the end, I had a defensible thesis, and in fact did defend it . . . twice—once orally toward the end of my ten-month stay in Moscow, and again, slightly more than a year later in Oxford. The Moscow defense, in Russian, occurred in the section (*kafedra*) on imperialism of MGU's history department. I should have known from the "Introduction to Daily Soviet Vocabulary," another of those informative items IREX supplied, that the *kafedra* would assign an official *opponént* to respond to my report. But either I hadn't read it or by March had forgotten, so that when Svetlana Voronkova, a student of Bovykin's, rose to give her assessment, it caught me by surprise. So much so, I could hardly follow what she had said—something about being within the school of "bourgeois objective historiography, like the esteemed E. H. Carr." Even then, I recognized this as praise, and belatedly expressed my gratitude when our paths crossed again in 2007.

In June, Leena and I boarded a train at Leningrad Station bound for Helsinki. I don't remember how we had located accommodation in advance of our arrival, but we did, at 14 Tehtaankatu (Factory Street), in the Eira district at the southern end of the city. The apartment had a loft for sleeping and a view of the sea from the large windows in the living room. During the day, Leena worked in a photoreprocessing plant and later for an academic journal, while I sat at a big blond wooden table and wrote my DPhil thesis. To break the monotony, I would take myself off to the Slavonic Library, which in the meantime had moved conveniently close to Tehtaankatu, sharing the building with the theological faculty of Helsinki University. I also enrolled in a Finnish class to learn my wife's native language. I did really well until, impressed by my progress, the teacher recommended I transfer to a more advanced class dominated by Swedish Finns seeking to perfect their second language. I thus went from being the best to the worst student and became so discouraged that I stopped going.

Sometime in March, toward the end of the long Finnish winter, I started going to the office where Leena worked, but after hours, to type my thesis on a first-class, red IBM Selectric typewriter. Her boss, Hannu Rautkallio, now a senior historian with many books to his name, deserves many thanks for permitting me to use the equipment. After having it copied and bound, I sent the thesis to Oxford and followed it several weeks later. My defense ("viva," from *viva voce*) took place on May 26, 1975. As per Oxford tradition, my advisor did not appear. In addition to Harry Willets, the economic historian Alec Nove arrived from Glasgow to examine the thesis. I much respected Nove's work. It seemed far less anti-Soviet than anything my professors at Columbia had published, to say nothing of the crowd at St. Antony's. Aside from his economic history of the USSR, he had drawn a lot of attention with his provocative essay, later published as a book, "Was Stalin Really Necessary?" which asked about the personal equation in the establishment of the Soviet planning system and the setting of targets impossible to reach.[36]

Formality prevailed at the occasion. We all wore full academic regalia, mine borrowed from another student. Shortly after we got underway, I suddenly had the urge to take off my cap, which, several sizes too large, swam on my head. "I hope nobody minds if I remove my cap," I nervously blurted out. "Not at all," Nove piped up. "And when you file your appeal against our decision, you can cite Harry Willets's brown shoes as also being in violation of the code." "Oh, no," I inwardly groaned. "Why would I want to appeal their decision unless they had rejected my thesis?" For the remainder of the viva, maybe an hour and a half in length, I gritted my teeth in defensiveness, responding with greater heat than warranted by the questions, and, speaking of heat, perspired profusely under my robes. I left the room ashen and wondering how I could bring myself to let Leena know I would have to rewrite the damn thesis. I waited in an adjoining room for what seemed an eternity, fully expecting the worst. Eventually, after receiving the examiners' report, Shukman bade me to his office. "Well done," he shouted, clapping me on the shoulder as I entered. "Congratulations!" Too dumbstruck to say anything but "thank you," I only later asked Harry why Nove had mentioned me appealing their decision. "Just a joke," he replied, "to try to put you at ease, I imagine."

CHAPTER 4

MELBOURNE AND LABOR HISTORY

Madam Eskola must have thought we had fallen off the face of the earth. "Write to me about Australia," she demanded on March 15, 1976, "and what there is besides kangaroos. I couldn't find your city—Bundoora—on any map, even in the library. Where is it?" A few months later, my mathematician friend Vadim wrote from Moscow asking, "How are you there in Australia, with your head down and your legs up? You have a different sky, different birds and animals, in general, you are living on another planet." Along with the text, Vadim included an illustration—a globe with a stick-figure image of him atop the USSR on the upper left holding a flag that says, "Long live American computers" while another figure below the lower right and upside down holds one that reads "Long live Russian history."

At the time, Vadim clocked in at the computer center of Stroibank, the bank that financed industrial, commercial, and residential construction, and he and his wife Irina were expecting their first child in August. The computer center, located in downtown Moscow near the main post office on Gorky Street, put him in close proximity to "many good stores with comparatively decent supplies [*neplokhim snabzheniem*]." "You, no doubt, will be surprised that I write about such strange things as 'supplies,'" he continued. "But our reality is not very pleasant. I recently read in *Literaturka* [short for *Literaturnaia gazeta*, the journal with a largely intelligentsia readership], a columnist's observation that 'gradually the word "to buy" is disappearing from use, and "to obtain" is taking its place.' This is why people have become nothing but consumers, spending too much time standing in lines, running around from one store to another . . . I am annoyed that I have less and less time to read good books."

When I read Vadim's letter, I might have felt sorry for him, but hardly gave it another thought. This new planet we had landed on in February 1976 consumed my life. Thanks to the information from Jack Gregory, chair of the History Department at La Trobe, I knew that Bundoora was an "outer suburb" of Melbourne. But otherwise, I didn't know much more about my new home than Madam Eskola did. I accepted the offer of a job at La Trobe basically because waiting for a better one had become intolerable. After two years in Moscow and Helsinki, moving in with my parents did not recommend itself. Never had the Long Island suburbs seemed duller and more confining. While Leena went to library school at the C. W. Post campus of Long Island University, I found a job as a stock boy at a local department store. I got along well with my workmates, most of whom had a high-school education, but the lack of prospects for academic employment depressed me. The market did not look promising and, as I had feared, the lack of a proper transcript and the understated letters of recommendation I assumed Shukman had written—not out of any ill-will toward me but because British academia knew no other mode of expression—didn't help.

"I may have to accept an interim research fellowship at one of the Russian centers (Harvard, Stanford, U. of Michigan) in the States," I naively reported to Yves Charbit in November 1974. If only. By April 1975, letters to me from history department chairmen contained statements that I quoted to Yves such as "our budget is stop, not go," and "we cannot afford to hire anyone in history." In fact, prospects for history PhDs hit an all-time low in the United States just as I began to search for academic employment. Between 1972 and 1973 and 1975 and 1976, American universities granted more than 1,100 doctoral degrees in history *each year*, while advertised job openings hovered between 620 and 780. According to an analysis for the American Historical Association, by the end of the 1970s, "only about 65 percent of those who received history PhDs in the 1970s had been able to find employment in the academy."[1] Would-be Russian historians faced more dire odds. Aside from the general retrenchment of area studies in the wake of the US defeat in Vietnam, the coming of détente saw a trailing off of the Cold War–induced expansion of the field. As Herbert J. Ellison, then director of the Kennan Institute for Advanced Russian Studies, wrote in 1984,

> Until recently, the general picture for both Russian and East European stud- ies has been bleak—diminishing financial support from private and public funds; severely limited opportunities in the academy and elsewhere for Ph.D. specialists . . . and a steady reduction of academic positions in many social science departments where places vacated by Russian specialists were claimed for other purposes.[2]

I keenly remember how bitter I felt when the State University of New York at Gen- eseo turned down my application for one of the few available positions in the field.

The law of supply and demand, economists insist, eventually reduces gluts by curbing overproduction. But what to do in the meantime? These days, the surfeit of PhDs created not so much by "overproduction" as by cutbacks in expenditures on unprofitable departments in the humanities has led to a burgeoning market in the precariat, academic proletarians working as part-time, non-tenure track adjunct professors. They gravitate to major cities with large numbers of academic institutions and spend inordinate amounts of time and money on the road between them teaching a class here, a class there. I should know because I have a son with a PhD in art history doing just that, and his sense of betrayal keenly reminds me of what I felt a few years before he entered the world.

Just when the offer from La Trobe arrived, I joined a project headed by the dean of the library school at C. W. Post. Nasser Sharify, an Iranian, had received a commission from Tehran to produce a blueprint for the Pahlavi National Library. He hired Leena and me along with four or five others to work with consultants from around the world. We edited their drafts on all manner of things—the architecture of the buildings, collection policy, storage, and staffing—working in a small office building rented for the purpose. Munificent funding for the enterprise meant Sharify could be generous with compensation; I even remember him asking what I thought I should be paid. Camaraderie among the staff could not have been better, and the entire experience proved enjoyable. Did I have any qualms about working on a venture designed to enhance the prestige of the shah, whose regime had grown increasingly repressive? Yes, I did. Did I try to rationalize it to myself? Again, yes. After all, I did not participate in the building of a military installation or some plaything for the idle rich, but a national library. Surely Iranians deserved one too. Such did I imagine the technical intelligentsia and other "third element" personnel associated with the WICs rationalizing their participation in an organization dedicated to improving the war effort and then deciding to work for the fledgling Soviet government after 1917.

I weighed the offer from La Trobe. On the one hand, it would disrupt Leena's pursuit of a library science degree; on the other, I had not received any other offers, and who knew how long it would take for another one to come my way? Besides, it would be an adventure. I sought the advice of Diane Koenker, who came up from Princeton to discuss the matter with me. Diane, who I think already had started a position at Temple University, advised me to go. As I would do more than once in the future, I took her advice.

It did not take me long to appropriate to my own circumstances the "tyranny of distance," the phrase used by the historian Geoffrey Blainey to describe what British settlers and other European migrants to Australia felt in the nineteenth century about their new home.³ I described it to Yves in a letter from July 1977 as "the gnawing sense that no matter how pleasant life is here, this is not where things happen," adding that "the fact we are not natives and that I am in a field which makes me something of an oddball . . . heightens this awareness." "To be sure," I went on, "the tyranny is not as great as it probably would have been ten or twenty years ago . . . Australia has made rapid strides in the last decade in becoming more cosmopolitan . . . breaking down the Anglo identification of most Aussies." The isolation seemed worse in retrospect. About ten years after I had repatriated to the United States, a graduate student responded to the news that I had spent seven years Down Under with the exclamation, "Wow, and that was before e-mail."

But to return to Vadim's letter, only after Mikhail Gorbachev identified the 1970s with the period of "stagnation" did I have a framework for understanding his complaint. By the mid-1970s the upward trajectory in the "supply" situation had flattened, but expectations of improvements had not. Vadim endured those years of stagnation along with everyone else, but when his mother and brother emigrated to California in 1983, he and his wife decided to join them. Irina received permission to depart with their daughter Alla but not Vadim. The authorities told him that his knowledge of computers included state secrets that barred him from leaving. The family faced an agonizing decision—give up the chance of a lifetime or split up at least temporarily. They chose the latter option. Compounding Vadim's misery, the security organs treated his application to leave as evidence of disloyalty, resulting in dismissal from his job and the impossibility of being hired in his field. He thus became a "refusenik," an unenviable category referring to Soviet Jews placed in limbo.

In the meantime, his marriage having frayed, Vadim met and fell in love with Lida, a Russian (that is, non-Jewish) woman. When I met her a few years later, they were living with their infant daughter in a spacious apartment just off Smolensk Square opposite the Ministry of Foreign Affairs. Lida worked in the reception office (*priemnaia*) of the Supreme Soviet, responding to letters that grew increasingly desperate as the planned economy started to unravel. Vadim had acquired an English bloodhound ("Sir Percival," or "Perce," for short), whom he took for walks along the Moskva River embankment to the astonished stares of passersby. To make ends meet, Vadim tutored students in math, prepping them for MGU's entrance exam. But he sorely missed his older daughter and his mother. With perestroika, it became possible for him to leave the Soviet Union, but this meant another dilemma because Lida refused to abandon her aged father. The plan called for her to follow Vadim with their daughter, but this never happened. And that is how Vadim found himself in California estranged from two wives and two daughters. The story has a mostly happy ending, which is that after a second divorce, Vadim met and married an affectionate and omnicompetent Filipino nurse. They live in Walnut Creek, CA and Vadim teaches math at a community college.

I spent seven-and-a-half years at La Trobe University. A relatively new institution, La Trobe attracted many academics from abroad, particularly the United States. Strangely, I spent little time with any of them outside the university. My closest friends came from Britain and Canada. Each had arrived several years earlier and, as is typical of how migrants integrate into their host country, helped me learn the ropes. Barry Carr, one of several Latin Americanists in the history department, had married an Australian woman and had every intention of remaining in the country for his entire career. Gordon Ternowetsky, a sociologist, came from Winnipeg with his wife Carroll. They threw themselves into the Aussie lifestyle, going so far as to buy some property down the Mornington Peninsula where they would spend weekends "in the bush." Leena and I first met them, ironically, at a Fourth of July Bicentennial dinner hosted by an American.

I look at my time at La Trobe as an extended apprenticeship in the history profession. I never taught a single class as a graduate student at Oxford, yet another negative factor in my search for academic employment. At La Trobe, I taught not only modern Russian history, but also more specialized courses on "Leninism and Stalinism," "The Social Bases of Stalinism," and "Soviet Society through Literature" (Aleksandr Blok, Vladimir Mayakovsky, Isaac Babel, Boris Pil'niak, Evgenii Zamiatin, Mikhail Zoshchenko, Mikhail Bulgakov, Iurii Olesha, Valentin Kataev, Pil'niak again, Nadezhda Mandelshtam, Anna Akhmatova, Aleksandr Solzhenitsyn, and Vladimir Maksimov). I also directed seminars on peasants ("cross-culturally"), and "the transition from feudalism to capitalism."

This last course, according to the syllabus, explored "the appropriateness of different *units of analysis* such as mode of production, social formation, world system, and class struggle"; "how concepts such as feudalism and capitalism originate and evolve"; and "the implications of an uncritical application of concepts defined by their western European origin to other settings." Its indebtedness to works I recently had read by Immanuel Wallerstein (whose graduate course in sociology I had taken at Columbia), Rodney Hilton, and Andre Gunder Frank should be obvious from the very verbiage I employed. Alas, so too is a tendency toward dogmatism. For example, I listed as an additional objective "an examination of the historical roots of the dissatisfaction with non-Marxist conceptualizations of feudalism and capitalism." "Why," the syllabus asked, "are such terms as 'social formation' preferred to everyday concepts such as 'society'?" Did it ever occur to me that not everyone had such a preference?

The course on "Leninism and Stalinism" reveals something else—a budding, though limited, desire to get beyond the politics of the Kremlin to explore Soviet life in all its messy complexity. The syllabus advertised week 9 as devoted to "Stalinism as a Way of Life." "Virtually every aspect of Soviet society," it read, "was transformed during the years of Stalin's leadership. Some have argued that this constituted the real revolution, a revolution in the way people lived, what their relations with other Soviet citizens were, etc.; others see these . . . changes as counter-revolutionary, as a step backwards from the 'advances' made . . . after 1917." At the time, I must have inclined toward emphasizing the negative—that "everyday Stalinism," to borrow Sheila Fitzpatrick's term, represented the triumph of counterrevolution. For I assigned Trotsky's *Revolution Betrayed*, which presented the most jaundiced view of this way of life. But I still evidently considered politics paramount and social processes derivative. Some twenty years later, when preparing the collection of documents I had assembled with Andrei Sokolov for publication by Yale University Press, I chose as the title *Stalinism as a Way of Life*. Not remembering that I had used the very same formulation in a course I taught at La Trobe, I now gave it an entirely different twist.

La Trobe's History Department boasted a large and diverse, though mostly young, faculty. Every department has its factions and ours proved no exception. To our credit, the factions cleaved around orientations instead of periods of history or personalities. The Marxists included Steve Niblo (1941–2008) and Barry Carr, both Latin Americanists, and Tom Spear, an Africanist. We occasionally gathered as a reading group to parse *Capital* with Sheila, Tom's wife and a non-academic, who outdid all of us with the perspicacity of her observations. The department's more numerous "ethnogs," as we playfully called devotees of Clifford Geertz's *The Interpretation of Cultures* (1973) and Greg Dening's *Islands and Beaches* (1980), included Inga Clendinnen (1934–2016), Rhys Isaac (1937–2010), Bronwen Douglas, and June Philipp.[4] Only my fractious identification with Marxism prevented me from taking advantage of their presence and learning more from them than I did. Inga, a woman of great intellect and energy who would have a splendid career as a historian and public intellectual, wrote on Aztec culture and contact with Europeans.[5] Rhys, a genial South African, won the Pulitzer Prize for history in 1983 for *The Transformation of Virginia, 1740–1790*.

As the department's only Russianist, I might have made greater efforts to establish connections with others in Melbourne who had similar interests, but generational, cultural, and disciplinary differences discouraged frequent contact. At the same time, in the absence of native Russian speakers and readily available recordings, my linguistic skills withered. This double exile—from my native country and from anything reminiscent of the country to whose history I had devoted my career—took its toll but also strangely liberated me to pursue whatever topics took my fancy in whatever way I chose.

For example, in the research for the dissertation I had come across the recruitment of Chinese and Korean "coolies" to replace coal miners called up by the army during World War I. Chinese? Koreans? I had no idea that migrants from northern China and the Korean peninsula had been crossing the Russian border on a regular basis. I really knew very little about that Far Eastern part of the Russian Empire, so why shouldn't I pursue the paths of these migrant laborers, gold miners, and market gardeners? Nobody cautioned me about engaging in Orientalism, a term unavailable until the publication of Edward Said's book by that name in 1978.

Aside from curiosity about a far-off past in a far-away part of the world, I also responded to a contemporary stimulus. In 1974, the second installment of Nikita Khrushchev's memoirs had appeared in English translation. I focused on the close of a chapter on Soviet relations with China in which Khrushchev mentions a conversation he had in the Kremlin with Edouard Daladier, the former French prime minister. Daladier, en route home from a visit to China, asked Khrushchev whether in light of the progress he had witnessed, the Yellow Peril worried the Soviet leader. "Frankly, the question took me aback, and I rebuked him sharply: 'I should tell you, Mr. Daladier, that we . . . don't discriminate among people according to the color of their skin.'" This section of the chapter is titled "Is There a Yellow Peril?" and it concludes with Khrushchev musing that if old Daladier had "lived long enough to see what's happened in our relations with China . . . he would have claimed that he, a bourgeois leader, was right." But Nikita Sergeevich adds, "it's not a 'Yellow Peril' which threatens the Soviet Union—it's the policies being conducted by Mao." Earlier in the volume Khrushchev refers to a proposal put forward in 1954 by a visiting Soviet delegation to Beijing. The delegation, which included Khrushchev himself, sought to overcome a labor shortage in Siberia by suggesting "a million or more Chinese workers be sent . . . to help us take advantage of the vast timber resources there." At first, according to Khrushchev's account, Mao demurred; subsequently, though, the two sides reached an agreement and some 200,000 Chinese laborers arrived, performed their labor, and returned home. Soon, "the Chinese themselves began pressing us to import more workers," Khrushchev claims. And then, "What had the Chinese been up to? I'll tell you: they wanted to occupy Siberia without war. . . . They wanted to make sure Chinese settlers in Siberia outnumbered Russians."[6] In short, another Yellow Peril.

So, innocent of professional advice, I proceeded to gather travelers' accounts from the late nineteenth and early twentieth centuries, availed myself of whatever

Russian contemporary sources I could find in the University of Melbourne library, ordered others on international interlibrary loan, and pieced together the story— but without acknowledging any relevance to more recent history, including that recounted in Khrushchev's memoirs. Why not? Because nobody advised me that making this connection could enhance the article's worthiness. My assumption to the contrary stemmed from the fallacy of scholasticism. I do not recall why I decided to send "Another Yellow Peril" to *Modern Asian Studies*, a venerable if stuffy British journal, but when I eventually received word of its acceptance, I experienced much pleasure.[7] My fondness for the article has only grown with the years. I admire the seamless combination of conventional political history and labor history, the recovery of information about Chinese institutions, and the argument that however much Russian settlers and businesses depended on Chinese migrants, they did not want them. Currently, the analogies with laborers from Central America migrating to the United States seem terribly obvious, but not so in the 1970s.

And then, in a pattern that would repeat itself in the early years of my career, I moved on—from *Modern Asian Studies* to *The Journal of Religious History*, where I published a slimmer article on "Peasant Disorders and the Myth of the Tsar: Russian Variations on a Millenarian Theme."[8] Inspired by my reading of Daniel Field's *Rebels in the Name of the Tsar* (1976), a fascinating excursion into how both tsarist officials and the revolutionary intelligentsia tried to manipulate peasant naïve monarchism, I wanted to get at the substantive reality of peasant belief. I read all I could about millenarianism before reaching the conclusion that peasants' "social-utopian legends" reflected their longings for emancipation. Such longings, often refracted through Orthodox Christian motifs, generated sectarian movements that I deemed millenarian. How, I now wonder, could I have assumed the capacity to know what "the peasants" really thought?

From a bowdlerized anthropological reading of religious history, I careened to economic history. Through Eric Jones, who taught economics and economic history at La Trobe from 1975 until 1994, I made the acquaintance of Malcolm Falkus, then spending a term as a visiting professor. Falkus, whose slim book *The Industrialisation of Russia, 1700–1914* (1972) I had found useful in teaching, mentioned to me the importance of the international grain trade to Imperial Russia's economic fortunes and even the growth of its cities. The idea of exploring this connection—of establishing causal links between grain exports and the growth of port cities—excited me for two reasons, I think. One had to do with the popularity of cliometrics, that is, the application of econometric techniques to historical processes, and my desire to connect with something new in the discipline. The other, more personal reason and the exception to the lack of interest I had in retracing the lives of my antecedents is that my paternal grandfather, Louis, originated from Odessa, the major grain exporting city on the Black Sea.

I thus began the research by reading whatever I could find on Russia's Black Sea port cities. British consular reports, held on microfilm at the Melbourne Uni library, proved extremely valuable. Myriad other sources I obtained in Helsinki in the winter of 1977–1978 and in the United States the following winter. Many proved deadly dull but some contemporary journalists' and travelers' accounts compensated. My heart would sing when I came across an observation such as, "in society even the women after normal greetings and meteorological observations turn the discussion to wheat." I counted every *chetvert* (a long obsolete Russian unit of weight) of wheat, barley, rye, and maize annually exported from Odessa, Nikolaev, or Kherson to France, Britain, Germany, and elsewhere, which I laboriously recorded on foolscap paper. I calculated numbers of enterprises, schools, workers, and Jews; chased down the global spread of grain elevator technology from its origins in Buffalo and Chicago; followed the spread of railroad lines across New Russia (a.k.a. Ukraine); and, when it came time to submit the article for publication, prepared tables, a graph, and a map that went into the appendices. The map (of South Russian ports and the grain trade 1880–1913) I obtained from an unpublished paper by Falkus, one of several kindnesses he showed me.

"The Odessa Grain Trade: A Case Study in Urban Growth and Development in Tsarist Russia" appeared in the spring 1980 issue of *The Journal of European Economic History*, a well-regarded publication of the Banco di Roma that—unusually for academic journals—paid contributors.[9] My only disappointment came from the fact that all the labor—and financial resources—expended on the research did not result in a book. A book is what I had had in mind when I applied in 1978 to the Australian Research Grants Committee (ARGC) to support research on "The Grain Trade and Economic Management in Russia, 1861–1914." Still, running to almost forty printed pages, the article represented, as I claimed in my report to the ARGC's secretary, "a substantial contribution to our understanding of patterns of urban growth and development in pre-revolutionary Russia." It propounded a simple argument—that the grain trade structured Odessa's growth and development, dictating where roads and railroad terminals, warehouses, port facilities, and other buildings would be located and providing the revenue that financed municipal services.

The most important lesson I learned from doing this article—and the reason it did not get expanded to book length—is that I should not pursue economic history any further. I could employ the categories and sling the data, but I could not develop a fresh perspective. It reminded me of high school mathematics: I could apply the formulae to solve assigned problems, but I had no ability to apply them to other kinds of problems. I rationalized my weakness by deciding that cliometrics was a bit of a con: it only heeded what could be counted, which led to the fallacy of assuming that what counted was what could be counted.

Reading over the article now, the passage that leaps out at me reads:

> Perhaps most importantly . . . the grain trade determined the structure of population according to occupation and sex. Aside from fortunes amassed by the major exporters, grain provided a means of livelihood for thousands of agents, commissioners, brokers, weighers and petty tradesmen, many of whom journeyed to the countryside in the summer and autumn to arrange contracts, buy up surplus stocks and sell their wares. It also attracted an even larger contingent of drivers, balers, bag stitchers, port and construction workers whose daily pay rose and fell depending on the size of stocks in the store houses and the price which wheat fetched. Between April and November as many as 50,000 peasants most of them male entered the city to work in these capacities. Those able to afford the expense stayed in basement flats or lodging houses. Others slept in the catacombs carved out of the limestone quarried for construction, or under the open sky. They frequented the taverns situated around the port and the prostitutes whose services were also in demand from merchant seamen.[10]

This resembled not so much economic as social history. Aside from substituting "gender" for "sex" in the opening sentence, I would write the passage no differently now. Curiously, it adumbrates the long-term trajectory of my career. The list of professions and occupations anticipates the labor history I would spend the next decade writing. The concentration on one particular commodity would recur in my work on the automobile. The 50,000 peasants who entered Odessa would appear again in larger numbers as migrants to the city in more recent work.

Not long after the article appeared, I began revising my Oxford thesis. That some four years elapsed before I took up this task can only be explained by my obliviousness to what the profession expected of recently minted PhDs. Nobody took me aside to suggest that my promotion and tenure depended on "the book," probably because at La Trobe they didn't. People of my generation may sometimes carp about mentoring of junior scholars as an unnecessary indulgence, but my experience suggests quite the contrary. I have no recollection of having contacted Cambridge University Press, but the statement in Archie Brown's letter to me of

May 2, 1980, that that publisher's editorial board had decided "not to publish your thesis as a book" means that somehow it got there. How he knew about it puzzles me still. Brown, who had joined the faculty at St. Antony's in 1971, also informed me that he had become editor of a new series Macmillan was publishing in association with the College. "While obviously I cannot promise a positive verdict," he added, "if you would like us to consider your thesis as a possible book in this series, could you please write to me at once by express mail." Writing back a few days later, I laid out prospective revisions and a timetable.

I much appreciated the encouragement I received from Archie Brown and later Michael Kaser, but the process of getting the book into print proved more complicated, slower, and less satisfying than I expected. The revisions did not amount to much. After receiving anonymous readers' reports, I wrote an introductory chapter, which, in the thrall of E. P. Thompson, I called "Russian Industry and the Making of a Russian Industrial Bourgeoisie." And, between the final chapter on "The Challenge of Revolution" and the epilogue detailing what happened to the war-industries committees after the October Revolution, I inserted a conclusion. This emphasized the mutually destructive results of the rivalry between tsarist bureaucrats jealous of their authority and the "industrial bourgeoisie" aspiring to translate economic into political power. As I argued in impeccably Marxist terms,

> This was not a matter of irresponsibility or treason, as each side accused the other both before and after the revolution. The state was not "blind" as Riabushinskii had alleged shortly before the war; it was structurally and ideologically incapable of legitimating national bourgeois interests. Neither were the people "orphaned." They became increasingly restless with the rule of their "Little Father," and, having brought about his downfall, refused to accept the bourgeoisie as their guardians.[11]

That I might have made more extensive revisions is undeniable. Hans Rogger, a professor of history at UCLA whom I had gotten to know when he spent a term at St. Antony's, thought I should "expand the book to make it a more general study of economic mobilization in Russia . . . and the politics of the war years." Do I wish I had taken Hans's advice about the revisions? Yes, but impatience, inherent to my nature and particularly so in my youth, impeded my judgment. I also lacked ready access to additional sources, already had embarked on research of a different nature, and therefore doubted I could pull it off.

So, at Macmillan's insistence, I arranged for joint publication with St. Martin's Press in the United States, and duly received Macmillan's proposed contract in

March 1982. The contract, I was astonished to see, limited the work to "not more than 256 pages," far less than I had anticipated. I immediately rang the editor, Tim Farmiloe, who reassured me that having discussed the matter "with our Production Manager, Mr. Bathe, and in the circumstances, we are prepared to extend the length from 256 to 320 printed pages." Then came the technical concerns—US as opposed to British spellings; appropriate daisy wheels for "word-processed camera-ready copy," and other now technologically obsolete arrangements. On a letter I received from Bathe dated June 18, 1982, I scribbled "corrections received. Will send on or about 25/2/83."

In his biography of E. H. Carr, Jonathan Haslam reports that Carr completed his manuscript of *The Romantic Exiles* by Christmas 1932, sent it to his publisher (Gollancz) on January 20, 1933, and received the printed copy on March 27 of that year. Carr's next book, a biography of Marx, sailed through with equal if not more impressively rapid dispatch: "By early March 1934 the first proofs of the Marx biography had arrived; and, at a pace that publishers now seem to find impossible even to approximate with high technology, it appeared in the bookshops in May."[12] Haslam's "now" referred to the late 1990s. My book reached me not in February, but in October 1983, two months after I had left Australia. That I grew impatient and frustrated by the delay is suggested by a draft of a letter to Macmillan's editor:

> I regrettably must write to you again seeking information about when I will receive the author's copy of my book and its date of publication [then a sentence crossed out followed by " . . . "]. The multiple delays which have beset the production of the book have caused me considerable distress and are now proving to be something of a professional embarrassment. I do not feel that I have made undue demands on Macmillan and if you are at all concerned about its good name, you ought to do everything possible to expedite this matter.

After all the hassles, the red, clothbound, camera-ready-copied item I held in my hands on that October day of 1983 gave me more relief than gratification.

From the distance of thirty-five years, it is difficult to know if my experience typified the vagaries of academic publishing at that time, though I suspect it did. Certainly, I laid it on thick by claiming the delays had caused "professional embarrassment." Unlike so many junior professors in the United States, my job security, that is, tenure, did not depend on "the book in hand." La Trobe already had promoted me to senior lecturer, the equivalent of associate professor in the US system, the year before the book appeared. The fact that my letters went to faceless *Brits* may partly explain their combative tone, a combativeness fueled by both my New York radical persona and absorption in the seven years I had spent Down Under of a certain chip on the shoulder toward the ex-colonial power. But that does not excuse their rudeness.

I have saved seven reviews of the book. *Russian Review*'s described it as "well written" and a "real contribution," but suffering from "a failure to develop certain themes" and having "a rather narrow understanding of political developments and issues." The review also claimed that the book treated the economic, political, and social dimensions of mobilization "all too separately." The reviewer in the *American Historical Review* considered it "a pity that the description and analysis of their role in the February Revolution itself was not developed even more." The more specialized journal *Technology and Culture* described the book as "fascinating," but managed to complain that "more emphasis could have profitably been given to . . . postwar reconstruction efforts." As with so many other books, the reviews read like palimpsests of the reviewers' own work or interests. A historian reviewing the book for *Soviet Studies* cited the book as providing "yet another proof that the Empire was not viable, and that revolution was inevitable," but also, and "more interesting[ly] . . . [proving] that the failure of the liberal revolution in March was also unavoidable." I didn't realize I had expressed myself in such categorical terms, but the last line of this review floored me and still seems risible: "An analysis of the secondary causes of the Bolshevik Revolution is a useful exercise but it lacks the real drama of the revolution itself." The book received a warmer reception from *Slavonic and East European Review*, but not as warm as in *The International History Review*. There, in contrast to the complaint in *Russian Review*, the book was said to "reveal an acute awareness of the interplay between politics and economics." "After reading Siegelbaum's analysis," the reviewer "inclines to the view that Moscow's 'liberal patriots' simply dressed profits and unregulated free enterprise in the imperial flag." I recount the less than stellar reception of my first book not to carp, but to suggest that the degree of one's success in this (or any other) profession depends less on the immediate approval of more senior gatekeepers than one's own willingness to learn and determination to do better the next time.

The front matter of the book described me as "a Senior Lecturer in History at La Trobe University . . . engaged on a study of Soviet workers in the 1920s and 1930s." For how long had I been so engaged? I remember being struck at the Second World Congress on Soviet and East European Studies, held in Garmisch-Partenkirchen, Germany in early October 1980, by how many other young scholars had begun to tackle topics on Soviet workers of those decades. John Russell, a working-class bloke from England, gave me a copy of his paper on shock brigades. I also met Don Filtzer, Vladimir Andrle, Francesco Benvenuti, and others—a whole collective, it seemed. I gave some sort of paper on the Russian bourgeoisie's vision of the future—a future never to be realized, for sure—but my interest already had turned toward workers. Not workers in Imperial Russia, but after the revolution, in the making of the Soviet Union, and particularly its industrialization drive under Stalin.

This represented two great turns—one toward Soviet history, as opposed to the history of Russia before the Bolshevik Revolution, and the other toward social history. Credit the great E. P. Thompson with providing inspiration for the latter turn. I mean not only *The Making of the English Working Class*; but several of his articles; his anti-war activism; the set of lectures he gave at Stanford University in the early 1980s reconstructing and reflecting on the brief life of his brother, Frank, which later appeared as *Beyond the Frontier*; and even *The Poverty of Theory* (1978), his angry and brilliant, but flawed and somewhat scurrilous attack against the French philosopher Louis Althusser. To encounter Thompson now, I think, is no less important and exciting than when I first did back in the late 1970s. I have taught several of his works repeatedly throughout my career and find students easily grasping the basic democratic decency of his outlook. The more distant in time and experience they are from "the poor stockinger, the Luddite cropper, the 'obsolete' hand-loom weaver, the 'utopian' artisan, and even the deluded follower of Joanna Southcott," whom Thompson so famously evoked and declared his intention to rescue "from the condescension of posterity," the more they are apt to appreciate these people's magical return to life in his prose.[13]

What might be a little more difficult for undergraduates to fathom is that Thompson rescued those "obsolete" folks not only from condescension but also from their transformation into numbers, patterns, tendencies, and other abstractions favored by economic historians of the 1950s and '60s, as well as continental Marxists at whom Thompson later took aim for their affinity for structures. It has become a cliché to assert that he gave "agency" to the past's ordinary people, thereby inaugurating the "new social history," but that does not make it any less true or significant. Thompson championed these people to the extent that though doomed, the causes they advanced gave them the hope and dignity of which their social betters seemed determine to rob them. His sympathy even extended to their religious practice—"even" because Marxists had long lamented the opiate-like disorientation (or to use the condescending phrase associated with Communists, the false consciousness) it bred among workers. Methodism may have contained an "incredible mumbo-jumbo" of "Hebrew genealogies, anathemas, and chronicles," but E. P. recognized that "the working-class community injected into the chapels its own values of mutual aid, neighbourliness and solidarity. . . . Here and there texts would spring to the eye, applicable to almost any context."[14]

The remarkable thing about Thompson's work is its perennial freshness. I recently read Joshua Clover's *Riot, Strike, Riot*, an analysis over the long term of dominant forms of protest correlated with changes in dominant forms of exploitation.[15] Clover frequently cites Thompson's work—"The Moral Economy of the English Crowd" more so than *The Making*—quoting at length to situate the transition from marketplace to workplace-based protests. But beyond the substantive dimension, the sheer bravado with which E. P. calls up his actors, puts them on the stage, and describes the action both takes one's breath away and at the same time inspires.

Of course, an enormous difference exists between making a class—a process that occurred in England between the French Revolution and the onset of Chartism—and making a socialist revolution. Yet, thanks to Thompson as well as the political currents swirling through much of the world in the 1960s and '70s, a cohort of recently minted PhDs with training in Russian history set their sights on applying the lessons of the new social history to the 1917 Revolution. They did not all agree about how Russian working-class formation and militancy "happened" (to use a Thompsonism), but they all told a Marxian story of experience of oppression leading to protest and higher levels of class and political consciousness. This literature epitomized what Ron Suny and I would refer to as the reinvigoration of labor history, which, as we observed, "shared in a general optimism about the political relevance of recovering experiences of earlier struggles."[16]

What happened to that class after the October Revolution? According to the standard Soviet narrative, it became the class in power, assailed by all manner of counterrevolutionary, bourgeois forces but triumphant over all of them. This line never persuaded practicing historians in the West, leastwise those who had caught the Thompsonian bug. Bolshevik betrayal, which some thought an appealing explanation, did not satisfy me either. In a survey of Western writing about Soviet working-class and labor history that I published in 2006, I tried to identify the key questions and answers submitted by my generation of labor historians.[17] The Thompson-inspired observation that Soviet workers participated in their own making as well as that of the Soviet Union, its work practices, culture, and institutions trumped all other explanations. They too needed to be rescued—from both the dismissiveness of an older generation of Western Sovietologists for whom only decision-makers in the Kremlin mattered as well as from assumptions among labor historians that only resistance mattered.

Before leaving Thompson, I want to refer to a letter my father wrote to me on November 29, 1982, the day "we buried grandma [Sadie]." "Death is always so physically final that it hurts," he wrote, although "the wonderful eulogy Stevie delivered" helped to lessen the pain. He then reported on his and Mom's move to the house in Huntington Station and associated activities—putting up shelves, looking for wallpaper, et cetera—but added that he had managed to get through about a third of *The Making*. "Why," he wondered, "don't 'marxist' leaders like in the USSR read the works of scholars and learn from them?" I wish I had asked him what he thought those so-called Marxists could learn, but what his comment now suggests to me is that, like Misha Lewin, he was still trying to save the Soviet Union, even if it had not personally saved him.

Curiosity about what it meant to be a Soviet worker animated my own work from this time forward. Along with my colleagues, I understood that age, gender, skill level, occupation, and geographic location played important and sometimes decisive roles. Like others, I put workers and shop floor politics at center stage in the drama of Stalin's industrial revolution, paving the way for enterprise-based studies that appeared in the 1990s. I will later discuss the limitations of this body of work of mine and others, but first wish to elaborate on its early manifestations.

I started modestly with an inquiry into the practice of socialist competition—challenges issued by groups of workers to others to meet or exceed their work quotas—during the First Five-Year Plan (1928–1932). Why, I wondered, would workers volunteer to work more intensively knowing that their quotas would rise as a result? Surely, neither the standard Soviet explanation of workers' enthusiasm for fulfilling the Five-Year Plan's ambitious targets and thereby building socialism nor Western historians' assumption of coercion seemed satisfactory. Still without access to Soviet archives, I began by wading into the trade union press, party literature, and secondary sources.

I had quite a bit to work with as far as Western historiography of the late 1970s was concerned, though little in the way of labor history. *Stalinism: Essays in Historical Interpretation*, an interdisciplinary edited volume based on a 1975 conference, heralded subsequent scholarship.[18] It pioneered the use of Stalinism as an analytical category, specific to a particular period of Soviet history. None of the essays surpassed for sheer brilliance "The Social Background of Stalinism" by Moshe Lewin, whose approach to social history was as idiosyncratic as it was appealing. The essay's opening sentence, phrased in that inimitable prose of Lewin's, still reads to me like a manifesto for integrating politics with "social factors":

The examination of social factors that were crucial in shaping or favouring the Stalinist phenomenon can safely begin from a study of the situation in which Bolshevism found itself at the end of the Civil War and the self-perception, or rather the ideological (theoretical, if one prefers) terms in which the leadership analyzed the situation at this point.[19]

Lewin already had published three books: his revised dissertation on collectivization, which appeared in French in 1966 and English in 1968, his account of the struggle to succeed Lenin, which appealed to a wider audience, and a more technical study of Soviet economic policy of the 1960s and early '70s that stressed its unacknowledged indebtedness to the thought of Bukharin.[20] He also had an essay in a collection on *Cultural Revolution in Russia* (1978), edited by Sheila Fitzpatrick.[21] Cultural revolution, a term that Fitzpatrick borrowed from the then contemporary upheavals in China, served as a convenient way of thinking about the radicalism that swept the USSR in the late 1920s and early 1930s—from legal theory, to educational strategies, "visionary town planning," and historical scholarship. Although workers hardly made an appearance in that collection, the book helped to contextualize some of the more contentious of the initiatives affecting them. Kendall Bailes's *Technology and Society under Lenin and Stalin* (1977) did the same by analyzing generational tensions among the technical intelligentsia.[22]

Soviet workers appeared more prominently albeit still largely as objects in Charles Bettelheim's *Class Struggles in the USSR: Second Period, 1923–30* (1978), and in an article by Sam Lieberstein in the journal *Technology and Culture*.[23] Like the output of those young historians I had encountered at the Garmisch-Partenkirchen conference in 1980, Bettelheim's and Lieberstein's work looked to the Soviet past to shed new light on contemporary concerns among Western labor movements—about the routinization of work and loss of workers' autonomy owing to the extension of Fordist and Taylorist methods of production.[24] Harry Braverman's *Labor and Monopoly Capital* (1974) represented the point of departure for many scholars, including myself.[25] The subsequent appearance of a firsthand account of subjection to piece-rates in a contemporary Hungarian factory suggested trans-systemic similarities.[26]

But I sought to distinguish forms of socialist competition that objectively subordinated workers to rhythms and incentive systems designed by management from others that enhanced workers' self-organization and mutuality. Socialist competition thus represented in my view an arena (or, as I might have been disposed to argue a decade later, a discursive field) in which the fate of the labor process as it had developed under capitalism hung in the balance. In a subsequent article, I argued that the possibilities of institutionalizing workers' control over their work died in the early 1930s with the party's decision to repress production collectives and communes.[27] At the time, I resisted endorsing the view of Bettelheim and others that no genuine transformation of the labor process had occurred in the USSR, but implicitly that is what I argued.

I chose to submit my article on socialist competition to a then-obscure Australian leftist journal.[28] Why? I assumed that the lack of archival citations and other deficiencies, judging by the academic standards of that time, jeopardized publication elsewhere. Or, I might have been trying to impress the Marxists I had met at La Trobe and elsewhere in Melbourne. The journal, *Thesis Eleven*, which describes itself these days as "Marxist in origin, post-Marxist by necessity," started publishing in 1980. It owed its founding to a group of sociologists ranged around the Hungarian Marxist philosopher Agnes Heller and her husband Ferenc Fehér, both of whom had emigrated in 1977 to take up positions in the Sociology Department at La Trobe. Among its long-time editors, Peter Beilharz and Peter Murphy are still on its board. Johann Arnason, now an emeritus professor of sociology at La Trobe, contributed an article to the same issue in which mine appeared. A recent look at this issue astonished me by the eminent company my article kept. In addition to Arnason, Janos Kornai, the Hungarian economist whose *Economics of Shortage* (1980) broke through a lot of obfuscation about the rationality of centralized planning in state socialist societies, contributed an article "On the Slowing Down of the Growth of Eastern-European Socialist Countries"; the French (originally Greek) ex-Marxist philosopher and polymath Cornelius Castoriadis (1922–1997) wrote on "The Impossibility of Reforms in the Soviet Union"; and Andre Gunder Frank (1929–2005), whose theory of underdevelopment in Latin America made such a strong impression on me, added a piece about "After Reaganomics and Thatcherism, What?" Such august company I never again would keep.

There is something poignant about revisiting publications of this sort. References to Reaganomics and Thatcherism, so characteristic of leftist literature from the early 1980s, optimistically implied that the massive shift in the economic regime of capital could be reversed after the next election, or, more optimistically, when socialism finally arrived. The innovativeness of the financial sector in using credit to expand and accelerate capital turnover, all the while battering down the walls of regulation erected as part of the recovery from the Great Depression, largely escaped notice at the time. This "globalization" of capital claimed among its first victims the factory and mine workers in the hitherto "advanced" capitalist countries then beginning to lose competitive advantage to other parts of the world. As factory-based labor withered, the instructiveness of looking at Soviet

Russian workers' militancy in defense of their control over production lost much of its potency. Referring later to this epochal shift, Joshua Clover would declare, "The conditions that historically enable the socialist vocabulary—real accumulation, a taut labor market, the possibility of gaining power by appropriating a share of that accumulation, an expanding industrial proletariat—no longer obtain."[29]

Gender hardly if at all impinged on my consciousness. That struggles in labor movements in the capitalist West entailed important gendered dimensions—maintenance of the "family wage," for example, or the connection between jobs requiring extensive physical labor and notions of masculinity—seems terribly obvious, but only in retrospect. The "maleness" of the Soviet workers I studied similarly appeared secondary to other characteristics—urban versus rural, skilled versus unskilled, for example. Aside from class, race had more purchase on leftists' analyses of capitalism's ills than did gender, at least in the circles in which I dwelt. Looking back from the era of Trump, it's all one ball of wax, each impinging on the other, but then we felt one had to emphasize class (in its reductively defined sense of being derived from relations of material production) above all.

My obtuseness toward issues of gender equality extended—of course—to my private life. In 1981 my first son, Sami, entered the world, giving his parents and grandparents much joy. The health care system in the State of Victoria made it as convenient as possible to raise a child, providing free and readily available clinic access. We also could not have been happier with the daycare facility Sami attended after his first year. Yet, Leena and I still managed to argue about childcare responsibilities—part of the long downward spiral in our marriage. It is now terribly obvious that we belonged to a generational cohort in which feminist consciousness-raising helped women to question all the assumptions inherited from our parents about respective spheres of work and domestic responsibilities. And, of course, they had every justification in doing so. Nevertheless, the disputes between us seemed entirely personal. Each of us calculated the time taken out of our respective jobs to look after our infant son and perform other mundane tasks, and then disputed those calculations. Instead of treasuring his upbringing, we bickered about it, as we would even more, when Sami's little brother, Sasu, came along five years later.

My unfairness toward Leena stares me in the face. I simply could not acknowledge that anything associated with her work as a librarian at the University of Melbourne, a position she obtained after completing her librarianship degree at the Royal Melbourne Institute of Technology, could be as important to her as travel for research was to me. I absented myself during parts of successive Australian summers (1981–1982, 1982–1983), thereby leaving Sami temporarily fatherless, to conduct research in the United States and Britain. I visited among other places Birmingham, then the center of Soviet studies in England. There, Bob Davies suggested what would be my next article—on the system of setting quotas or work norms so crucial to the piece-rate system of payment that originated in the United States as Taylorism (or in Frederick Winslow Taylor's words, "the principles of scientific management") and came to predominate in Soviet industry. This project proved to be not so much labor history as the history of the conditions under which workers performed labor, debates over how to determine skill, appropriate incentives, and other matters constituent of labor management in the USSR.[30] Somehow, I missed the irony of studying debates among Soviet experts about the quality and quantity of work even while I became embroiled in precisely such debates in my own home.

"Soviet Norm Determination" argued that no matter how strenuously the party sought to apply science to determining output norms, human agency in the form of negotiations between management and workers and especially foremen's "rule of thumb" intervened to subvert the effort. This meant that "wages, in effect, determined norms rather than the reverse." Aside from conscious sabotage, it seemed to me that even the most expert of norm setters confronted limits to their knowledge. Workers themselves often had a better grasp of requisite times for fulfilling tasks. But the story did not end there. The party soon identified individual workers on whom it could rely to bust rates to outflank managers who had established a modus vivendi with their labor force. These they dubbed shock workers, and then Stakhanovites, after Aleksei Stakhanov dug 102 tons of coal during his shift on the night of August 30–31, 1935. Yet, even then the general application of norm increases proved elusive. I now acknowledged explicitly that "the labour process as it emerged in the course of Soviet industrialization was in essence identical to that which had developed in the capitalist world," because "workers' formal control over job tasks, the classification of their work, and the intensity of the production process was systematically eliminated in the course of the 1920s and 1930s." "But," I concluded, looking ahead and striking a note of defiance, "the battle front . . . still exists, although the fighting is largely subterranean."[31]

As suggested by these quotations, I had begun to find my own voice as a labor historian. In this and other respects I received considerable assistance from those who, like me, were trying to figure out what went on in Soviet factories of the pre–World War II era. Some were senior to me—quite senior, in the case of Bob Davies who provided useful feedback on a draft I sent him and invited me to Birmingham to present my work to the Economic and Social History Seminar he ran; less so in the case of Sheila Fitzpatrick who, in the midst of moving from Columbia University to UT Austin, not only offered to read my work in draft but replied to numerous queries and promoted my fledgling career in other ways. Others, my age or younger, comprised our cohort—Paddy Dale, then still finishing his dissertation at the University of Birmingham but already keen to collaborate with me; J. Arch Getty, then, like me, just starting a family as he started out at UC Riverside; Bill Chase, Arch's good friend from graduate school who revised his dissertation into a book at the same time I did; Wendy Goldman, with whom I shared so much in common politically; Hiroaki Kuromiya, a graduate student at Princeton whose mania for tracking down relevant sources exceeded even mine; David Christian, a fellow Oxonian teaching at Macquarie University in Sydney, who provided me with three single-spaced pages of comments on a draft of the norm determination article; and above all, Diane Koenker, whom I can never repay sufficiently but who would insist that I need not do so. We all entered into it together, helping each other overcome self-doubt and other anxieties, a real, if far-flung community without the dubious benefit of e-mail.

In my determination to map still more of the Soviet factory floor during the Stalin era, I later would write an article on foremen. I submitted it to a Festschrift to honor Misha Lewin and I included it in a volume on which I served as coeditor.[32] Meanwhile, I had uprooted the family, returning—in my case—to the land of my birth. Before taking leave of La Trobe in this memoir, I want to close out this chapter by honoring the best students I taught there. Brad Allan, sardonic and smart, remained in touch with me after I left Australia and would meet me in Melbourne on my return there in 2015. Pauline and David Fry became fast friends. Leena and I visited them "in the bush" of eastern Victoria, where, after graduating, they lived with their baby daughter. But before then, we spent a memorable night and early morning in July 1980 watching on their TV the five-set Wimbledon men's final between Björn Borg and John McEnroe. Meryl Hinkson, an extraordinarily gifted mature-aged student and the mother of three young children, wrote an impressive honor's thesis on the Donets Basin in the late nineteenth century based evidentially on British consular reports, and conceptually on categories derived from Marxist political economy. David Blazer expertly put together a radio program on which I appeared with Barry Carr to discuss the history of May Day from its pagan roots up through its Marxist/communist appropriation. Peter Vodicka wrote an outstanding tutorial paper on whether Leninist Bolshevism or Russian socio-cultural conditions gave rise to Stalinism. Paul Bartrop, only six years my junior and now a well-known historian of the Holocaust and genocide studies, contributed a paper in 1976 on "Russian Peasants in the Factory." Kate Mustafa, a friend of David's and another mature-age student, gave me a fond farewell party.

Only once did I have the privilege of relying on a graduate teaching assistant. Roger Markwick, then completing his doctorate at the University of Melbourne under Lloyd Churchward, turned out to share my political outlook and scholarly interests, becoming a life-long friend.[33] I mustn't fail to mention Michael ("Mick") Morgan. Mick submitted his honor's thesis on "The Tsarist State: A Critical Comparison of Several Approaches to Its Study" on November 5, 1982. A work of sixty-nine pages, it surveyed how Richard Hellie, Richard Pipes, George Yaney, and a few other American historians of Muscovy and Imperial Russia misrepresented the relationship between the state and society, namely, in block-like, antagonistic terms.

Mick and I would collaborate on what became an article in *Radical History Review*.[34] Overly rhetorical, frequently quoting out of context, and clunky in its use of historical materialism, it is a source of some embarrassment now. I wish I could attribute its weaknesses to Mick's relative youth and lack of experience, but most of the blame is mine. If "Soviet Norm Determination," which I composed at the same time, had a confident authorial voice, here it smacks of stridency. Yet, some of the criticisms it makes of Pipes' *Russia under the Old Regime* and Hellie's "The Structure of Modern Russian History" still strike me as valid.[35] Their representations of the patrimonial/totalitarian/garrison state remain a distorting lens through which to view Russia's history, crowded out social forces among other things, and, as we noted, "fulfill[ed] an obvious function in the . . . revival of Cold War thinking." But aside from the neoconservatism (for which Pipes became well-known as the head of the Ford administration's Team B), what now seems no less obvious are the neo*liberal* implications of their antistatism. Pipes's assertion that tsarist patrimonialism crushed the bourgeoisie's entrepreneurial spirit seems like something right out of Friedrich von Hayek or Thomas Friedman. His attribution to the Mongols of Russia's aberrant "patrimonialist" political ideology and structures now seems painfully orientalist.[36] Hellie had his own peculiar version of Russian deviancy. In a work published in 1982, he attributed endemic violence in the Muscovite state of the fifteenth and sixteenth centuries to a vitamin deficiency; later, he would correlate "long hours of winter darkness" with attenuated left-brain development.[37]

My embarrassment also stems from my awkwardness in engaging in criticism of *longue durée* history without offering a reasonable alternative. We only platitudinized against ideological explanations and recommended Perry Anderson's *Lineages of the Absolutist State*, via a long quotation that obviated the need for explanation. From this side of the linguistic turn, I can't imagine referring to state and society in terms of "the membership of each component." When, ten years later, I published a book with both categories in the title, I stood on firmer ground, or so it seemed at the time.

CHAPTER 5

LABOR HISTORY AND SOCIAL HISTORY VIA THE CULTURAL TURN

When Leena and I went to Melbourne in 1976 we assumed it would be for three years, no more. That corresponded to the duration of my initial appointment. When three became four and then five years, I started applying in earnest for Soviet history positions in the United States. Rutgers emerged as the first possibility. For some reason, I took my mother along when driving down from my parents' home on Long Island for the campus interview. Disappointment seems to have wiped from my memory anything else about that unsuccessful venture, as well as the other one at the University of Texas at Austin where Sheila Fitzpatrick got the nod instead. Then, late in 1982 Michigan State announced a job in Soviet history. I knew two and only two things about MSU: it had had very successful football teams back in the sixties coached by Duffy Doherty, and during the same era hatched the so-called Vietnam Advisory Group made notorious by a *Ramparts* cover illustration in April 1966 that depicted Madame Nhu, de facto first lady of South Vietnam, as a Michigan State cheerleader. Only later did I learn that both previous Russian historians—Arthur E. Adams (1917–2007) and Robert M. Slusser (1916–1997)—had worked for American intelligence organizations.

Diane Koenker, who had been keeping me abreast of the US job market even while she sought to leave Temple University, reported in April 1983 that MSU offered her the job but she had turned it down because she and her husband had accepted offers from the University of Illinois. "I fervently hope," she wrote, "that they [MSU] are making you a better offer and that you will be brought out." Third time lucky. A phone interview with Harry Reed, the chair of the search committee, during the short window of a mutually convenient time, led to the invitation for a campus interview. In May 1983, I flew from Melbourne to Lansing. This trip I do remember. When I arrived at the airport late at night and seriously jetlagged, Harry stepped forward to introduce himself. I tried not to betray my surprise at being greeted by an African American, for on the phone Harry who hailed from Los Angeles did not "sound black" like the kids I had grown up with in Lakeview. I might as well have been sleeping like Rip van Winkle during my effective absence from American academia, because ten years earlier one rarely encountered African Americans as senior professors. Harry conveyed me to the Kellogg Center, which accommodated guests of the university. The campus itself—traversed by the Red Cedar River and dotted with thousands of giant oaks, elms, maples, and many other varieties of trees then putting out their shiny springtime leaves—exceeded my expectations. So too did the size of the football stadium, or "the cathedral," as one faculty member sardonically referred to it.

At my job talk, Vladimir ("Volodia") Shlapentokh (1926–2015) of the Sociology Department sat directly to my right next to William McCagg Jr., who had a severe hearing impairment. Several times, Shlapentokh, a Soviet émigré with enormous energy and an ego to match, leaned over and in more than a stage whisper told Bill, "This guy doesn't know what he is talking about." What I talked about concerned my research on the Stakhanovite movement, or as I insisted on calling it, "Stakhanovism." The rest of my visit went by in a flash and on the return flight somewhere over the Pacific, I passed out in the aisle of the plane—from exhaustion, I suppose—and had to sign a waiver in Honolulu that the airline bore no responsibility should I require hospitalization or fail to survive the connecting flight. I got the job, Shlapentokh notwithstanding.[1] In August 1983, I returned to East Lansing with family in tow.

We arrived in the midst of what I conceived of as Reagan's counterrevolution. Previous visits had exposed me to it but only fitfully. In December 1980 during Australia's summer break and a month after Reagan's election as president, I joined over 200,000 others in Central Park not only to honor John Lennon but to mourn the end of an era of hopefulness. The breaking of the air-traffic controllers' strike, the launching of the Strategic Defense Initiative, the deployment of the Marines to Lebanon, and Reagan's "evil empire" speech all preceded our arrival in Michigan. The US invasion of the island of Grenada, the beginnings of the Iran-Contra affair, and Reagan's landslide reelection followed it. Full of "Reagan Democrats," Michigan occupied a crucial role in the counterrevolution.

I found reintegration into American society difficult for additional reasons. When the chairperson of my department told me about healthcare options, he repeatedly referred to "HMOs" as if I knew what he meant, but I hadn't a clue. Disoriented about a lot of things, I also found myself disappointed with the students during the first semester of teaching. They did not lack courage to speak up in class, at least compared to students at La Trobe, but they possessed shockingly poor writing skills. I guess things did not go well otherwise because by December when I flew to San Francisco to give a paper at the American Historical Association's conference, I told John Salmond, a senior La Trobe professor in attendance, I wanted to return to Australia. "Give it another couple of months, Lewis," he told me. "It's too soon to decide." Sage advice, as it turned out.

Leena also experienced a rough transition, indeed rougher if only because up to that point, she only had lived in the United States for less than a year, and that with my parents on Long Island. She found a job in the library of the State of Michigan's Department of Transportation. Having been trained and worked in Melbourne as a Slavic librarian, she felt like a fish out of water. Eventually, after about eighteen months or so, the library at Michigan State accommodated her, and she took up a position analogous to the one she had left in Melbourne. How many marriages in our generation foundered because one spouse (usually the husband) dragged the other from one end of the world to the other? Count ours as one of them.

Ambition to advance my career also caused friction. My parents, particularly my father, must have detected the tensions when visiting us for the first time in our new home. On May 18, 1984, shortly after returning to Long Island, Dad wrote to me "wonder[ing] why you are still turning out articles and reviews" rather than "a full-fledged book." "You must not and cannot allow your home chores to get in the way," he admonished.

> Your family . . . simply must cooperate in freeing you up to be as productive as I know you can be. You never required or really got any pressure whatsoever from mother or me during your growing-up years to study & do well in school. It was all your own drive. So I know you can do it. It just demands Leena's understanding and cooperation. Something you have got to get.

As someone who worked so hard to make his family comfortable while his wife stayed at home, my father seemed generationally incapable of understanding that Leena had a career in which she wanted to advance too. Like many male spouses of my generation, I was having trouble making the transition to a dual-career family. The stress of our generation hit home.[2]

During my first few years at Michigan State, I had the good fortune to come under the guidance of Bill McCagg (1930–1993), one of the gentlest and most generous of souls whom it has been my privilege to know in the profession.[3] Bill and his wife Louise, a talented sculptor, had raised their daughters in nearby Bath Township. They lived in a most unusual house built around a giant tree, the trunk of which stood somewhere between the kitchen and the living room. An accomplished historian of Habsburg Hungary, Bill also had a strong interest in the Eastern Bloc. His increasing deafness motivated him "to put the disabled of Russia and more generally Eastern Europe on the historical and sociological map," as I would remark at the AAASS annual conference in November 1988. From this specific interest came the idea of hosting a conference on the subject. The conference—"The Handicapped in the Soviet Union and Eastern Europe"—met on the MSU campus in April 1985. It brought together an eclectic group of scholars from a variety of disciplines. Some, like me, had to be cajoled to deviate from their main scholarly concerns; others had been writing about the disabled or the professions that claimed expertise in their treatment; still others were themselves disabled. We experienced more than a little discomfort and miscommunication. But I think we all came away with the feeling that something of an intellectual breakthrough had been achieved.

The conference served as the basis for *The Disabled of the Soviet Union: Past and Present, Theory and Practice* (1989), a volume that Bill and I coedited for the University of Pittsburgh Press.[4] The volume turned out to be foundational for the study of disability in the context of communism.[5] Working with Bill proved foundational in another sense: it set a standard for many other such collaborative efforts during my career. For the conference and the volume, I prepared a paper on industrial accidents and prevention during the 1920s and '30s.[6] An obscure topic, it nonetheless sensitized me to Soviet authorities' manipulation and eventual suppression of data, a useful reminder as I turned my attention otherwise to those Soviet super-performing workers from the 1930s.

My interest in Stakhanovism grew out of my work on socialist competition, my curiosity about the social bases of support for Stalinism, and my desire to figure out what motivated these workers. I received an additional stimulus from Andrzej Wajda's film *Man of Marble*, which although made in 1977 only arrived in Australia in September 1980. I recall seeing it with my mother who came half way around the world to meet her new grandson in March 1981. The film, set in 1970s Poland, tells the story of a cinema school student who decides to make her diploma movie about a Stakhanovite bricklayer, Mateusz Birkut. Memorialized in marble in the 1950s, Birkut subsequently disappeared. In an attempt to track him down, the student interviews people who knew him—a senior filmmaker who had recorded Birkut's record-breaking stints, an erstwhile Communist activist turned nightclub manager, a fellow brigade member and close friend, and Birkut's estranged wife.

When he made the film, Wajda already had become quite jaundiced about Polish communism but could still be nostalgic about its early promise. Birkut is represented as a naïf, who genuinely believed that if he and his mates laid bricks more efficiently, workers would receive apartments sooner. The repression of his friend, who had fought in the Spanish Civil War on the side of the Republic, sets Birkut on a downward spiral. Ironically, his friend, released from prison during the amnesties accompanying de-Stalinization, winds up as director of the major construction project at Nova Huta outside Krakow. Although fictionalized and specific to Poland's tortured postwar history, the film gave me food for thought.

In truth, I am not sure whether I found Stakhanovism or it found me. As a boy whenever I performed some physical task, Grandma Sadie would exclaim "*Er iz a schwerarbeiter.*" Whether she meant it as a compliment I am not sure, but I assumed so at the time. To be a *schwerarbeiter* meant not being a *zhlob* (a dullard, a yokel), but rather, someone who exerted oneself, sweated (*schwitzed* in the Americanized Yiddish my grandmother spoke) to get things done. The more I exerted myself, the greater the reward—a taller glass of milk, more praise, or later in high school and college, excellent grades. Who is to say I wasn't a Stakhanovite even before I had ever heard the word?

While working on *Stakhanovism*, I presented papers at conferences and published articles on aspects of the movement and its prehistory.[7] Among the articles, the one on production collectives and communes most successfully combined my political perspective with (an albeit positivist) methodological rigor. I submitted the manuscript to *Slavic Review* in August 1984. It opened with two epigraphs to illustrate the main point—that an enormous distance separated Stalin's determination of the "imperatives" of Soviet industrialization from the consciousness characteristic of members of the collectives and communes:

> There cannot be any doubt [about] the confusion in the minds of . . . our "Leftist" blockheads, who at one time idealized the agricultural communes to such an extent that they even tried to implant the commune in the factories, where skilled and unskilled worker, each working at his trade, had to put his wages into the common fund which was then shared out equally. We know what harm these infantile egalitarian exercises of our "Leftist" blockheads caused our industry. (Stalin, 1934)

> Now, brother, we don't toady. Nobody sucks up to the foreman. (N. Pogodin, Bakunin commune, Baltic Shipyards, 1930)

Workers formed production collectives and communes, I argued, not so much as attempts to leap into the utopian future, but as practical mechanisms designed for particular ends, among which less dependence on immediate bosses figured prominently. This argument went to the heart of what socialism meant—it expressed my belief in the importance of recovering alternative collectivist, egalitarian meanings paradoxically suppressed in the name of building socialism.[8]

My father, whom I described in the dedication of *The Politics of Industrial Mobilization* as "my sternest critic," had read a draft of this article. It "deals with a fascinating aspect of Soviet (not socialist) development," he wrote noncommittally on the cover page. Otherwise he limited his remarks to a few question marks in the margins and a laconic "don't understand this" at the beginning of the conclusion. I came to realize that I was writing not for my father but for a different, more eclectic audience, although at a more fundamental level, I now realize, I was writing for myself. Rarely if ever during this period of my career did I turn down a request to provide journals with book reviews or encyclopedias with subject entries based on my previous work on the WICs and my new endeavors in labor history.[9] To what purpose? Memorialize my authoritativeness on these topics? Add to or pad the accomplishments I listed on the department's annual review form? I will not claim to have been above such pettiness. But a more legitimate purpose drove me as well: writing in such a focused way within a prescribed word limit helped me to distinguish the important from the incidental or trivial.

Stakhanovism, the main fruit of my efforts in the mid- to late 1980s, listed in its bibliography archival materials but none in the Soviet Union. Lord knows I tried to penetrate the sanctum sanctorum of sources on the topic. Indeed, as I wrote in frustration to the director of IREX in 1986, "This is not the first, nor the second, but the third time I have been denied a visa to undertake archival work on the subject."[10] Instead, I used the Smolensk Party Archive available—thanks to its capture by the Nazis in 1941 and seizure by the Americans at the end of the war—on microfilm from the National Archives in Washington, and the Harvard Interview Project on the Soviet Social System then housed in the basement of the Russian Research Center at Harvard. My attempt on one of the few research trips I made to Moscow to order factory and local newspapers at the Lenin Library proved abortive. "*Zashtabelirovan*" (obstructed, or literally piled up) the librarian had written across my request slips. A trip out to the suburb of Khimki where the newspapers were stored proved no more successful. The policeman stationed at the entrance did not accept my reader's ticket because Khimki, as I well knew, was off-limits to foreigners. But, desperate, I stood my ground, making something of a nuisance of myself until a librarian waived me in. After presenting my list of newspapers to her, my hopes soared as she started to process the order. Soon, however, someone with more authority overruled her. So instead, I relied on a lot of national, regional, and industrial newspapers obtained elsewhere, chased up journals of various commissariats, trade unions, and other organizations, and read every book from that time onward that had to do with the subject.

Some of this research happened in Helsinki, where I traveled in those years, sometimes with Leena and Sami, but also alone. After the birth of Sasu in 1986, we became a family of four. Fares to Finland depleted our budget, but the boys' Finnish grandparents deserved to see them, so we packed our bags and drove to Detroit airport one June day in 1987 when Sami was six and Sasu a little over a year old. Halfway there, we discovered that we had left Sami's passport at home, whereupon I frantically turned around and drove back doing eighty miles per hour on I-96. We made the flight, only then to be subjected along with other nearby passengers to poor Sasu screaming his head off for much of the next eight hours. I doubt I got much work done on that particular trip, though I made the most of every opportunity. Such visits—and there couldn't have been more than a total of two or three—had their compensations: strengthening connections among the boys with their mother's country and Finnish relatives; improving my Finnish language ability (a little); getting to know Leena's parents better, particularly her father, a war veteran, who didn't seem to mind that his son-in-law devoted his career to studying the Soviet Union.

Besides, one did not need to travel with one's family for mishaps to occur. During a solo trip to Helsinki, I wrote much of what would become "Stakhanovites in the Cultural Mythology of the 1930s," the penultimate chapter of *Stakhanovism*. Inspired by Katerina Clark's *The Soviet Novel* (1981), it would be quite different from the other chapters in its emphasis on non-working life and on what later I would call "discourse" with less hesitancy. Ready access to Soviet newspapers facilitated the writing, much of which I did in the library. A few days after arriving back home in Michigan, I intended to take up the chapter again, but could not find the yellow foolscap pad on which I had composed the draft. It dawned on me that I must have left it either on the plane or in the Frankfurt am Main transit lounge where I had changed flights, because I had the distinct recollection of working on the chapter en route. I wrote to the airline (TWA) inquiring if anyone had turned in the missing pad and enjoined my colleague in German history to write a similar letter to the airport authorities in Frankfurt.

In the meantime, I started reconstructing what I had written. There cannot be any more painful task for an author than to try to reproduce an unfinished text that has disappeared. It is the "old-school" equivalent of when a computer crashes and files not backed up are destroyed. (Gulp, time to hit the "save" button!) Well into this process, I had all but given up hope of retrieving the draft when it arrived in the mail. It turned out I had a false memory of working on the chapter on the trip home. I undoubtedly had been thinking about it, but that is not the same thing. The chapter sat for weeks untouched on the broad newspaper reading desk where I had left it. The library's staff assumed I had taken a break and would return. Finally, they must have realized I had left the country and somehow—possibly through my brother-in-law whom I had informed about my loss—obtained my address. Painful though it was, the additional reflection and revision improved the chapter.

Stakhanovism opened the same way the article on "socialist competition" did—with a quote from Lenin: "The Russian is a bad worker compared with the advanced peoples. . . . The task the Soviet government must set the people in all its scope is—learn to work."[11] The entire book concerned how the Soviet government tried through the panoply of its instrumentalities to teach workers to work better and how workers responded to those efforts. In the book's final paragraph, I gestured toward the present by citing Mikhail Gorbachev's use of the Stakhanovite movement's fiftieth anniversary (1985) to promote the "acceleration" of industrial processes, and expressed skepticism that "advanced workers, the 'Stakhanovites of the 1980s,' could draw inspiration" from their earlier counterparts.[12] Indeed, the production of new labor heroes proved no less of a bust than Gorbachev's other increasingly desperate measures.

Ironically, just as I explicated the Soviet mania for industrial progress and the inculcation of an appropriate mentality, globalized capital was executing a shift toward a deindustrialized version of itself. Containerization and the invention of new financial instruments, so indicative of capital's nimbleness, doomed the industries that had undergirded American economic paramountcy in the twentieth century—coal, steel, and auto production. The traditional factory-based working class correspondingly shrank as did the unions that defended them and the communities that depended on their incomes.

Compounding the irony, I had company. The same year Cambridge University Press published *Stakhanovism* saw the appearance of Hiroaki Kuromiya's book on Stalin's industrial revolution, Vladimir Andrle's on industrialization and social change, and Francesco Benvenuti's entry into the sweepstakes on Stakhanovism.[13] Two years later, yet another on the same subject came out in German.[14] This cluster, initiated in 1986 by Don Filtzer's *Soviet Workers and Stalinist Industrialization*, represented a paroxysm of productivity on Soviet labor and working-class history. This literature succeeded in identifying which labor practices repeated older arrangements, which borrowed from the contemporary capitalist world, and which were Soviet inventions. It helped clarify the possibilities and limits of social transformation during the 1930s, and, as several of the titles suggested, expanded awareness of the interface among the social, economic, and political registers of life under

Stalin. Nobody pursued this line of inquiry and focus on Soviet workers more dog-gedly than Filtzer. Combining loads of aggregate data with telling examples of labor exploitation and contestation, he produced over a period of fourteen years four suc-cessive volumes covering Soviet workers up through "the collapse of Perestroika." Totally reliable, these are go-to books for anyone interested in Soviet labor history.

But fewer and fewer scholars had such an interest. Labor history in general started to lose its preeminence in the 1980s, a process that accelerated in the 1990s. I would explain this trend partly as a function of the postindustrial age in which class lost its immanence while other relationships and identities—gender, ethnic-ity, race, and sexual orientation—gained in salience. Moreover, with the coming of the cultural and linguistic turns, historians also became more enamored with interrogating ("deconstructing") the narratives *about* people than with people's lives. Retrospectively, they regarded their earlier work as epistemologically naïve, and prided themselves on their new astuteness.[15]

Misha, an intellectual lodestar as well as a quipster, dismissed these new trends as "deconstruction." I regarded them with more ambivalence. Even if I had only just become comfortable as a labor historian and enthusiastic about the work I was doing, I didn't want to be left behind the intellectual vanguard. I associated that vanguard with the reading group hosted by Ron Suny and mostly consisting of his colleagues at the University of Michigan. Once every six weeks or so through-out the academic year, we would gather at Ron's to discuss a work of history or a cognate discipline (anthropology, cultural studies, sociology) that someone—most frequently, Geoff Eley—had recommended. During the summer, we met less often, and usually to discuss a novel. The MSG (Marxist Study Group, a name chosen with tongue in cheek) first assembled in 1984 and despite Ron's tempo-rary shift of academic home to the University of Chicago, his sabbatical leaves and other disruptions, it still continues. Its longevity has everything to do with Ron's geniality as a host.

At the outset, we read Karl Polanyi's classic work of political economy *The Great Transformation* (1944), Eric Wolf's *Europe and the People Without History* (1982), and Michael Burawoy's two books *Manufacturing Consent* (1979) and *The Politics of Production* (1985). At the time, Burawoy's books excited me most, and indeed the latter served as a source of inspiration for the subtitle of *Stakhanovism*. Now, it is Polanyi's warning about unrestrained markets destroying democracy that seems most pertinent. Labor history, social history, and political economy continued to appear among our readings in succeeding years. In 1987, we read Mike Davis's *Prisoners of the American Dream* (1986) followed by Moshe Lewin's *Making of the Soviet System* (1985). The next year's menu included *Working-Class*

Formation (1986) and *The Brenner Debate* (1987), both edited collections, and Tim McDaniel's *Autocracy, Capitalism and Revolution in Russia* (1988).

I identify 1989, Europe's annus mirabilis, as the year the balance shifted. Joan Landes's *Women and the Public Sphere in the Age of the French Revolution* (1988) and Barbara Taylor's *Eve and the New Jerusalem* (1983) augured a feminist/gender historical thread. Hayden White's *Metahistory* (1975) introduced us to narrativity. From then on, cultural studies/history—represented by Lynn Hunt's *New Cultural History* (1989), Natalie Zemon Davis's *Fiction in the Archives* (1985), and Andrew Ross's *No Respect: Intellectuals and Popular Culture* (1989)—began to crowd out our earlier emphases. Like embers from an extinguished fire, Peter Linebaugh's magnificent *London Hanged* (1991) and Thomas Sugrue's *The Origins of the Urban Crisis* (1996), occasionally would remind us of our earlier interest in social history.

It is tempting to see this turn toward culturalist pursuits as a turn away from political engagement. Such an interpretation would cast us as erstwhile leftist intellectuals, incapable of understanding that the death of communism presaged, in Francis Fukuyama's now infamous phrase, "the end of history." But I resist the temptation. For one thing, interest in narrative construction and the power of discursive formations need not be a retreat from politics. I prefer to think of it as enriching one's appreciation of power dynamics. For another, I am not sure we understood quite so clearly that the events unfolding in Eastern Europe spelled the end of communism—as opposed to its retrenchment. Specialists on Poland, Hungary, Czechoslovakia, and other east-central and eastern European countries had a leg up on Soviet scholars in this respect. For, to an astonishing degree, we Soviet specialists—whether historians like myself or political scientists who studied contemporary affairs—failed to grasp that by 1989 the country operated on borrowed time.

I personally still had a hard time imagining myself as anything but a labor or social historian rescuing workers from others' condescension. Between 1987 and the turn of the millennium, I pursued quite a few projects that reflected this tension between the new cultural history that had increasing cachet and an outmoded social history. Some projects never got beyond the stage of musing and a bit of research. Others, originally intended as components of a macro-project that I ultimately abandoned, came to fruition as discrete articles. In the meantime, I welcomed a few collaborative ventures, the offer to do a synthetic book, and the chance to meet real live Soviet workers.

To begin with the aborted undertakings, in May 1987 I applied to the associate dean of Michigan State's College of Arts and Letters for an All-University Research Grant. I requested funding for "a study of anti-religious activism in Soviet Russia . . . tentatively titled 'Without God: The League of Militant Atheists and Anti-Religious Activism in Soviet Russia, 1917–41." I described the interface between the prescriptive culture of Soviet authorities and the traditions, values, and symbols of the Soviet people as "one of the 'growth areas' of Soviet studies." I forecast working in Soviet libraries and archives in 1989–1990 and in the meantime gathering materials from libraries in the United States, specifically the universities of Michigan and Illinois. Scarcely had I begun to pursue this scheme when I abandoned it, not because of a failure to receive funding, but because of a lack of sustained interest in questions of religion on my part. When a book on the subject appeared in 2000, I gave it a cursory reading at best.[16]

Other ideas floated through my head in the next few years. "Hooliganism and Social Transformation in the USSR, 1917–41" inspired a one-page neatly inked outline. I imagined six chapters starting with tsarist Russia, then 1917, "revolutionary justice," town life under NEP, in the village, and in industrial enterprises. That seems to be as far as I got. Nothing about discourse here except for an indication of hooliganism in the factories "as redefinition of go slows and other traditional practices." Books on hooliganism in late Imperial Russia and under Khrushchev appeared in 1993 and 2012.[17] At one time, I had a notion to write a biography of Aleksei Stakhanov, whose instant celebrity, booziness while attending an industrial academy in Moscow, and inconvenient alcoholism during the remainder of his life as a minor official in the Ministry of the Coal Industry suggested a Soviet tragedy. Or maybe not. I also became intrigued later in the 1990s by "Gigant" (Giant), the aptly named first state grain farm established in 1928 in the Sal'sk district of Rostov oblast to serve as a model farm for grain production. Here an American connection existed: not the 1952 novel by Edna Ferber from which the better-known 1956 Hollywood movie emanated, but Thomas D. Campbell, a Montana wheat farmer, who served as a consultant on the application of factory techniques at Gigant.[18] This one I regretted abandoning, though years later I would have ample scope to examine American technical assistance in connection with the automobile.

I sacrificed Gigant for a macro-project that would explore the theme of work in Russian history. "Work," as I observed in one of my first requests for financial support, "has served as an index of modernity, or the lack thereof, and an important though problematic component of a Russian national identity."

> Beginning with efforts to reform serfdom in the mid-nineteenth century and extending up to the post-Soviet present, work has figured as a key site in Russia for scientific investigation, literary and artistic representation, organizational experimentation and assertions of both national inferiority and superiority *vis-à-vis* the West.

I conceived of the project as a series of essays each devoted to "a particular episode or moment when work assumed a high degree of political salience and its meanings provoked contestation." The book, in my imagination, would consist of seven chapters, later expanded to nine. It is difficult to explain why it never saw the light of day, other than that my impatience got the better of me (again!), so that instead of waiting until I had completed all the episodes, I decided to publish them separately. The notion that they would work well in comparison to each other must have faded along the way.

I had more success in following through to completion projects that involved collaborators. Some of these fell into my lap and did not require much new research. For example, Bill Chase and I contributed an article on the Soviet experience up to 1941 for a volume on work time and industrialization.[19] By the time of our collaboration, Bill had published a number of articles and review essays on Soviet labor history as well as his book on Moscow workers in the 1920s.[20] Our respective chronological concentrations dictated the division of labor, and the contribution almost seemed to write itself. Other collaborative efforts emanated from conferences and ensuing volumes, one coedited with Bill Rosenberg and the other with Ron Suny. In April 1988, the fifth and final seminar in the series sponsored by the Social Science Research Council (SSRC) on twentieth-century Russian and Soviet social history met at the University of Michigan in Ann Arbor. The brainchild of Misha Lewin, this series did more to put social history on the map of Soviet studies than anything else except for the work of Sheila Fitzpatrick and of Lewin himself.[21] I had failed to appear at previous seminars, either because I resided in far-off Australia or had yet to become identified as a historian of the interwar period. For this seminar, I prepared the paper on foremen to which I already have referred. The collaborative aspects of this volume consisted of editorship duties, which I shared with Bill, and the first chapter, which I coauthored with Ron, Bill's colleague at the University of Michigan.

I don't know whether Bill Rosenberg had me in mind to coedit from the start, but I much appreciated his invitation. Bill did most of the work, corresponding with contributors, arranging with a graduate student to do the index, and drafting the introduction.[22] The process went so smoothly it is hard to recall much about it. The theme that social forces (workers' mentalities, cultures, institutions, expectations, and so on) powerfully constrained Soviet leaders' plans for and methods of industrializing the country coursed through the volume. Contributors represented a who's who of Western historians working on Stalinism at the time—from senior scholars such as Bob Davies, Misha Lewin, and Peter Solomon, to those beginning to hit their stride such as Sheila Fitzpatrick and Katerina Clark, up-and-comers like Hiroaki Kuromiya and David Shearer, and the youngster in our midst, Stephen Kotkin. Kotkin had made a big splash at the conference. Having come straight from the archives in Magnitogorsk, and full of Foucauldian zeal, he characterized with typical bravado all our conceptual frameworks as antiquated. His essay, "Peopling Magnitostroi," foreshadowed a chapter in his then-forthcoming *Magnetic Mountain* (1995) and ran to about double the average length of the other contributions.

The article with Ron, "Conceptualizing the Command Economy," represented my first foray into historiography since the *Radical History Review* muddle back in the early 1980s. My judgment in the interim had become more circumspect and Ron helped me to refine it still further. We overwhelmingly approved of the trends we analyzed, I with more reservations than Ron. Toward the end, we wrote that "the discursive as well as sociological dimensions of labor and management's experiences are only now beginning to be mapped out," which meant that the discursive no less than the sociological dimensions *needed to be* mapped out. We then referred to a conference we had organized at Michigan State in November 1990 where discussants subjected older conceptions of class to vigorous interrogation and criticized "the inadequate attention to the relationship between gender and class, class and ethnicity, and the influence of cultural representations in general."[23]

Among the discussants at the MSU conference, Bill Sewell most adamantly threw down the post-structuralist, anti-positivist gauntlet, asking an unfortunate paper-giver who had referred to events or processes as "unfolding," "who folded the event in the first place?" Geoff Eley and Kathleen Canning pushed the presenters in the direction of cultural studies already being pursued in German history. And Laura Engelstein, pointing out that "the world of the noble worker activist represents male solidarity, fraternity, individualism," chastised us for ignoring the gendered nature of class consciousness and identity.[24] Other commentators such as the Berkeley sociologist Michael Burawoy, Yale's renowned US labor historian David Montgomery, and Bill Chase hewed much closer to labor history's conventions. We had spirited discussions. Pity we did not reproduce them, for they would have served a useful function as a time capsule of some of the best minds in the business at loggerheads over a sea change in the profession.

Ron and I coedited the volume, having persuaded Cornell University Press to publish it. The change in title from the conference's "The Making of the Soviet Working Class" to the volume's *Making Workers Soviet* occurred one evening over dinner at a Vietnamese restaurant in East Lansing. It reflected the shift away from the Thompsonian paradigm to one in which "class formation is not only open-ended but as much in the eye of the beholder as in the 'experience' of the actors."

If, as we wrote in the introduction, "class is more than social stratum, more than wage level or position in the social relations of production, then . . . the discourses in which it is constituted must be brought into a study of its constitution."[25]

We thought we were charting the future for Russian labor history by enriching it with insights that Gareth Stedman Jones, Bill Sewell, Jacques Rancière, and Joan Scott had adduced from the linguistic turn. But, as suggested by those who presented papers on workers before the revolution, not everyone agreed with that agenda. While Reginald Zelnik invoked Rancière's example of a "massive rethinking of labor history" whereby power is shown to operate "through mechanisms of categorizations and social control," Mark Steinberg stressed proletarian creativity in appropriating bourgeois values. Heather Hogan emphasized broad proletarian consciousness while Steve Smith stuck to the factory floor. The book's eight essays on workers in the 1920s and '30s even more resembled a collage. Victoria Bonnell offered a richly illustrated survey and analysis of visual representations of Soviet workers. Stephen Kotkin contributed another piece of his not-quite-yet-published book, the piece containing what would become the best-known neologism in the field—"speaking Bolshevik." "If ever there was a case where the political significance of things said, or discourse, stood out," Kotkin argued, "it was in the articulation of social identity under Stalin."[26] Most contributors ignored this perspective.

"Taken together," wrote Bill Chase in an encomium that appeared on the paperback edition, "the essays define the contours of future work in Russian and Soviet labor history." Not quite. The book may have been a "benchmark volume" as Chase predicted, but instead of marking future contours, it appears in retrospect as Soviet labor history's swan song. Is this judgment too harsh? No, in the sense that never again would such a renowned and talented group of historians gather to deliberate on this subject. Yes, if we take into account a lot of subsequent work, including my own, that remained within the social history of workers. Surveying the landscape of that work, factory-based studies of working-class formation predominated. I am thinking in particular of David Hoffmann's *Peasant Metropolis* (1994), Kotkin's *Magnetic Mountain* (1995), and Kenneth Straus's *Factory and Community in Stalin's Russia* (1997). To these one might add later publications such as Kevin Murphy's *Revolution and Counterrevolution: Class Struggle in a Moscow Metal Factory* (2005), which like Hoffmann's and Straus's centered on Moscow's Sickle and Hammer Factory, and Jeff Rossman's *Worker Resistance under Stalin* (2005) about a strike at the Teikovo cotton mill in 1932.

Once in the vanguard of Soviet studies, histories of laboring men and women up to 1941 receded in importance in the 1990s. Aside from the "internalist" explanation of new trends in the humanities, two other external factors seem obvious.

Deindustrialization in the West, to which I already have alluded, made Soviet working-class formation that much more remote. De-sovietization, that is, the collapse of the Soviet Union itself, inspired a host of new historical questions about nationality and the imperial nature of the USSR, putting workers and labor history in the shade. Finally, and irrespective of these developments, I would argue that a point of saturation had been reached about the working lives of Russian workers in the first decades of the century.

Yet, I carried on. In fact, I caught something of a second wind. Thinking that meanings of work could enable me to combine elements of labor and cultural history, I embarked on a succession of ventures lending themselves to such an approach. The first took me to the years immediately following the October Revolution; the second, further back to the late Imperial period. Finally, I returned to the middle 1930s, my chronological comfort zone since the book on the Stakhanovite movement. What in retrospect links these three studies, aside from their common origin as parts of a larger but never-to-be-completed whole, is their shared concern for narrative and representation, and in two of them, the ways that working people represented themselves before figures of authority. Their voices, encountered in successive returns to the archives, did not arrive unmediated. Still, it is hard to convey the excitement I felt discovering them. Part of that excitement had to do with their materiality. Handwritten on paper of usually poor quality, these documents allowed me to touch in the most literal sense a past otherwise out of reach. Under no illusion of serving as a conduit for their messages, I did not shrink from trying to decipher them.

"Here," I wrote a few pages into one of two articles I published on comrades disciplinary courts, "are early Soviet analogues to the sixteenth-century French letters of remission encountered by Natalie Davis." Thanks to the MSG session devoted to *Fiction in the Archives*, I had become acquainted with Davis's fascinating treatment of documents containing usually successful pleas for mercy from the king.

> Like the "fictions" contained in those documents, the discursive strategies employed by violators of labor discipline can be studied for evidence of what they "thought a good story was, how they accounted for motive, and how through narrative they made sense of the unexpected and built coherence into immediate experience."[27] But the Soviet records of appeals include more than that: . . . often they include the rhetoric of the revolution, sometimes expressed as an unfulfilled promise, sometimes as a device to persuade the court of the guilt of the accused and no less often as an accusation against

the accusers. The terminology employed—"working class," "proletarian," "discipline," "exploitation," "bourgeois," "*chinovnik*" [bureaucrat]—is familiar to students of the period but it is often infused with personal nuance and recollections of a prerevolutionary past.[28]

So, at last I had absorbed enough of the linguistic turn to stress the importance of language in how people represented themselves. But could I take the next step and acknowledge the agency of language itself? Not really. I could argue that "labor or work discipline is a discursive category which has its own rich and varied history in Russia,"[29] but to ascribe power to that discourse over workers and management alike went too far. I now think that is all right. Had I gone to the lengths that, for example, Bill Sewell did, I would have been an entirely different historian. I would have abandoned my materialist foundations and compass, only later to recognize the error of my ways, as Bill acknowledged in his case.[30]

Rather than stepping back to analyze the discursivity of their rhetoric, I sought emotional closeness to these contentious workers. I stood right there with Natalia Alkhimova when she explained her truancy from her job at Moscow's AMO factory by citing inter alia an implausible decree from the "Council of Labor Defense."[31] "So now," she added in appealing the decision of a lower court, "I turn to the Union in which I thought I could find support as the defender of the working class to explain that I am not guilty." Or poor Drogunov who, citing his difficult family situation as the reason for stealing three pounds of flour from Moscow's Bakery No. 5, begged the court "not [to] make my guiltless family suffer." In addition to Natalie Davis, I cited Jean-François Lyotard and, yes, Jacques Rancière. But that was so much window dressing. My real animus was "to explore how the issue of labor discipline spilled over into a range of other issues . . . issues often intensely personal, revolving around conflicts between individuals' expectations, resentments, identities and material needs, on the one hand, and the claims of collectivities . . . to their loyalty and obedience on the other."[32] I liked this article so much that I published a modified version of it five years later. I called the new version "Narratives of Appeal and the Appeal of Narratives."[33]

My fondness for these articles' subjects made the research appealing. In addition to trade union newspapers, journals, and other publications I read in Moscow libraries, I worked with materials from the Central Council of Trade Unions (*fond* [repository] 5451) and the Central Committee of the Textile Workers Union (*fond* 5457). The Central State Archive of the October Revolution (TsGAOR), as it was still known when I conducted the research there in 1990–1991, housed all the material.[34] This, my first time back at the big gray complex on Bol'shaia Pirogovskaia since 1974, occurred in radically different circumstances, namely, a Soviet Union in free fall. I also worked in the Moscow provincial archive (TsGAMO) located in an unobtrusive building in the city's southern district where I read disciplinary court transcripts to my heart's content. This archive practiced a more domestic (*podomashnemu*) regimen, but not at the expense of efficiency of service.

On days when TsGAOR opened at noon, I would work at TsGAMO in the morning, and then take the metro, lunching on Georgian khachapuri (cheese bread) purchased on the way. Like a skilled craftsperson long deprived of his or her favorite tools, I couldn't get enough of these sources and couldn't have been happier. I still at this time in the early 1990s took notes by hand—on 4 x 6-inch cards or sheets of paper I cut up to that size. Conversion to the computer had to wait until my return to Michigan. As for methodology, deciphering the handwriting of each appellant served as the crucial criterion: if I could understand what I read, I could use it, if not, "*fuhgeddaboudit*."

I presented "Narratives of Appeal" at a conference on "Soviet Letters to Authority" that Sheila Fitzpatrick organized in April 1996 at the University of Chicago. I then worked it up into an article for a special issue of *Russian History* on petitions and denunciations that she edited. Davis and Rancière still appeared in the footnotes but now so did Bill Sewell and Peggy Somers, both members of our Ann Arbor reading group. In the interim, Sewell had published an article suggesting a new "theoretical figuration of the social world" that would consist of "mutually constitutive complexes of meanings, scarcities, and power relations." Somers, a historical sociologist, helped me to understand different "narrativities."[35] I analyzed the appeals of workers before comrades disciplinary courts—some that appeared in the previous article and some new ones—within this framework. Now, I did not just grant these workers the right to defend themselves but analyzed the narrative structures of their defenses. At the end, I observed that they "can be interpreted as evidence of a complex process of trial and error" during what Diane Koenker had referred to as the "liminal period of the definition of socialism."[36]

In between these two versions, I got interested in a different kind of narration—one that told about what it meant to be Russian through exhibits of peasant craftwork (*kustarnaia promyshlennost'*). I must have already begun thinking about this subject when I submitted my report on my comrades disciplinary courts research to the American Council of Learned Societies in August 1991. "Further trips," I wrote, "will be devoted to tracing earlier (pre-revolutionary) expressions of concern about what Russia lacked in the way of a work culture and, to borrow a phrase, what had to be done." By the summer of 1992, thanks to internal funding from MSU, I had already started researching in Helsinki's vast holdings of Russian journals, debates among rural investigators in the 1870s and '80s over the origin, nature, and viability of handicraft industries. I perceived early on that these debates went to the heart of anxieties among educated society over the destabilizing effects of capitalism in rural Russia. In such rural-based craft industries as lace-making, embroidery, handloom weaving, woodworking, and toy making, educated Russians discovered–or invented—representations of the premodern harmony they wanted to believe existed before its disruption by industrial ways and the middlemen (*skupshchiki*) connecting peasants to those nefarious forces. To acquire the vocabulary associated with these crafts required a steep learning curve.

I think back on that summer's research with great fondness. I had both boys with me, part of the arrangement my increasingly estranged wife and I worked out. Then ages eleven and six, they were accompanied by Sami's friend Noah, who had persuaded his parents to let him come. We occupied a two-story house set back from the road in Jollas, a metro and bus ride from the city center. The house belonged to Ilmari Susiluoto, an old friend of Leena's from her student years, who spent the summer with his family in the United States. Among the many people whom I have run across in my travels through the world of Sovietology, none surpassed Ilmari in eccentricity and giftedness. Whimsical, a jokester, and contrary to the stereotype of Finnish males, a very warm individual, Ilmari had written a pioneering study of systems thinking (a.k.a. cybernetics) in the USSR, locating its origin within the orbit of one of Lenin's early Bolshevik rivals, Aleksandr Bogdanov (1873–1928).[37] He then pursued a most unlikely career in the Finnish diplomatic corps as that country's leading expert on the Soviet Union before taking up the writing of books on, among other subjects, Karelia, alcohol in Russia, and Russian humor.

A forested area bordered the Susiluoto's house to the south while the shore, studded with tiny islands, lay to the southwest. Walking along the moss-carpeted paths would take us past some large wooden houses dating from the late nineteenth or early twentieth century. Although much the worse for wear, they evoked those imagined dachas where Chekhov's *Three Sisters* pined for Moscow. While I worked in the library, the three boys spent their days idyllically rowing to some of the islands, hiking in the woods, and coming into the city to meet me for lunch and shopping expeditions. Finnish speakers thanks to their mother's insistence that they learn her native tongue, Sami and Sasu did well, enjoying their role as translators for Noah and occasionally for me. The only untoward incident I can recall occurred when I stood over an outdoor grill preparing dinner one evening for guests, and Sasu came running out of the house. "Dad, dad, come quickly," he yelled. He had gotten hold of some matches and ignited a towel in the wood-paneled bathroom.

Interrupted by other pursuits, the research on exhibitions of peasant crafts stretched into 1994 when I spent a month in St. Petersburg. My hosts, a family I met through an American graduate student and his Russian wife, accommodated me with much warmth in their cozy apartment on the Petrograd Side's Karpovka River Embankment. Serezha, an auto mechanic who moonlighted by repairing TVs, his wife Lena who sold them, and their teenaged son remained friends for years thereafter. I became more intimate with Lena's sister, a divorcée with an adult daughter. Of course, it is painful to recall this marital infidelity. If nothing else, I feel awkward being associated with the stereotype of the American male on the loose in a country where, as I discuss below, many women prostituted themselves. Irina, who had a nice if insecure income from her involvement in some sort of commodities exchange, was not among those women. But still.

I worked in the Russian State Historical Archive, RGIA, then still located in the old Senate building. It combined faded imperial splendor with a touch of domesticity that included the archivists sharing hard-boiled eggs, cookies, and tea with readers in the afternoon. I had at my disposal the papers of committees that had organized successive craft exhibitions or sponsored exhibits at World Exposi-tions in Paris and Chicago. Material abounded. Here, for example, is a list of files I read on a single day (May 24):

> f. [*fond*] 401 (Cottage industry office of Ministry of Agriculture and State Prop-erties, All-Russian Industrial and Artistic Exhibition in Nizhni-Novgorod, 1896), op. 1:
> > d. 1—rules for participation;
> > d. 5—journals of sessions of the cottage industry section's experts commission;
> > d. 6—letters, announcements, correspondence, etc.;
> > d. 8—petitions from zemstvos and craftspeople;
> > d. 13—list of awardees

I probably overdid it in collecting an enormous amount of material that clutters my filing cabinets still. The argument I developed correlated the mixed and even conflicted messages conveyed by exhibitions of peasant crafts with late Imperial Russia itself. No matter how hard organizers tried to regulate who could exhibit their wares, "anomalies abounded." Wise to the rules, applicants tailored their descriptions of themselves and how they made their goods accordingly.

Many peasants welcomed what a professional artist involved in craft revival called "the unfortunate influence . . . of urban and factory civilization." The benign, aestheticized versions of Russia's heritage embodied in the goods and their display masked this tension between producers and their upper-class sponsors. The two all-Russian exhibitions of peasant crafts in 1902 and 1913 came off as "highly choreographed occasions symbolizing homage to the sovereign . . . *tableau vivants* of enlightened officials, philanthropic nobles, *zemstvo* [institutions of local self-government created after the Emancipation of the serfs] instructors and diligent peasants surrounded by a cornucopia of goods." Nevertheless, despite the best efforts of the organizers, the contradictions between art and labor, elite versus popular consumption, originality versus familiarity, and the Russian national character as opposed to those of the empire's other peoples could not be resolved.[38]

As the footnote reference attests, I published the results of my research in a collection based on presentations at the quadrennial world congresses of Eastern European and Russian studies in Warsaw. I traveled to the Polish capital with fourteen-year-old Sami in August 1995. We had spent a week in France's Loire region staying in an eighteenth-century stone cottage rented from an American couple whose advertisement in *The New York Review of Books* Sami had spotted. We then boarded a train in Paris for Krakow, following the same route that Jews deported from France to Auschwitz had taken in cattle cars more than half a century earlier. Having recently seen *Schindler's List*, which made a great impression on him, Sami wanted to visit all the sites that appeared in the film. We also spent a day in Zakopane, a lovely resort town in the Tatra Mountains, which satisfied my yearning to see where Birkut reconnected with his estranged wife in a key scene from *Man of Marble*. Fourteen marked the age limit when Sami could bear spending a vacation with his dad, which helps explain why I am so nostalgic about that trip.

Prior to its publication in the conference volume, the *kustar* industry article had undertaken a journey of its own. Sometime in early 1995, I submitted a bloated version, running to fifty-nine pages replete with illustrations, to *The American Historical Review*. In due course, I received comments from three readers and a cover letter from the editor. "Research is impressive; argument, however, is not fully formed . . . author is trying to link this research to too many existing interpretations . . . trying to do too many things in the space of one article." Yep, that about sums it up. The editor encouraged me to revise, observing that the new draft would stand a good chance of acceptance. I did revise and resubmitted. Readers liked the second version more, but, as the new editor of the journal wrote, "significant concerns remain about the effectiveness of the presentation." I had had enough. What devil had possessed me to submit to the *AHR* a confused, overly long manuscript

I do not know. What is clear is that whatever fascination the subject once held had dissipated under successive bouts of criticism. The conference volume served as a fallback option.

Fortunately, by this time, I had found a very engaging episode in the meanings of work that became one of my favorite compositions. "Dear Comrade, You Ask What We Need" came about almost by accident.[39] Searching for material in the State Archive of the Russian Federation (GARF, formerly TsGAOR) on state farm workers, I came across references in the finding guide (*opis'*) to correspondence between instructors from the Union of Livestock and Dairy State Farm Workers of the Center and South—a truly obscure institution—and 145 prize-winning milk-maids and cowhands. The correspondence, much of it handwritten, dated from 1935–1936, years most familiar to me from my research on the Stakhanovites. Letters sent to the prizewinners asked them to report on their family situation, material conditions, food regimen, literacy, and state of health, explicitly asking "what do you need in terms of housing, furniture, and clothing?" "Dear comrade, you ask . . . ," the salutation used by many of the recipients, gave me my title.

I instinctively knew this exchange contained something significant, but what? The rhetorical strategies of these mostly semiliterate prizewinners are only part of the story. After all, the exchange of information touched off another exchange—of material goods and services in return for gratitude and a commitment to perform the role of model Soviet citizens. This I labeled the "politics of distribution," something if not unique to, then prominent in state socialist societies where, especially in the Stalin era, the state engaged in "socialist paternalism." I now see that the politics of distribution occupies a middle position between my earlier immersion in the politics of production and the next decade's absorption in consumption and material culture.

Throughout the 1990s I remained something of a production machine myself. My productivity served as a coping mechanism—an escape—that at the same time exacerbated the situation I was escaping from. I am referring to the increasingly strained relations in our marriage. Time away from home, and when at home in my study, avoided confronting the bitterness and emptiness we both felt. Of course, escaping also took its toll on my sons. Recently, I uncovered among a pile of notebooks and letters yellowing in my basement the following note to Leena from "Susan," a childcare worker, dated 7/28/89: "Sasu was so sad this morning—he really missed his dad. It made him feel a lot better to make this picture for him. I told him you would send it/save it for him. Thanks." Alongside the note Susan had drawn a big frowny face. A paper clip attached the note to the picture on which she had written in the upper left-hand corner "To: Dad, we love you!" The picture consisted of two triangles atop two circles. In one of the circles Susan had written "Sami" and in the other "Sasu." Sasu, then not quite three, had scribbled with different colored pens in each circle. I don't remember if Leena showed this to me when I returned from my three-week trip to Donetsk, but coming across it now, my heart aches. I never did take the boys with me to the Soviet Union, a source of regret later in life, but a relief at the time.

It is also true that I was driven. My yearning to tell a different kind of story about the Soviet Union's formative decades, one in which working people occupied the center of the drama, remained undimmed by the collapse of the Soviet Union itself. Soviet elites may have decided they had been stuck with communism long enough, but I was still stuck *on* it. In this respect, I resembled those well-meaning but deluded sponsors of craft-producing peasants who wished to keep capitalist development at bay—they, at the dawn of that process cut short by the October Revolution, I at its second dawn. I tried to save the Soviet Union not from itself but from the condescension of wiseacre scholars. Toward the end of the nineties, however, these always problematic motives began to wane. A sign of maturity or emotional exhaustion? Hard to say. More likely, belated recognition that, at long last, the game was up.

The larger process I have traced in this chapter, moving from labor history toward a broader social and cultural historical perspective, produced four projects in the nineties. Each had a different cast of characters, and each helped me better understand how the Soviet Union took the shape it did. Understanding that seemed even more important in the aftermath of its demise than during its lifetime. The first of these, *Soviet State and Society between Revolutions*, I described in a grant request as "a survey of the New Economic Policy [NEP] period (1921–29) . . . intended for upper-level undergraduate and graduate students." I already had tried my hand at such a synthetic overview by contributing a piece on "State and Society in the 1920s" to a volume on reform in Russian history.[40] Of course, reform-talk had proliferated in the midst of perestroika. Writing a book on the twenties thus presented an opportunity to assess a previous bout of reforms and even learn a thing or two about why they ended so tragically in Stalinism.

Preparing to write this book meant acquainting myself with the ever-growing amount of literature by historians of the period and combing through primary (including archival) sources I needed to substantiate my arguments. It also behooved me to keep abreast of the ways Soviet journalists were employing the "lessons" of NEP. Articles appearing in *Novyi mir* (New World) in 1988 made a particularly strong impression on me, as did transcripts of roundtable discussions among Soviet historians.[41] The bibliography consequently listed a cavalcade of works, both well-known and obscure. When, where, and how did the book get done? Between 1988 and 1991, along with teaching, traveling, bickering with Leena, and trying to be a father to my sons, I wrote the book in the portion of the basement that served as my study.

In seeking to avoid presentism and also to strike a balance between a synthesis of others' work and my own perspective, I received assistance from Mary McCauley. I had known Mary since my years at Oxford when I visited her at the University of Essex to chat her up about, of all things, factory committees in 1917. I had recalled that she dedicated her first book to them and, intrigued, I wanted to find out why.[42] Mary, who had a long and brilliant career as both a scholar and a human rights activist, popped up periodically to lend a hand, fairy godmother-like. In this case, she edited the series in which *Soviet State and Society* appeared, read drafts of early chapters, and gave sage advice for improving upon them. Did I express my gratitude? I hope so. If not, I do now, albeit belatedly.

In the course of the writing, the "survey of the New Economic Policy period" became a book about a great deal more. I confined NEP itself to a mere 35 of the book's 229 pages of text. "State" and "society" now functioned as "building blocks of historical analysis . . . force-fields marked by the complex interplay of attractions and aversions, and thus dynamic, transmutational structures."[43] The book moved from what the revolution and civil war had "bequeathed" to Soviet Russia to the crisis of 1920–1921, the perils of "retreat and recovery," living with NEP, and the dangers and opportunities of the late 1920s. The sections on marriage, religion, making workers productive, and the agrarian and industrialization debates drew on material I had gathered for previous projects—including the abandoned one on anti-religious activism. As the old idiom has it, much cited in radical Left circles of my youth, "nothing ventured, nothing gained."

The reviews pleased me as much for the seriousness with which reviewers treated the book's conceptual framework as for their praise. I faced more direct feedback from fellow historians at the November 1994 convention of AAASS in Philadelphia where Wendy Goldman presided over a roundtable discussion of the book. Steve Kotkin cleverly referred to it as an "anti-synthesis synthesis"; Wendy noted my use of social history to alter the traditional political narrative but worried that my focus on class had minimized gender; and David Hoffmann expressed alarm that the linguistic turn endangered social history. For many years after its publication, I could not look at the book, probably because it reminded me of an unhappy period in my life. But more recently, I have reached for it often when teaching graduate courses on Soviet history and the history of communism, which is to say I couldn't think of anything better to assign on the 1920s.

Some projects have a way of initiating others, even if the links are not obvious or immediate. While reading for *Soviet State and Society*, I came across material on workers' clubs and palaces of culture, institutions designed to concentrate and control the leisure activities of workers. The debates about the appropriate architecture for such structures interested me as much as the kinds of activities that went on inside them. These two dimensions related to each other in fascinating ways—function shaping form, and popular culture squaring off against avant-garde culture. Addressing the relationships therefore gave me a way of extending myself beyond class formation in the workplace to the setting where cultural activities occurred and the activities themselves. But the story transcended the 1920s to encompass the '30s as well, and so I shelved the idea until later when I turned out a modest fourteen-page article for *International Labor and Working-Class History*.[44]

More so than anything else in the post-Soviet nineties, historians welcomed the declassification of documents in Soviet archives and the publication of a series of guides to archive collections. The Russian Archive Series (RAS), based at the University of Pittsburgh's Center for Russian and East European Studies, provided the latter service in cooperation with the Russian Archive Administration's director Sergei Mironenko. The guides, which covered both Soviet state institutions and the former central party archive, were easy to use and, in my experience, totally reliable.[45] Bill Chase and Arch Getty, both members of RAS's editorial board, edited several of them. Arch also facilitated housing for foreign scholars via Elena Drozdova and Leonid Weintraub, a Moscow-based couple with seemingly infinite connections among apartment owners willing to lease them. After my friend Vadim had left Moscow for California, I relied exclusively on Arch's operation, officially known as Praxis International.

At the same time that the Russian Archive Series got under way in 1992, Jonathan Brent of Yale University Press founded its Annals of Communism series.[46] This entrepreneurial endeavor typically paired historians and archivists in Russia with scholars from North America with the objective of publishing documents with linking commentary. With support from the National Endowment for the Humanities and the Soros Foundation, Yale provided the Russians with some desperately needed income and both sides with money to cover travel expenses. Among those whom I already have mentioned, Chase, Getty, Fitzpatrick, Gorodetsky, and Pipes would coedit volumes in the series.[47] Also in 1992, Andrei Sokolov of the Institute of Russian History in Moscow submitted a proposal to Yale for a volume he tentatively called "Soviet Social Life in the 1930s: The Personal Experience from Documents." Andrei previously had established extensive connections with archival personnel, participated in Pittsburgh's Russian Archive Series, and knew Chase and Getty well.

Bill Chase recruited me for this volume in February 1993. My first task consisted of translating and providing commentary on Sokolov's proposal. With the press's financial support, I spent several weeks that June in Moscow assisting in the identification of documents from the party archive (then known by its Russian acronym as RTsKhIDNI, the Russian Center for the Preservation and Study of Documents of Recent History; later RGASPI, the Russian State Archive of Socio-Political History) and GARF. Brent soon learned of my enthusiasm for the "incredibly rich" material I had seen. Indeed, the wealth of documentation was a researcher's dream come true. That material mainly consisted of four types of documents: letters of praise, complaints, and suggestions addressed to Soviet and party leaders, state organs, and editors of newspapers concerning "socialist construction"; denunciations/"unmaskings"; protocols and resolutions of meetings of primary party organizations, trade unions, and the Komsomol; and summaries of reports from the secret police on conditions, attitudes, and manifestations of discontent among the general population. The next spring, Sokolov wrote via e-mail—a technology he had just started using—that he and his team of archivists had "practically finished with the selection of documents." But this assurance proved overconfident. I returned to Moscow in September 1995 and while there, suggested adding some of the documents I had seen relating to those prizewinning livestock and dairy state farm workers. Judging from a letter sent to me by Sokolov's junior partner, Sergei Zhuravlev, the selection process continued well into November. "In general," Sergei wrote, "the more one works in the archives, especially in recently declassified documents, the more one is convinced how little we know of the history of the 1930s and how much is still 'virgin,' untouched territory."

I already had suggested to Brent that Yale arrange for Sokolov to visit me in the summer so that we could work unimpeded on the volume. That visit finally occurred in the fall semester of 1996. We worked well together, discussing the order of the documents and each other's drafts of connecting narrative. Midway through the visit, we held a "conversation" between the two of us for my colleagues in the History Department about "Doing the Social History of the Stalin Era in the Light of New Archival Materials." A more painful memory of Andrei's visit relates to the evening I took him to watch Sami play indoor soccer. Midway through the game, Sami broke both his tibia and fibula when his leg crashed into that of an opposing player. The collision produced the noise of a tree's dead limb snapping, a never-to-be-forgotten sound. I also will not forget Andrei's good humor, patience, curiosity about American Midwestern ways, and intellectual agility.[48] As agreed by Yale, he published a Russian version with ROSSPEN (Russian Political Encyclopedia, founded in 1991) in 1998, listing himself as editor-in-chief and me as a participant in the book's creation.[49] Despite having the services of two of the best translators in the business in Thomas Hoisington and Steven Shabad, the English version that I oversaw required nearly two years more.

The introduction defined the book as a work of social history, one that allowed

> peasants and workers, intellectuals and the uneducated, adults and children, women and men, Russians and those of other national groups, the downtrodden and the elite to tell their own stories in their own words. They "speak Bolshevik" (some better than others), as well as other languages. They complain and beseech, and are both elliptical and shockingly blunt. They proclaim their unswerving dedication to building socialism and their horror at some of the things that are done in its name. Taken together, they reveal, unwittingly for the most part, the social values, codes of conduct, stereotypes, pathologies, and yes, hopes and fears that produced and were produced by this most traumatic decade in Soviet history.[50]

I don't think I ever wrote with more confidence and fervor. A most appreciative review understood the point:

> This book allows those people who lived through the turbulent decade of the 1930s to speak for themselves. Most of the documents are written either by ordinary citizens or about them. . . . With their circumspect commentary, Lewis Siegelbaum and Andrei Sokolov do a superb job of carefully leading the reader from document to document and not stealing the limelight from the voices of the past.[51]

By repeatedly assigning portions of the book to students in my Soviet history classes, I grew more familiar with many of the people who produced the 157 documents. The young Leningrad worker who wrote to his Uncle Fedya from Magnitogorsk; the rural soviet chairman who complained to Soviet president Mikhail Kalinin about feeling "like you're on the edge of a straight razor"; the seventy-year-old who, thanking Stalin for "a bit of a happy life," urged the constitution "not [to] forget about us old people"; the Leningrader who offered amendments concerning natal policies that would have made Aldous Huxley incredulous; the seventeen-year-old kulak's daughter who, "burning with shame in front of my girlfriends," petitioned Lenin's widow Nadezhda Krupskaia to enable her to continue her studies—they evoked all kinds of associations and emotions. In their values and the words they used to express them, though, they all exhibited how Stalinism could indeed be a way of life.

Even while completing this book, I threw myself into quite a different plan. Instead of collaborating with a senior Russian historian, I went solo. Instead of dealing with a panoply of sites across the country, I focused on only one; instead of an entire decade, a couple of months; instead of the complications and contradictions of building socialism, a construction site to dig a canal. Suddenly, I had returned to labor history, but with a twist. The "romance of the Soviet worker," as I later termed it, had ended for me, but a different kind of romance—with the Soviet East—had germinated.

The inspiration came from photographs taken by Max Penson (1893–1959) in 1939 of the construction of the Great Fergana Canal, which I first saw at an exhibition in New York.[52] The panoramic photos of thousands of Uzbek peasants wielding hoes (*ketmeny*) under the broiling summer sun conjured up pharaonic times.[53] Soviet propagandistic literature described their efforts as a "people's construction project" to build a 270-kilometer irrigation canal. Draining waters from the Syr Daria River, the canal would achieve "cotton independence" for the entire Soviet Union and not incidentally initiate the catastrophic desiccation of the Aral Sea. Sheer curiosity drove me to try to find out how the project originated, how Soviet authorities organized the labor to dig the canal, and whether it resembled colonial endeavors elsewhere in the world. I also had become aware that the project inspired the great Soviet director Sergei Eisenstein to try to make a full-length feature film (to be called *Fergana Canal*). Eisenstein envisioned using actual footage of the canal's construction and having the movie culminate with scenes of water flowing into the completed construction site. What happened to that film?

I spent September 1998 in Moscow reading several Soviet dissertations out at Khimki, no longer off limits to foreigners. I worked in the Russian State Archive of the Economy (RGAE) reading materials from earlier irrigation projects (f. 2276) and the Commissariat of Agriculture (f. 7486) on the Fergana Canal. Immersing myself in Eisenstein's personal papers and looking at films and photographs at the archive in Krasnogorsk outside Moscow proved a delight.[54] As I wrote in October to Eisenstein expert Joan Neuberger, "I too have been bitten by the Eisenstein bug." But Eisenstein's fascination with the Soviet Orient had its limits. After shooting footage at the canal site, he abandoned the project because funding restrictions made his grandiose plans moot. Undaunted, I returned to East Lansing determined to apply to IREX to facilitate research in Uzbekistan.

Then, while giving a talk at Harvard to the Russian history seminar, I made a serendipitous connection with a graduate student from Uzbekistan. She happened to have the e-mail address of the daughter of Rakhima Aminova, the author of a dissertation I had read in Moscow. Aminova, the first Uzbek woman to receive a doctorate in history, defended her dissertation in 1953 on "The Great Popular Movement in Uzbekistan's Irrigation Construction (1939–1940)." In my message to Aminova's daughter, Dinora Azimova, I indicated my intention of continuing research in Tashkent "but first of all would like to know if it would be possible to meet your mother."

IREX informed me in March 1999 that it would be supporting my research in Uzbekistan. Even while I entered into the blizzard of e-mail exchanges to obtain a visa, locate housing, and make other arrangements, a reply came from Dinora. In her capacity as "Head of Department of International Relations of the University of World Economy and Diplomacy," she could assure me that "all members of our family will be glad to meet you here," including her mother. Dinora proved most hospitable. She treated me to a sumptuous dinner at her family's spacious apartment, attended by two other guests: an American woman from Notre Dame and an Indian gentleman who was acquainted with my Oxford friend Madhavan from Delhi. Unfortunately, the speech capacity of Dinora's mother Rakhima whom I subsequently met at the family compound outside the city suffered from the advanced stages of Parkinson's, and she could only communicate through her two daughters' translations, which made for an awkward interview.[55] But I also interviewed Dinora's father-in-law who recalled witnessing the canal's construction as a fourteen-year-old Komsomol activist in Kokand.

The archival research in both Tashkent and Fergana went well. I read materials in the Uzbek state archives (f. 2702) that documented progress along the route of the canal, and in Fergana became fascinated by the papers (f. 546) of the chief hydrologist, Klavdii Siniavskii. Yet, I could only do so much in a few weeks. As I wrote to IREX in my report, "While standing at the canal, I suddenly realized that if I were going to seek out people who worked on the construction project, I could do worse than make inquiries in the villages (kishlaki) ranged along the canal," but I realized "this will require further preparation and assistance." "Thus," I added, "it would appear that another research trip, perhaps next spring or summer, is in order."

That did not happen. After I had worked up a paper to present on Eisenstein's *Fergana Canal* to the AAASS convention in Denver in November 2000, I archived the materials I had collected and hardly gave them another thought. Why? Could I have become discouraged after submitting a revised version of this paper to the new journal *Kritika* only to have the editors tell me to revise it again? Why so easily discouraged? The admittedly more convenient explanation is that I became chairperson of the History Department at MSU in 2000 and the responsibilities proved greater than anticipated. Convenient, but probably insufficient. What I think happened is that having transformed myself from a labor to a more broadly social historian via the cultural turn, I felt incapable of transforming myself once again. That I did just that a few years hence might belie this explanation too, except it begs the question of what kind of historian I refused to become.

The initial idea of trying to determine what motivated those Uzbek peasants to flail away under the hot sun for forty-five intense days seemed somehow naïve and also elusive. I also worried about engaging in Orientalist exoticism, and that not knowing the local language would make me a fraud. An alternative approach, actually written up as a proposal, I called "Constructions of the Great Fergana Canal." It would have been as much meta-historical as historical, focusing on how three individuals "constructed" the canal: Eisenstein, his co-scriptwriter Petr Pavlenko, and Rakhima Aminova. This would have turned me into the cultural historian that, by the turn of the millennium, I knew I did not want to become. Should anyone at a future date be interested in doing something with the material, I would be happy to oblige.

If I could do it all over again . . . Such is the lament of the disappointed. Yes, I confess to disappointment. As I write this, I have just finished coediting a book (with a much younger scholar expert in the area) about the Eurasian borderlands of Imperial and Soviet Russia.[56] This is a field I might have plowed two decades earlier. Why couldn't I have understood the engineer Siniavskii, a Russian dispatched from Moscow to transform the Uzbek landscape, as a colonial type? Perhaps my inability to take up postcolonial studies signified a retrograde unwillingness to regard the Soviet Union in this light.[57] Now that I have conceded the Soviet Union had imperial qualities, the prospect of returning to Fergana to comb through Siniavskii's papers again seems too daunting.

CHAPTER 6

CENTERS AND PERIPHERIES

When we speak of the shelf life of books, we usually do not consider how long they stay vibrant for their authors. This undoubtedly varies from one author to the other depending on the time in their lives when the books were written, their reception by others, and other factors. As already mentioned, *Soviet State and Society* did not stay with me beyond its publication until nearly two decades later, when, like a prodigal child who suddenly returns to the fold, it inspired newfound affection. With *Stakhanovism*, things were different. Sometime in the winter of 1990 Frank Smith, the editor at Cambridge University Press with whom I worked, informed me that the press had decided to do a paperback edition. We discussed and he agreed to a new preface that would relate the book to events occurring since the publication of the hardbound edition in 1988. I wrote this preface with blinding speed and sent it to him.

I had returned months earlier from Donetsk, the principal city in Soviet Ukraine's Donets Basin (Donbass), where I had spent three weeks among coal miners and their families as a member of an oral history video crew. We had arrived quite serendipitously just after some 400,000 miners throughout the country had suspended their strike against the Ministry of the Coal Industry to give it time to meet their numerous demands. Not since the 1920s had workers struck in the Soviet Union for more than a few days. This strike produced strike committees out of which developed workers committees, reelected councils of labor collectives, and a real sense among the miners of their own empowerment. "*Perestroika* from below" was how I described it in the preface and how the hour-long documentary film I helped make would be titled. "For the first time in fifty years," I wrote,

the coal miners had become the center of national and indeed international attention. But now, unlike the past, it did not stem from production feats that made awkward heroes of a few and created difficulties for many. In resorting to the strike weapon, Soviet miners were partaking of an older tradition, one in which workers dared to express their aspirations through collective forms of self-organization.

The old refrain, this time not of lamentation but of hope. And so, having originally dedicated *Stakhanovism* to Sami and Sasu, I decided to rededicate the new edition to the Donbass miners. Not until I received my copies in the mail did I discover the preface's absence. Profoundly apologetic, my editor confessed he simply forgot to add it. Who now remembers the miners' strikes of 1989 and the early 1990s? Who these days associates the Donbass with the dynasties of its coalminers? Within a few years after Ukrainian independence, *The New York Times*, *The Washington Post*, the BBC, and other Western media stopped reporting from the region . . . until 2014 when they started reporting about the Donetsk and Luhansk People's Republics and the "little green men" from Putin's Russia who supported them. Nationality sells more than class. Back in the late 1980s and early 1990s, nationality meant little to me, for class was all.

The miners project began when Bill Chase contacted me to ask if I could substitute for him as the expert Russianist on a project launched by Larry Evans (1947–2014), a sometime steelworker and founder of an alternative quarterly magazine in Pittsburgh, *The Mill Hunk Herald*.[1] Winding up that operation and restless for something different, Larry decided to take advantage of Pittsburgh's sister city relationship with Donetsk by launching a video project to interview steelworkers in both towns. By the time I came on board, Larry already had recruited the other members of the team that would spend three weeks in Donetsk that summer. They included about six labor studies students from Rutgers; Ruth Needleman, a labor historian from Indiana Northwest (in Gary); Ted Friedgut, a senior Israeli historian with whom I would share interviewing responsibilities and collaborate on an account of the strike and its immediate aftermath; and Danny Walkowitz.[2] Danny, an American labor and urban historian at NYU, had film experience of his own that he would draw upon to radically transform Larry's project.[3]

No sooner had the Pittsburgh-Donetsk Oral History Video Project gotten off the ground than the miners in Donetsk and elsewhere in the Donbass joined others throughout the Soviet Union in striking against the Ministry of Coal. The strike lasted from July 18 until just before we arrived in Donetsk on the 30th. Thanks to our guide Slava, a former Komsomol activist, we had carte blanche at the Kuibyshev mine, one of twenty-one within the Donetsk city limits. We donned hard hats and overalls and went down the mineshaft, ate and drank with the miners in the mine's cafeteria as well as in their homes, played soccer with them, attended meetings, and conducted interviews. The first interview I did, on August 3, was with Ivan Moskalenko, a sixty-two-year-old pensioner, who came to Donetsk from Zaporozhe in 1947. The interview took place in the garden outside his white stucco home, "and a magnificent one it is too," I wrote in my notes: "peonies, gladiolas, chrysanthemums, apple, pear and apricot trees, bees, and glorious tomatoes." And so, "under a bright burning sun, with 4 camera technicians, the project director (Danny), a translator, and assorted other folk looking on," the interview proceeded for an hour in three twenty-minute takes. "It is exhausting," I wrote, "and I am extremely nervous throughout."

Why so nervous? Because I had never interviewed anybody before, because I lacked confidence in my ability to follow what Moskalenko was saying and feared he would regard my questions as ill-informed and badly expressed, and because I had never before encountered a real live Soviet worker. And yet I also recorded a state of "elatedness." That word appears in my work diary alongside these semi-coherent, ungrammatical "reflections":

> This is all so unexpected and unbelievable that I know it can't last. This city and its people are very Soviet but also very eastern Slavic, their rurality, especially the miners who live in villages near their mines amidst the slag heaps digging in their gardens, are a strange and to my mind, beautiful people.

Two days later, I and several other members of our team crowded into the balcony of a large hall where about two hundred workers and administrative personnel from the Kuibyshev and Panfilov mines met in conference. *Perestroika from Below*, the one-hour documentary film directed by Danny Walkowitz, concludes with about twenty minutes of this meeting.[4] The climax is a vote to remove the "honored miner of Ukraine" status from the trade union boss Viktor Efimov after several miners heatedly relate stories of their ill-treatment by him. My notes contain several observations not captured in that film. I noticed that the stage no longer accommodated the mine's director and party organizer, who now sat in the first two rows down below. Members of the strike committee including several of our soccer-playing friends now sat above them, a physical manifestation of status reversal. Voting occurred by closed ballot, a more time-consuming process than by show of hand but one that prevented retaliation.

The meeting lasted almost the entire workday, as one speaker after the other mounted the podium to denounce Efimov, and people in the audience fired questions at him: why were autos distributed only to management? Why were you not here when refrigerators were being distributed? Why do people who do not work here get to go to the rest home on the Black Sea? Who decides who gets apartments?

FIGURE 6.1 "We donned hard hats and overalls and went down the mineshaft," 1989.

They made demands too: abolish separate showers for engineers and workers; do not count sick days as absences; we must choose our own representatives instead of confirming those sent from above; socialist competition must be organized by worker collectives themselves.[5] To paraphrase a slogan I have chanted at many a rally in the United States, "this is what Soviet democracy looks like."

I admit that the last demand, for workers themselves to organize socialist competition, fills me with nostalgia. So too does seeing in my notebook the names of miners—sometimes written in their own hand, sometimes in mine—whom we considered as candidates for interviewing but who now remain just names on paper. And then there are the photographs—of me, a forty-year-old historian dressed in miner's gear, playing at being a miner; of a quiet residential street with tall poplars lining one side and on the other, a solitary Lada parked in front of an old two-story building with a man leaning against it engaging in that favorite of Soviet pastimes, smoking; of a group of saffron-robed

FIGURE 6.2   Gennadii Kusch and Valerii Samofalov with other strike committee members, 1989.

Hare Krishnas, wearing sandals and chanting as they proceed past a Lenin statue on Artem Street, Donetsk's main thoroughfare; and of six members of the Kuibyshev mine's strike committee strung out on a long bench affecting different poses. Among them, I easily recognize Gennadii Kushch, with his impressive Lech Walesa–like mustache, and Valerii Samofalov, blond and ruggedly handsome. Both sat for extensive interviews and welcomed us into their homes and families. Both were beefy guys, in their forties, and—not unusually among miners—already grandfathers.

Aside from the Kuibyshev miners and members of their families, we took the opportunity to interview elderly people, pensioners whose life stories, now that I have developed an interest in migration history, fascinate even more than they did in 1989: Narsis Melikian, son of refugees from the Armenian genocide, who spent the war years in Nizhnii Novgorod and on the Moscow front before returning to Stalino (Donetsk's name until 1961) and becoming a mining engineer; Tatiana Nikiforovna Artemova, born in 1913 in Kursk oblast, arrived in Stalino in 1932 to work in the mines; Marfa Ivanovna Limonets, born in 1915, went into the mines at age fifteen to carry lamps to the miners, her work interrupted by the war when she "fell into the hands of the Italians." We encountered the latter two sitting on a bench outside their apartments. During the interviews, they brought out apples ("our own special Ukrainian apples") and expressed *their* gratitude for the time and attention we gave *them*.

During that trip, I visited the smoke-belching Donetsk Metallurgical Factory (DMZ) to interview steelworkers, spent time in art and historical museums searching for remnants of Stakhanovites, journeyed to a pebble-strewn beach on the Sea of Azov, met some Soviet Jews speaking "a beautiful clear Russian," played tennis with the husband of Danny's translator, stole a few hours now and then to work in the regional archives, and on "the hottest day of the summer, as a thick haze hung over the city of Donetsk, . . . sat with Yuri [Iurii] Boldyrev on a bench in a park shaded with acacia trees." I am quoting here from my first excursion into journalism, an article called "Behind the Miners' Strike" that I wrote for *The Nation*.[6] Quite a character, Boldyrev had smarts and knew it. He had earned a degree in physics at the local university but decided to go into mining primarily because it paid so well. When I met him, he chaired the strike committee at the Gorky mine, one of Donetsk's largest and most productive. He embodied both the contradictions and achievements of the strike movement, a new phenomenon on the Soviet scene. It would not be our last encounter.

Among those of us who journeyed to Donetsk in the summer of 1989, only Danny and I returned a second, and then a third, time. In May 1991, we went back primarily to share *Perestroika from Below* with the miners and our friends at DOKA TV who had generously supplied us with newsreel clips from the 1930s onward. How we expected them to understand the English-language narrative and voice-overs, I don't know. Things in general had gotten very complicated. A general election among miners now chose the director, though strike fever still existed. Valerii, assistant to Gennadii on the mine's Council of Labor Collectives (STK), was already tired of issuing demands, trying to mobilize the comrades, and repeating the cycle. As he put it, "What surprises me is that we already have been through all this. In 1917 we were told, 'Let's get rid of the rich and distribute it among the poor and all will live well.' History had taught us nothing. Now we say, 'Let's take everything away from the party,' and by extension, 'Let's set up new gulags, but for Communists.'"[7] Tensions also had arisen between the Kuibyshev STK and the city strike committee whose members we also interviewed.

While still in Moscow before flying to Donetsk, I contacted the miners' interregional strike committee, the body set up to coordinate strategy among miners in (still Soviet) Ukraine, Siberia, and the Far North of the Russian republic. As I entered the committee's headquarters "in the Hotel Rossiya, literally within a stone's throw of Red Square," my eyes teared up from the blue haze of too many cigarettes and too little ventilation.[8] But among the delegates, I managed to make out Iurii Boldyrev. Speaking even more rapidly than I remembered, Boldyrev told me the miners would never see improvements until Mikhail Gorbachev resigned and new elections occurred. Toward what end, I wondered? From whom did the miners think they would get a better deal? Three months before the coup attempt against the Soviet president, Boldyrev and his comrades demonstrated to me the total rupture between Gorbachev's version of political liberalization and economic reform (perestroika) and what the miners wanted. Whatever bonds of trust had existed between them and Gorbachev during our first visit to Donetsk in 1989 had snapped.

After a year's absence, we returned to Donetsk in June 1992, this time accompanied by a Moscow sociologist Evgenii Romanovskii and Stephen Crowley, a political scientist from Oberlin College whose research project compared the degree of political activism among miners and steelworkers in Donetsk to the Kemerovo region of Siberia.[9] A lot had changed since our last visit. Ukraine now had become an independent state and many people we knew were having a hard time adjusting to the new reality. In *Workers of the Donbass Speak* we documented apprehensiveness about compulsory Ukrainianization, and a strike that sought to pressure the government in Kiev to adopt a more federalist political structure and to release additional funds for wage increases. "What has become worse? Everything," Iurii Makarov, cochair of the Donetsk city strike committee, told us. "The Center has just moved from Moscow to Kiev."[10] I previously have quoted Tatiana Samofalova, Valerii's wife, on what Ukrainian independence meant to her and do so here again because, with much of the Donbass unreconciled to a Ukraine tilting west, it movingly reveals another orientation:

> I was born in Ukraine and I've lived here all my life. My father, my husband's father, my grandparents are buried here. . . . But it's not enough to live in independent Ukraine. My relatives, my aunt, my cousin, live in Russia and it has become a problem now to go and see them. We cannot meet with each other very often, and letters don't get delivered. Why should I want such independence? What am I independent from? From my own relatives? What for? I don't want such an independence.[11]

In "The A.F.L.-C.I.O. Goes to Ukraine," Danny Walkowitz and I tried to expose the strong-arm tactics that that organization's Free Trade Union Institute (FTUI) used to make the Donetsk strike/workers committee more compliant with its agenda for greater "democracy."[12] Strong-arming included suggestions about dropping Iurii Boldyrev from the Donetsk city strike committee and retrieving a printing press it previously had lent. We singled out for criticism Adrian Karatny-cky, a Ukrainian American, who served as FTUI's point man for Ukraine. An ardent supporter of the Ukrainian nationalist organization Rukh from its found-ing in 1989, Karatnycky would go on to head Freedom House where "he developed programs of assistance to democratic and human rights movements in Belarus, Serbia, Russia, and Ukraine," and then served on the board of the Atlantic Coun-cil's Eurasian Center.[13]

Though short-lived, this engagement with on-the-ground labor politics was exhilarating. I felt, among other things, that I had taken up the cudgels for the same struggle Dad had fought in the late 1940s and early 1950s. The forces ranged against him and his comrades in the teacher's union consisted of anti-communists of both liberal (or, as he never tired of repeating, social-democratic) and conser-vative stripes. Boldyrev and others we tried to defend hardly could be accused of being Communists, but their hostility toward the siren song of nationalism and FTUI's version of democracy earned them the same opprobrium. Moreover, despite various insurgencies in the 1970s against the aging, accommodationist AFL-CIO leadership under George Meany, Lane Kirkland, who led the organiza-tion from 1979 to 1995, proved a worthy successor.[14]

We too had our differences with Boldyrev and other local activists. Our awareness of how corporations, particularly in the energy sector, had manipu-lated market forces made us far less optimistic than our friends in Donetsk for whom the market had a magical aura. When we interviewed Makarov and other leaders of the Donetsk strike committee in May 1991, we asked them about their attitude toward the marketization of the coal industry. "Positive. Our attitude is positive," one of them replied.[15] And no wonder, when, as I later analyzed "the miners' dilemma in the Soviet Union and its successor states," "the price of coal was administratively set at a level that bore no relation to demand or the costs of production." Part of the Soviet policy of providing cheap energy to its enter-prises, the system of "planned losses" meant that miners depended on subsidies ("handouts") from the Ministry of the Coal Industry, a dependency they bitterly resented and characterized as "ministerial feudalism."[16] Hence, the importance they attached to the demands for permitting mining associations to market their product "at world prices" and the retention by the mines of a greater proportion of their proceeds.[17] For them, the value of their product was self-evident and so too should have been their reward. As one activist told Stephen Crowley, "A market is this: I earn my own, I buy my own, having sold my labor power."[18]

I don't think anyone, leastwise the miners themselves, gave a thought to what now seems self-evident—environmental considerations. Wind, solar, and other sources of energy already were challenging coal's hegemony in Western Europe and North America, and environmentalists in those parts of the world were putting coal executives on the defensive. But in the Soviet Union and its successor states, environmentalists had plenty of other issues to pursue: safety at nuclear power stations in the wake of the accident at the Chernobyl power station in April 1986, reversing the desiccation of the Aral Sea, stopping loss of habitat for wildlife, and opposing a bizarre scheme to reverse the course of northward-flowing rivers. Coal thus remained king even while those whose livelihoods depended on it added to the political turmoil.

The situation of the miners did not change appreciably during the 1990s; it mostly deteriorated. Instead of a shortage of soap—one of the most galling effects of the regime of perestroika—they labored after the implosion of the Soviet Union under a regime of deferred wages. Wage arrears reflected a stalemate between the collective power of labor capable of extracting subsidies through strikes and the threat of further disruptions on the one hand, and the nostrums of global advisory bodies keen to bring fiscal discipline to new, post-Soviet budgets on the other. Nobody could know exactly when or how that stalemate would be broken by the time I finished "Freedom of Prices and the Price of Freedom," but I could see "the spectre of the Iron Lady [hanging] over the 'bloated' mining industry, the miners' movement and the miners themselves."[19]

In subsequent years, I occasionally turned my attention back to the miners of the Donbass. In 2004, I revisited and updated the themes addressed earlier in the form of a ten-year retrospective.[20] Ten years further on, the war in eastern Ukraine between Ukrainian government forces and those of the Donetsk People's Republic (with support from those shadowy Russian irregulars) occasioned a despairing reflection about nationalism and its casualties. Referring to Tatiana Samofalova's "complicated affinities," I asked, "Will the Ukraine that emerges from this war be able to accommodate such indifference to nationalism?"[21]

I recently attempted to reconnect with Tatiana's husband, Valerii. "I am writing this letter," I told him in Russian, "with little or no hope that you will receive it. I write, nonetheless, because I owe you a letter. You wrote to me on February 9, 1993. I don't know why I did not reply and now ask your forgiveness."[22] Valerii's letter, which I had uncovered among my papers, mentioned worsening living conditions and the hope that if not his children then his grandchildren might witness "the triumph of democracy over totalitarianism." Enclosed I found two photographs of me in their apartment, images that, he wrote, evoked cries from his grandson of "Liusia, Liusia!" Valerii's grandson would now be about twenty-five and draft-eligible.

To this account of my Donetsk visits and the writing that eventuated from them, I am moved to add a coda. In November 1992, just weeks after my article about the AFL-CIO and the meddling of Adrian Karatnycky had appeared in *The Nation*, I encountered at the annual convention of AAASS, that year in Phoenix, an American professor of Ukrainian origin whom I knew casually. We had always exchanged pleasantries over successive conferences, but this time as we alighted from elevator we had shared, he turned to me and with a thin smile asked rhetorically "And who are you, Siegel*baum* and Walkowitz, to defend the Ukrainians against Karatnycky?" It may have been the only time in my life that I felt the cold chill of anti-Semitism directed at me personally. Nevertheless, I cherish my experience in Ukraine. It not only made me a better historian, but a better human being.

In retrospect, it seems incredible that in addition to traveling to Donetsk I managed to fit in service to the Holocaust Memorial Museum, but I did. In early January 1990, I spent ten days with Raul Hilberg on a mission to identify archives in Minsk and Kharkov related to the Holocaust. A memo distributed before the trip described our purpose as "gather[ing] information on records in Soviet archives in the areas occupied by the Nazis so that we can efficiently organize a program to microfilm the most important of them." Although the museum claimed to be "mainly interested in German records captured by the Soviets," it welcomed information about Soviet-originated records, particularly the records of the Extraordinary State Commission to Investigate German-Fascist Crimes.[23]

The invitation from the museum came as a surprise. At forty-one, I was considerably younger than other consultants, had never worked on anything related to the Holocaust, and had limited Soviet archival experience. Perhaps at this stage, some three years before the museum opened its doors to the public, it had tried to get others before settling on me. As for Hilberg, although a renowned expert on the Holocaust, he had never been to the Soviet Union and did not have Russian. I therefore acted as translator whenever we encountered anyone without English (or German, his native language).[24] Despite the vast gulf between us in age and experience, we got along all right.

In Minsk, the Central State Archive of the October Revolution (TsGAOR-BSSR) shared with the oblast archive the same building, one of few in the central part of the city that had survived from before the war. One morning, I came across a photograph in one of the files of the Nazis' Generalkommissar for Weissruthenia, Wilhelm Kubbe, standing on a balcony above the courtyard from which the photographer had snapped the image. A little while later we stopped for lunch, and I emerged from the building into what turned out to be that very same courtyard. I could barely lift my eyes to look at the balcony. Kate Brown has noted in her brilliant book about "places not yet forgotten" that "often places ostensibly rich with meaning have, at first glance, little power to narrate history and its significance." This is why, she adds, "place often disappoints."[25] Granted, but in my case, something like the reverse happened. The co-incidence of seeing the photograph in the same building where the new Nazi ruler of Minsk had been headquartered, and then finding myself in the same courtyard over which he had gazed powerfully narrated the specificity of what had taken place in that city between 1941 and the summer of 1944.

Both Raul and I reported that the archivists in TsGAOR-BSSR had not been very helpful. For example, as if a time machine had brought me back to Moscow in 1973, they did not permit us to consult finding aids. I did nevertheless manage to spend a few hours with *fond* 861 (Extraordinary State Commission for Investigation of Atrocities by German-Fascists) for 1944–1949, making such laconic entries in my notes as follows:

Op. 1, ed. kh. 12, l. 25: KALINKOVICHI (15 Dec. 1944) Rounding up of Jews in town and conveyance by freight trucks 1½ kms outside of town (NE) where they were shot. Among those participating—LISTED are 3 'police'; 12 trucks with 50–60 people.

Op. 1, ed. kh. 12. l. 93: KOPATKEVICHI (1948–9) Includes reference to Aug. 1941 "German punitive expedition in Sekerichi, Kolkov village soviet, seizing 4 and shooting them, "only because they are Jews;" Dec. 1941, 8 in Ptich + 25 shot; March 1942, 12 in Kopatkevichi burned alive in cemetery.

Op. 1, ed. kh. 12, l. 162: AKT (17 Dec. 1944)—Aug. 1941 census of Jewish population; assigning to them of most dirty work; seizing of property— shooting of 96 Jews.

Natalia (archival contact) says there is film of ghetto in KINOARCHIVE division: 222720 Dzerzhinsk, Minsk obl., ul. Moprovskaia, 1, dir. Murmylo, Stanislav Ivanovich

The Extraordinary Commission, headed by the two prominent Soviet Jewish writers Vasilii Grossman and Il'ia Ehrenburg, compiled testimony of this sort throughout territories of the Soviet Union formerly occupied by the Third Reich. The tortured path by which the commission's findings eventually reached the public is now well known, but was not in 1990.[26] I remember Hilberg's surprisingly dismissive response (something like, "Well, it's only witnesses' testimony") to the astonishment I expressed about such horrifying details as those cited here. What is no less surprising to me, is that after filing these notes away, I completely forgot that I had ever made them, until they reappeared in connection with my preparations for writing this memoir.

Raul had greater appreciation of what I located in the other archives. The Minsk oblast archive (f. 688, the papers of the Minsk City Commissariat, essentially the collaborationist city administration from 1941 to 1944) included lists of Russians and Germans receiving goods, chits to receive the requisitioned property of Jews, passes issued to Germans stationed in Minsk, personnel lists of apartment rent payers, lists of clothing requisitioned from Jews, and requests from local inhabitants for material assistance. Unlike in the central state archive, we enjoyed full access to the finding aids. In Kharkov, where the director put herself at our disposal, I saw records of educational institutions under the occupation (a subject badly in need of research to this day), and of the city administration. The latter (f. 2982) contained the biggest find: a color-coded list of residents by street, alphabetically arranged as per the census of December 1941, with Jews' names on yellow pages and those of Russians, Ukrainians, Poles, and Germans on white. The occupying forces used this list to assemble the city's Jews—some 10,000 individuals—on the grounds of the tractor factory where units from Einsatzgruppe C proceeded to execute them.[27]

Our trip exposed us to a Soviet order rapidly unraveling. While waiting at the airport in Kharkov for the flight to take us back to Moscow, I wandered into the lounge where a group of young people had gathered around a television. As I got closer, I could see Gorbachev pleading with a crowd in Vilnius to oppose Lithuania's secession from the Soviet Union. "Over fifty years," he told the crowd in Vilnius' Lenin Square, "we have become tied together whether we like it or not." I could not assess the crowd's reaction on the screen, but the television viewers' ridiculing giggles were unmistakable. Then, after learning that our flight had been canceled because of a snowstorm, I stood outside trying to figure out what to do. A couple of leather-jacketed guys approached me offering to drive us to Moscow—through the snowstorm. "Aren't the roads too dangerous?" I asked incredulously. "No problem," one of them said before naming a price in dollars. Not interested in risking our lives, I attempted to wave them off, only to provoke them to reduce the price more than once and then, in desperation, convert it to far less valuable rubles. In this manner, I inadvertently discovered an elementary lesson in bargaining.

The price of our cautiousness was to spend an extra night in Kharkov, sleeping uncomfortably in something calling itself a "motel," near the airport. By the time we arrived in Moscow the next day, we had missed our flight home. We thus had to check into a hotel—the venerable Natsional on Gorky Street. After we presented our passports to the woman at the desk, she commented that our visas had expired, which indeed they had. The remark prompted Raul to explode at her, with denunciations of bureaucracy and other distasteful things. "She's only doing her job," I recall telling him, instantly regretting my choice of words that he undoubtedly had heard before in a different context.

Hilberg, who wrote to me shortly after we went our separate ways at JFK airport that "it was good having you along on this trip," died in 2007. In 2013, nearly a quarter century after I had traveled with him to Minsk and Kharkov to help identify material in Soviet archives for the Holocaust Museum, I undertook research in the museum's library of an entirely different nature. I had learned from a graduate student at the University of Chicago that the museum had obtained digitized copies of Soviet archives including material from the Evacuation Council and its regional subsidiaries.[28] Formed less than a week after the Nazi-led invasion in June 1941, the council had assumed the Herculean task of evacuating eastward strategic installations and their personnel numbering in the millions. I don't know who identified these materials as appropriate for the museum's collection—they certainly did not only concern Jewish evacuees—but digitized for reading in the museum's library, they represented a real boon.

It is hard to exaggerate the disorientation one felt in those last Soviet and first post-Soviet years. Each new violation of an old taboo—Gorbachev pleading with those Lithuanians on television and being laughed at in public, miners' delegates calling for Gorbachev's resignation, the declaration of an independent Georgia just two months before I arrived there from Donetsk in 1991—required an adjustment to a new reality. Aside from trying to keep abreast of recent developments and incorporate them into one's teaching, one's research agenda and family responsibilities (in my case, the raising of two sons) also impinged. So many adjustments coming in rapid succession produced excitement but also a certain amount of mental and emotional fatigue. To be sure, many of my North American and European colleagues suffered from the same condition.

But what about Soviet citizens? How well do we understand what they went through? When did elation at unexpected and, in their lifetimes at least, unprecedented opportunities lead to anxiety, insecurity, and disorientation? Or did some people experience reverse trajectories—from anxiety to elation? Some did, although I suspect they comprised a tiny minority, the notoriously crude, undeserving New Russians. Of them I only caught glimpses. One such rare occasion found me in 1994 at Le Gastronome, an unbelievably expensive restaurant that took its name from the food emporium previously occupying the space on the ground floor of the late Stalin-era apartment building at Krasnopresenskaia. As *The Moscow Times* described the fare, citing the restaurant's new director, "Crocodile steaks, goose confit, sushi starters and expensive wines are just some of the exotic foods that the restaurant serves to meet the demanding tastes of New Russians, who now make up 65 percent of the restaurant's clientele."[29] Jonathan Sanders, CBS's correspondent in Moscow, whom I had known as a graduate student in history working at Columbia under Leo Haimson, took Dan Orlovsky and me to dine there on his employer's dime. Asked by Jonathan to choose a wine, I balked because every bottle on the menu had at least (!) three figures—in dollars—next to it.

Russian television, as a recently published book argues, both registered and contributed to the disorientation.[30] Every weekday night beginning in December 1987, Aleksandr Nevzorov of the program *600 Seconds* would recount the day's toll of murders, each "killing" (an instantaneous loan word from the English) presented in more gruesome detail than the previous one. In 1986 as glasnost gathered steam, a Soviet Russian woman sitting in a Leningrad studio could affirm to an audience in Boston via a "tele-bridge" that "we don't have sex in the USSR," meaning it was not a subject fit for public discussion or visual representation. Within a few short years, sex became mainstream.

For my money, though, Svetlana Alexievich's *Secondhand Time* best captures what being Soviet meant in those last chaotic years before 1991 and then in post-Soviet times.[31] Even in translation, we can hear her interlocutors' bitterness, anger, and (less often) bemusement. "There's a commercial on TV for copper bathtubs that cost as much as a two-bedroom apartment," a forty-nine-year-old former party secretary tells Svetlana. "Could you explain to me exactly who they're for? Gilded doorknobs . . . Is this freedom?" Later, she complains that "the great Russian language has grown unrecognizable: 'voucher,' 'exchange rate corridor,' 'IMF tranche' . . . It's like we speak a foreign language now."[32] Visiting Moscow or Petersburg during the 1990s, one came across a lot of obvious misery—women and men of all ages standing in front of entrances to railroad stations selling their family's clothing, rolls of toilet paper, shoes, cigarettes, and other items; mothers with small children sitting on the marble floors of metro stations holding out their hands, keening, or sleeping; and roving gangs of youths, the late twentieth-century equivalents of those early Soviet-era kids without a future (*besprizorniki*). I did not have conversations with these people. I never got to hear their life stories; nor, before Alexievich bothered to listen, were they represented in the literature about that time.

As a frequent visitor from abroad accommodated in neither the most luxurious nor the cheapest of hotels, I encountered two young women exhibiting a different kind of misery. Let us call them the Natashas, because that is what both called themselves. It happened in Minsk and in Leningrad: I would receive a telephone call in my hotel room. The voice at the other end introduced herself as Natasha and asked if I wanted to meet her—not in the hotel but in her apartment. How did these Natashas get the phone number? How did they know that a man would answer the phone? Would this have been a straightforward one-off transaction—sex for money—or did they envision longer attachments (and more money)? I don't have answers to these questions, but what should not be in question is the desperation that would have driven these and undoubtedly many other women to invite complete strangers—and foreigners at that—into their homes for the likely purpose of giving them access to their bodies.

By contrast, my collaborator and friend, Andrei Sokolov, never gave the impression of being either desperate or miserable. I actually do not remember him complaining at all. Whenever he wanted to indicate that he considered something absurd or irritating, he would wave his hand in the air and say *"ëlki palki."* A chain of popular restaurants in Russia serving middlebrow cuisine bore this name, but Andrei's imprecation predated their opening in 1996. At the time, I had no idea what he meant by this expression and never heard it from anyone else; I since have learned that it is an all-purpose equivalent of "darn" or "fiddlesticks," a euphemism for far ruder profanity that also begins with the sound "ë/yo" and refers to what would be done to one's mother. Comparatively, Andrei did not have that much to complain about. He lived with his wife, Natasha (!) and her mother in a modest apartment in Tëplyi Stan, a residential community in the far southwestern part of Moscow on the Kaluga-Riga (orange) line of the metro. Six stops separated the Tëplyi Stan metro station from Profsoiuznaia, the station nearest to where he worked at the Institute of Russian History. It also lay in the direction of the Sokolovs' dacha where the family raised vegetables that they brought back with them in Andrei's slightly beaten up white Lada hatchback.

But Andrei did not only work at the Institute. He also taught at Moscow State University, gave classes at the Russian Humanities University, and served as a dean of I don't remember which institution. Only on Tuesday afternoons when he held his "reception hours" could I see Andrei at the Institute. As I entered his office on the third floor at the short end of an L-shaped corridor, he invariably would let out an "ooooh," followed by some ironic remark like "esteemed colleague, Dr. Siegelbaum." There would follow drinks, usually beer but sometimes harder stuff, accompanied by sausage and crackers, exchanges of articles and books, and visits from colleagues in the Institute. We would thus sit around Andrei's cluttered desk, bantering with each other and ridiculing just about everyone as afternoon imperceptibly became evening. On those occasions, I felt privileged to be among such genial people who didn't take themselves or their diminished circumstances too seriously and seemed genuinely glad to share with me what they had. These are among the happiest memories I have of Moscow.

Among Andrei's colleagues, I got to know Sergei Zhuravlev best. Andrei's protégé, Sergei became his closest colleague and eventual successor as senior social historian at the Institute. Like Andrei, Sergei could not afford to work solely at the Institute. He wrote local histories for district administrations, taught evening classes, and, again like Andrei, participated in joint ventures with foreign academics. They, I want to stress, could count themselves among the fortunate ones—academics who had learned to survive without party-approved agendas and central state funding that had all but disappeared.

How did the Soviet Union's end affect my own agenda? I don't mean my research projects but in the larger sense of how to understand the Soviet project. If one might define the purpose of studying Soviet history as gaining a better sense of what *they* were about, and thereby obtaining a more complex or rounded picture of what being Soviet meant, wasn't that still worthwhile? It may not have mattered any more to the American national security establishment, which had sponsored "know thy enemy" studies since the beginning of the Cold War in the 1940s. But I never gave a fig for those people and *their* agenda. What I mean is, did Soviet history have any importance aside from the political threat the USSR had posed to American hegemony? From one perspective, it mattered no more than ancient Roman history, Song dynasty China, or Medici Florence. Nor should it have. Whatever advantage we who studied Soviet history had enjoyed by our association with the existential enemy, we had not earned it. The loss of such distinction did not seem unfair but merely unfortunate. From another perspective, debates about Soviet history never limited themselves to that country; they implicitly dragged in the entire history of Marxism, socialism, and the global Left—past, present, and future.

Once, possibly at an MSG session, I expressed alarm at liberal triumphalism, most famously represented by Francis Fukuyama's "end of history" essay.[33] Geoff Eley waved off my concern by pointing out that the end of communism logically meant the end of anti-communism. I suppose Geoff anticipated that without communism the national security state would lack its raison d'être (and collapse of its own accord?). I did not share his optimism. Nor did I agree with the view Sheila Fitzpatrick propounded one day as we strolled in Moscow's former All-Union Exhibition of the Achievements of the National Economy that "we" (meaning we social historians) had triumphed, and Richard Pipes and his ilk had become irrelevant. She may have even put it in terms of us now being at the center, the insiders, or the establishment. I didn't feel that way, and still don't.

Figuring out what defined "us" in the wake of the Soviet Union's disappearance inspired "Alternatives." Beginning in 1992, those of us interested in exploring alternatives to the dominant narrative of the inevitable triumph of capitalism and liberal values met as a caucus at AAASS conventions and sponsored sessions. We also published a newsletter twice a year. The initiative for creating this informal organization belonged to Joan Neuberger and Wendy Goldman, though I, Ron Suny, and several others participated in preliminary discussions. Among my papers relating to Alternatives are a mailing list of ninety-three names, a letter from Joan from December 1993, and the first issue of the newsletter for 1994. The list, compiled on the basis of people signing up at the caucus meeting or subsequently, contains the names of many I already have mentioned: Reggie Zelnik, Ron Suny, Bill Rosenberg, Joan Neuberger, Moshe Lewin, Stephen Kotkin, Diane Koenker, Heather Hogan, Mark Harrison, Wendy Goldman, Arch Getty, Sheila Fitzpatrick, Don Filtzer, Laura Engelstein, Bob Davies, Katie Clark, and Bill Chase. In what might have been a gesture of solidarity or just curiosity, three Russians from Moscow signed up too. Joan's letter referred to the next "LA Newsletter," which did not mean Los Angeles but Left Alternatives, the name of the organization. It urged me "to include in the next issue a short introductory paragraph describing in some general terms what the newsletter is for, how people can get on the mailing list . . . and encouraging readers to contribute."

Volume 3, number 1 for 1994 indicates that I did follow Joan's suggestion. The issue contained three substantive contributions: an extended version of my contribution to a roundtable discussion called "The Problem of Class in Soviet History," Mark Steinberg's "Cultural Theory and the Category of Class," from the same roundtable, and a fascinating, full-length article on Vorkuta by Michael Burawoy and Pavel Krotov based on their six weeks in that northern Russian mining town. The prefatory editor's note indicated that Ron Suny would edit the next issue and that written contributions should be sent to him. But no subsequent issue appeared. Left Alternatives died as quietly as it had been born.

We all went our separate ways. Some, like Sheila, refrained from any further association with the Left. Mark Harrison, who had joined the British Communist Party in 1973 after returning from a year of research in the Soviet Union and who rose thereafter quite high in the Midlands regional party organization, decided that communism had no future and shifted gears.[34] Others continued fighting the same fight but on different fronts. I am thinking in particular of Joan Neuberger who rose to national prominence by leading the effort among the University of Texas faculty to oppose the presence of firearms on campus. Still others left the profession or passed away—Reggie Zelnik, from a freakish accident on the UC Berkeley campus in 2004; and Misha from complications associated with the onset of Alzheimer's in 2010, two years after my father had succumbed to the same wicked disease.

I distracted myself by developing an interest in the building of that canal in Soviet Uzbekistan, and it is there, in what my previous work would have defined as the periphery, that I want to end this chapter. I already have introduced Dinora Azimova, daughter of the historian who wrote her dissertation on the Great Fergana Canal's construction. Dinora, an academic in her own right, clearly had adjusted well to the new conditions in the country, as had the rest of her family. When I went to the family compound outside Tashkent to interview Dinora's mother, I also met Dinora's brother, Uzbekistan's minister of finance. This Uzbek family had sufficient means to employ Russian chauffeurs and house servants, an interesting reversal of colonial arrangements, I thought. No less surprisingly, when Dinora introduced me to her sister-in-law as a professor at "Michigan University," the woman asked, "which one?" "Michigan State University," I answered. "Oh, I spent two years as a student at Central Michigan University in Mt. Pleasant!" she exclaimed in flawless English.

IREX, the sponsor of my visit to Uzbekistan in 1999, occupied a downtown Tashkent office that employed locals who all exuded kindness and helpfulness. At least ten years my junior, the American in charge of the office was affable enough. I ran into him one night at a gathering of expats doing their best to imitate those notoriously hysterical party animals in Moscow best described by Matt Taibbi and Mark Ames in *The Exile*.[35] In Fergana, IREX had set me up with Fauziya Ablyakimova, an IREX alumna who spent a semester at the University of Illinois Champaign-Urbana and taught English at Fergana State University. Fauziya arranged for me to stay in the apartment of her in-laws who were away. She accompanied me to the archive the first morning I worked there and provided me with dinner each night. And, although I did not mention it in my report to IREX, she not only arranged for a driver to take me to the Fergana Canal, but sat alongside me in the rear passenger seat and when we arrived at the canal, climbed up its banks eager to show me details of the bas relief statues. Think of how many ways this extraordinarily agreeable occasion violated the canons of religious fundamentalism—a married Muslim woman spending the day on an excursion with a non-Muslim American man in a completely isolated part of the country engaged in the pursuit of historical reconstruction.

Although a Muslim, Fauziya had had a Soviet upbringing. Both she and her husband, a gym teacher, were raised in Ashkhabad (Ashgabat), Turkmenistan, the children of displaced Crimean Tatars. They came to Fergana in the 1970s for the most ordinary of reasons—job opportunities. In 1999 when I met them, their backgrounds struck me as nothing more than a curiosity. Not until a decade later when I started concentrating on migration did it become apparent that the entire Soviet Union consisted of people displaced for one reason or another. I already have mentioned some of Donetsk's elderly residents, but many others hailed from elsewhere: Larissa Sartania, who translated for Danny, came from Georgia; Alevtina Voronshchova, who worked for one of the local television stations, migrated from Siberia and claimed Polish ancestry; and my host in Tashkent, a Jewish woman who accompanied her parents as evacuees during the war, had decided to return to Russia with her daughter.

I did not maintain contact with Fauziya, but Dinora, employing the language of fictive kinship, maintained contact with me. In the summer of 2004 she reached out to her "American brother" by e-mail to ask if I could assist in the translation into English of a Russian-language script for a movie she had written about the visit of the poet Sergei Esenin to Tashkent in the early 1920s. Though unfamiliar with the story, which had a basis in fact, I obliged. I don't know if anything came of her ambition. A few years later, while in Moscow, I received via e-mail an urgent request from Dinora to meet her at the Borovitskii Gate to the Kremlin where one of her "children" was performing in a concert hall attached to the armory. I duly turned up at the entrance where I discovered that she had left a ticket for me. After finding my seat, I began craning my neck to see if I could locate Dinora, expecting her to appear at any moment. Meanwhile, young people from various countries in the "Near Abroad" performed pieces of classical music—a Belarusian girl played Mozart, a Georgian boy rendered Beethoven. Then, an Uzbek boy walked on stage accompanied by an older woman who at first I thought must be Dinora. The boy sat down at the piano and sight-read a piece of music unfamiliar to me, the woman obligingly turning the pages.

After the concert, I approached these two, praising the boy's performance and inquiring if they knew Dinora Azimova. "Yes," the boy answered brightly. "She is the reason I am here. She paid for me to come." The woman, the boy's real mother, beamed. "Had she also intended to come?" I asked crestfallen. The boy replied that indeed she had, but at the last minute something important had come up. Many strands are woven into this encounter. The daughter of a pioneering indigenous female academic, herself a success in her profession, lands on her feet after the breakup of the country that made possible her family's upward social mobility.

Having accumulated a great deal of cultural capital, she invests some of it in a grateful child prodigy (her "son") who, born after Uzbekistan had become independent, travels to Moscow to perform with other children from former Soviet republics. She thereby helped to perpetuate the ties—let's call them imperial—that bound these far-flung nations to the center, that is, to Moscow, and to each other, via the medium of European high culture.

CHAPTER 7

ONLINE AND ON THE ROAD

The website Seventeen Moments in Soviet History (www.soviethistory.msu.edu) has existed for almost two decades. For much of that time, it has played a key role in how students in North America and elsewhere in the world access Soviet history—what they see, hear, and read from the Soviet past. Seventeen Moments was the brainchild of Jim von Geldern, a professor of Russian studies at Macalester College in St. Paul, Minnesota. Jim's previous collaborative efforts in producing collections of documents had done well, but the new technology of the Internet intrigued him, and he wanted to try something new.[1] I hardly knew Jim when, in October 1998, he approached me about developing the website with him. He made his pitch simple: "you know the sources, and our particular interests are complementary, enough so that you seemed the natural choice." He also had excellent timing, for I knew I would be chairing the History Department the following fall semester, and the notion of a joint project of this kind seemed just the kind of distraction I could use.[2]

From the start, Jim had conceived of the website as consisting of discrete, chronologically defined components. Fond of the 1970s Soviet television series *Seventeen Moments in Spring*, which followed the escapades of a Soviet mole inside a Nazi German espionage agency, Jim eventually adapted the title to make it correspond to seventeen discrete years within the seventy-four of Soviet history. Each "moment" would be an orienting year—say, 1917, or 1929—containing corresponding content. The year 1943, for example, would have units on the nine-hundred-day siege of Leningrad, the Battle of Kursk, the end of the Comintern, and the new national anthem. The year 1956 would house sections not only on Khrushchev's famous secret speech to the Twentieth Party Congress, and the Hungarian uprising, but also the launching of Sputnik and the explosion at the plutonium facility near Kyshtym. Although the latter two events occurred not in 1956 but a year later, they "belonged" to 1956, because the next moment we chose did not happen until 1961.

At first, we only had hunches about what content would go in what years. The first unit that occurred to me concerned a relatively minor event—the transfer in 1954 of the Crimean Autonomous Oblast from Russian to Ukrainian republic administration. "The Gift of Crimea," as we called it, proved to be not very rich in source material: two documents, a couple of photographs, a few paintings of the peninsula, and three songs with rather tenuous connections to Crimea and virtually none to the event.[3] Little could I have imagined when I drafted the lead-in essay that it would figure as one of the few readily available sources of information in English on the background to the Russian Federation's annexation of Crimea in March 2014.[4]

The viability of any unit depended on the availability of materials—textual documents, photographic and other images, and video clips. We had at our disposal our respective institutions' libraries plus the ever-expanding resources available on the World Wide Web. But we realized early on that we would need to expand our resource base beyond what we knew and could lay our hands on. In December 1999, we sent e-mail messages to dozens of historians requesting that they provide: "(1) five to ten documents you particularly like to use when teaching Soviet history; (2) several documents important to your particular area of specialization; (3) several documents from the post-1960 era, as well as something from the post-Soviet period." Many replied with excellent suggestions. We also recognized the need to travel to Russia to expand our resource base, especially video, but that presupposed money and connections. Fortunately, Jim, who had far more technical expertise and experience with grant writing than I, put together a brilliant proposal that he sent in our names to NEH's Educational Development Demonstration Project, thereby garnering $150,000 for our project. He described the final product as twofold: "Documents . . . formatted in HTML for distribution over the internet via a website, and a CD-ROM produced by an academic publisher," the latter to "feature a more focused navigational scheme including thematic arrangements and lesson plans."[5]

The academic publisher should have been Indiana University Press, which produced a CD-ROM for *Entertaining Tsarist Russia*, Jim's second book, coedited with Louise McReynolds. But its editor-in-chief passed on the opportunity, evidently skittish about committing the press to a sourcebook whose sole presence would be online. Consequently, we decided to fold the lesson plans into the website. The Internet has yet to find its historian, but when it does, I hope the contingencies about its shape and direction will be recovered. As recently as the turn of the millennium, most book publishers hadn't a clue about how to respond to the new medium; their failure to seize its opportunities has hurt them badly.

Jim perceptively argued in the proposal that the recent availability of Soviet archival material—including audio and visual resources—meant that "the study of Soviet history no longer needs to be limited to officially published documents and dissident writing smuggled to the West." The Soviet Union turned out to be multivocal, and the new medium's capacity to display "new types of 'documentary' evidence, such as film, graphics, and music, which have stretched traditional means of publication to their limits," gave it a distinct advantage. Jim indicated that we intended to travel to the Russian State Documentary Film and Photo Archive (RGAKFD) in Krasnogorsk outside Moscow to acquire previously unavailable materials for the collection. This would be made possible by our connections to Abamedia, a Fort Worth–based company founded by J. Mitchell Johnson "to produce television, film, and new media programming for the international market."[6]

In March 1998—that is, six months before Jim approached me—Abamedia had held a planning conference in the Library of Congress to discuss with academic advisors and potential funders strategies for expanding the holdings of ROCK (Russian Online Culture and Knowledge), Abamedia's digital library of Russian cultural materials. I attended as did about twenty other "academic advisors." We advised Johnson to work on expanding accessibility to the Krasnogorsk archive, advice that, I suppose, we based partly on self-interest. How much self-interest did not become apparent until Jim and I plotted the itineraries for our two trips to Moscow. Thanks to Abamedia and its Russian Archives Online program, we enjoyed carte blanche status in the film and photographic archive. And thanks to the archivist Elena Kolikova and her staff, the canisters of celluloid kept on coming almost as fast as we could feed them into the sprockets on those large machines that looked like they had done service during the Great Patriotic War. Watching hours and hours of astonishing and sometimes unintentionally humorous newsreel from *Sovkinozhurnal*, and thumbing through thousands of photographs in a room on the second floor proved among the most rewarding experiences I had in decades of working in the archives.

I also fondly remember those times in Moscow because Leslie Page Moch accompanied me—the first of our trips together to Russia. I had known Leslie even before she became a colleague in the History Department in 1996, but we only became intimate after admitting to each other that our respective marriages were irreparably broken. We started living together in September 1999 after her marriage had ended and I had filed for divorce. On that first trip to Russia in 2000, Leslie and I shared an apartment with Jim in the Sokol'niki district of Moscow. The following year, a spacious apartment in the southwestern district at the end of the metro's Sokol'nicheskaia Line accommodated the three of us plus Jim's tremendously bright Bulgarian student Emilia Simeonova, now in economics at Johns Hopkins. One could not have wished for a better companion than Leslie. She got a reader's ticket at the Russian State Library (that is, the former V. I. Lenin State Library of the USSR, popularly known as "Leninka"), independently renewed a slight acquaintance she had made years earlier at an international conference, and always seemed ready to experience another adventurous outing.

Once on the metro, I noticed Jim reading something that prepared aspiring law students for the LSAT. It turned out that he intended to supplement his career as a Russianist by becoming an immigration lawyer in St. Paul. And that, after another couple of years at the University of Minnesota's law school and successfully passing the law boards, is what he did. Meanwhile, we both beavered away at writing entry essays for each unit and selecting corresponding video clips and photos for Seventeen Moments. While Jim did all the coding, I did most of the essay writing—approximately eighty essays. Some exhibited more elegance than others. Some played to my strengths; others stretched me in new directions. Jim tended to take the more cultural topics; I did the political and economic ones. We debuted the website in time for the fall 2001 semester, as promised in the NEH application.

By this time, I had served two years of a five-year stint as chair of the History Department at MSU, presiding over department meetings, composing annual reviews of the performance of each of my fifty or so colleagues, attending chairs' and directors' meetings and the occasional retreat, representing the department at annual Big Ten chair gatherings, making the case (mostly unsuccessfully) to the dean for positions to replace retirees or those who found positions elsewhere, and strategizing with the university's provost, vice-provost, and medical officer about how to persuade a psychologically disturbed and potentially dangerous colleague to resign. That last task took up about as much time and certainly fortitude as all the others combined. I subjected myself to performing these tasks for the most mercenary of reasons: I needed the extra income to help pay for Sami's tuition at NYU, plus alimony. I did not do a great job, but I tried to be conscientious.

The Seventeen Moments archive/online sourcebook today includes "more than 600 primary source texts, 270 video clips, 1,100 songs and 1,400 images representing the incredible breadth and variety of Soviet life in the way that ordinary people experienced it."[7] It is used in hundreds of colleges and universities as well as not a few high schools throughout the United States, Canada, and in many other parts of the world, transforming (I don't think it is an exaggeration to say) how teaching and learning about Soviet history takes place. Seventeen Moments first went online years before "DH" (digital humanities) became a widely used term, no less an expected field of endeavor for historians and others in the humanities.

I am proud that the site received a Classic Award (although I'm not sure what the "classic" means) in History from Multimedia Educational Resource for Learning and Online Teaching (MERLOT—oh those acronyms!) for 2006.

Nevertheless, I am philosophically opposed to the online teaching (OT) part of that award as a substitute for live teaching in a real classroom, whether that classroom is located in a conventional "bricks and mortar" building or anywhere else. Of course (and this point has been made so often, it is tiresome to repeat it), for people who live in remote areas and are otherwise incapable of getting to a real classroom, online teaching is a boon—providing they have the wherewithal and self-discipline to learn in isolated conditions. But the investment of universities in DH is out of all proportion to this actual need. It represents a disinvestment in actual faculty, especially tenure-stream faculty. For a few years, MOOCs (massive open online courses), with their promise of putting the "great professors" on everyone's screens, threatened to sweep academia. One enthusiast writing in *The New York Times* celebrated its "disruption" of traditional models and the "shimmery hope . . . that free courses can bring the best education in the world to the most remote corners of the planet, help people in their careers, and expand intellectual and personal networks."[8] University administrators salivated over the prospect of dispensing with pesky tenure-stream faculty altogether and relying on temps to grade students in courses "taught" by the stars. Fortunately, adverse publicity about stupendously high dropout rates from MOOCs slowed and even reversed their growth. But they continue to enroll large numbers of students in a multitude of courses and are among a bevy of other bad, profit-driven ideas afflicting higher education.

Designing websites for use in class is distinct from—and in fact at odds with— designing an entire class on the web. It also is intellectually challenging. Early in the process of designing Seventeen Moments, we discovered that plotting out the site involved more associative thinking than either of us had ever done before. For the unit on "The Khrushchev Slums" (1961), our somewhat jaundiced take on the mass housing program of the late 1950s and early 1960s, we located a wide variety of images from the Concise Housekeeping Encyclopedia published in 1954 but also visual renderings of the "ideal metropolis of the Soviet future" from the popular science fiction journal *Tekhnika molodezhi* (Youth technology), a fabulous clip from the 1962 cinematic operetta *Cherëmushki* with music by Dmitrii Shostakovich, some raw footage of a village outside Moscow undergoing transformation into a forest of high-rise apartments, and "We Move into Our New Home," a jazzy pop song from the mid-1960s.[9] Each offers a different dimension of the urban housing scene relating laterally rather than linearly to the others. Each of us felt our minds stretching as we embarked on successive units.

The pace of adding units inevitably slowed after the first burst. Eventually, we began recruiting new ones from colleagues whose work lent itself to the multidimensionality of the site. Kristen Edwards, a tech-savvy Stanford PhD, provided one of the first, on wartime evacuation, the subject of her dissertation. Kristen also gained access for us to the Hoover Institution's rich collection of posters and served as a sounding board and sympathetic ear when we ran into difficulties or lacked confidence about how to proceed. In 2008 the site underwent its first redesign thanks to a research grant from Macalester College and the technical input of Christian Meister. Between June 2010 and July 2014, Deborah Field, Amy Randall, Christine Evans, and Steve Harris contributed units that strengthened our offerings in gender, the media, and technology. More recently still, Kate Brown provided an essay based on her intrepid research into the Soviet plutonium processing industry.

Among the site's numerous users, nobody has been more creative than Amy Nelson of Virginia Tech. I've known Amy ever since she acted as one of the graduate teaching assistants in a Soviet history course I taught in 1986 at the University of Michigan. Amy, whose interest shifted from the history of music in the Soviet Union of the 1920s to animal history, contributed a wonderful article on pet keeping to a volume I edited on private spheres in Soviet Russia.[10] Amy's inventiveness in using Seventeen Moments came to my attention at a session devoted to the website at the ASEEES convention. A glance at the website for her Soviet history course for spring 2017 (http://amynelson.net/soviethistorys17/) will give the reader a good sense of how she uses the site to explore Soviet history with her students. In 2014, as some South Asian guys who had come in as the lowest bidders for upgrading the site for a second time seemed to be taking us for a ride, Jim and I gratefully accepted Amy's assistance and made her a third partner in its administration.

On January 14, 2015, a week into Michigan State's spring semester, Doug Priest, a graduate student appointed to teach the undergraduate Soviet history class in my stead, sent me an urgent e-mail message: "Today in class," he wrote, "one of my students alerted me to the fact that the front of www.soviethistory.org appears to have been vandalized by a hacker."[11] After commiserating with Doug, I contacted my colleague who runs H-Net, the Humanities and Social Sciences Online network that hosted Seventeen Moments. "At this juncture," he informed me, "it appears that the hacker achieved database access and was able to acquire 93,000 user accounts with names, affiliations, and passwords, which he announced on Twitter and managed to post publicly." Wow! Pride at the extent of the Seventeen Moments viewership combined with horror at the hubris of the hacker as I tried to take in the next part of the message: "I hope [this information] will help you in your search for programming services to fix the code and a host to provide a new home to remount it for public use."

While teachers of Soviet history—including poor Doug Priest—scrambled to find alternative sources for their students, Jim, Amy, and I pondered our options. I first inquired if H-Net really had cast us adrift as its director's message to me strongly implied. It had. Oomph. I spent a few days feeling miserable, but self-pity did not rescue the site. Amy meanwhile put a few of the geeks she knew on the case, which proved helpful. She also scouted out the possibility of hiring a commercial operation to upgrade and host the site. Ultimately, we decided to place Seventeen Moments under the umbrella of MATRIX, the Center for Digital Humanities and Social Sciences at Michigan State. The site has been running again since September 2015 with only minor disruptions. And the gratitude and praise expressed by users both online and in person as well as the tangible benefits experienced by students in my own classes make it all worthwhile. As I write, Amy, who has assumed primary responsibility for the site, is applying to NEH to help fund its upgrade.

We know only too well from the presidential election of 2016 that the Web has occasioned an exponential increase in the flow of easily accessible—and sometimes intentionally disseminated—misinformation. An early case of misinformation spread via the Internet—far less sinister but still eye-opening—occurred in the wake of the explosion in Baghdad of a truck bomb on August 19, 2003, which killed twenty-two people including the UN's special envoy to Iraq Sergio Vieira de Mello. Every account of the incident I consulted online referred to the truck carrying the bomb as "Soviet-made." Russian sources proved no exception.[12] Many quoted FBI agent Thomas Fuentes who identified the vehicle as a "Soviet-made military flatbed truck known as a Kamaz."[13] This description intrigued me because I had become interested in Soviet-made vehicles and also because I had become sensitive to blaming the Soviet past for everything wrong, deficient, or dangerous in post-Soviet Russia.[14] I therefore wanted to know whether Special Agent Fuentes had determined the truck indeed dated back at least twelve years or did he use "Soviet" in this loose and misleading way? Fuentes, I hasten to acknowledge, did have his detractors. Indymedia UK, which described itself as "a network of individuals, independent and alternative media activists and organizations," claimed that neither a Kamaz or any other truck had caused the explosion, but rather a "remote-detonated sub-surface weapon, in all probability planted days in advance."[15]

As I explained in *Radical History Review*, the forensics of the case concerned me less than what Roy Rosenzweig, founder and director of the Center for History and New Media at George Mason University, described earlier in 2003 as the "simultaneous fragility and promiscuity of digital data."[16] My search for the "phantom Soviet truck" thus became an exercise in assessing the advantages and dangers of relying on the Web and its primary search engine, Google, as a source of information. On the plus side, had Google not led me (via "Kamaz truck bomb") to other instances in which Kamaz trucks had figured in explosions, I would never have known how frequently it had served as the weapon of choice in the Chechen Wars. This discovery led to others (via "Kamaz Middle East") about the uses of these vehicles, including their prominence among Hajj participants from Dagestan and Azerbaijan, some of whom employed them to transport handmade rugs to and electronic equipment from Saudi Arabia. On the negative, whether accurate or not, information once reported can get magnified (or in the parlance of the Web, "go viral") and the lateral thinking that Google encourages makes causation a secondary concern and relevance an ever-expanding concept. I found myself, not uncharacteristically, ambivalent about the digital revolution, and remain so.[17]

But I never had any ambivalence about studying the Soviet automobile. Several things conjoined to awaken my interest. First, one would be hard pressed toward the end of the millennium not to notice the proliferation of cars in Moscow. Suddenly, it seemed, traffic jams occurred everywhere. Infrastructure—both physical and legal—could not keep pace, which meant that chaos reigned on and sometimes off the road. As with so much else, it seemed that the Soviet-era suppression of the desire for wheels of one's own had produced a vengeful reaction among post-Soviet citizens. This aroused my curiosity about cars in the Soviet era: what made them so incompatible with Soviet socialism? Did their status as the most iconic consumer item of twentieth-century capitalism have anything to do with it? Were Soviet cars really as inferior to those made in the West as their reputation suggested, and if so, why? Who owned cars? How did they acquire and service them? The questions piled on top of each other and helped me formulate a book-length project. The fact that I had grown tired of working on the interwar period and Stalinism more broadly contributed to my enthusiasm. I yearned to write about something that would span the entirety of the Soviet experience and frankly something less depressing. Finally, cars offered the opportunity to return to consumption and material culture, arenas I enjoyed exploring in connection with exhibitions of cottage industry in late Imperial Russia.

Even before pursuing the phantom truck, I had done some research on the arcane topic of automobile rallies (*avtoprobegy*). Here something presented itself that I hadn't expected—trucks and cars racing each other through steppe and desert on dirt roads or no roads at all to test the capacities of the vehicles and the endurance of their drivers. Rallies had another purpose: to rouse popular interest in these mechanical beasts in parts of the country where they had never been seen before. I will admit that some of the photographs and descriptions in Soviet newspapers I encountered as well as books devoted to particular rallies such as the Moscow-Kara Kum-Moscow rally of 1933 fired my imagination in a way similar to the Fergana Canal.[18] And in El-Registan (1899–1945), born Gabriel' Arshakovich Ureklian, an ethnic Armenian writer who grew up in Central Asia and adopted an Uzbek persona, I had discovered the quintessential Soviet Man present at both the rally and the building of the Great Fergana Canal.[19] I also confess that being the first historian in the English-speaking world to take notice of these Soviet high jinks behind the wheel appealed to me. Cars in the desert spoke to me as well because having reached an advanced stage of my career, I wanted to have some fun, and this seemed like fun.

Coincidentally, I turned to those cars barreling through the remote regions of the USSR in the aftermath of 9/11/01 and the onset of George Bush's "war on terrorism." I cannot deny that they afforded considerable relief from news of the United States once again exercising its military might, this time ostensibly in pursuit of terrorists but inevitably at the expense of a lot of civilians. Still, like so many other veterans of the '60s anti-war movement, I actively resisted the drumbeat of war from the White House, joining with millions seeking to prevent an American invasion of Iraq. Peter McPherson, MSU's president since 1993, provided an additional, more local incentive. When, backed by most of Congress and it has to be said, many liberal intellectuals, George Bush ordered the invasion, McPherson was ready to lend a hand. Indeed, after serving in the Office of Reconstruction and Humanitarian Assistance in Iraq for a few months, McPherson told a reporter from the school's newspaper that he was having the time of his life: "I think this must be heaven. . . . It's fun to put together a country's budget."[20]

McPherson's "service" disgusted me. How much did it resemble MSU's notorious Vietnam Advisory Group headed by political scientist Wesley Fishel in the late 1950s and early '60s? What, I asked myself, would we students at Columbia have done if Grayson Kirk had volunteered to perform such tasks in Vietnam? But of course, the times and students' circumstances had changed. I limited myself to a letter to the editor condemning McPherson for "playing the colonial officer," and, when the university's administration invited National Security Advisor Condoleezza Rice to address graduates and receive an honorary degree in May 2004, I organized a protest outside the building where she spoke.

Yes, through those Soviet car rallies, history provided my escape from the grimness of the US invasion of Iraq and the ineffectualness of the resistance in this country. The more esoteric the subject, the better. The research led me to the pages of the contemporary press, which covered the rallies sometimes via breathless en route reports. It also brought me to Moscow where I read in Leninka bound copies of the monthly *Za rulem* (Behind the wheel), the flagship journal of the Society for Cooperation in the Development of Automobilism and Road Improvement (Avtodor). This voluntary organization sponsored most of the rallies of the late 1920s and 1930s, and in GARF I read through its *fond* (4426). I thus became acquainted with and quite taken by Avtodor's founder and president, Nikolai Ossinskii. Born into a noble family as Valerian Obolenskii, he served in a number of capacities in the Soviet government, and tirelessly worked toward the production of automobiles in the country. He eventually succeeded, overseeing an agreement with Ford in 1929 to produce Model As in Nizhnii Novgorod.

The 2003 convention of AAASS in Toronto gave me the first opportunity to present the fruits of my research. Diane Koenker organized a panel with the inventive title of "Verbs of Motion: Driving, Biking, and Hiking in the Soviet Union and East Germany." The commentator, Anne Gorsuch, and the audience responded warmly to the presentations. A few months later, in April 2004, I "workshopped" the paper at the University of Chicago's graduate seminar in Russian history. Presided over by Sheila Fitzpatrick and attended by graduate students and her colleague, Richard Hellie, the seminar offered congeniality and thoughtful criticism. I felt I was off to a good start.

Mention of this seminar prompts a few reflections on graduate education in Soviet history and my own efforts to advance it. Academic heaven is a graduate seminar in which the students are teaching each other and the professor(s). This has happened only a few times in my career, most memorably at Berkeley in 1998 when I came up from UCLA (where I taught the spring quarter) to visit Dan Orlovsky. As a visiting professor, Dan had attracted to his seminar a bunch of bright graduate students interested in the literature on Soviet nationality policy. One could learn from Chicago's students too. I got to know many of them at Midwest Russian Historians Workshops, which began in the late 1980s and continues to the present. Meeting biannually at mostly Big Ten schools, the workshop has given graduate students the opportunity to present chapters of their dissertations in progress and faculty to present drafts of articles and book chapters.

Like other graduate students, those at MSU working under my supervision benefited from presenting their work-in-progress and meeting their peers and faculty from throughout the region. I likewise benefited. Through the workshop I got to know better Mark Steinberg, Christine Evans, and Christine Ruane (who came regularly all the way from Tulsa), and to renew acquaintances with Ben Eklof and

John Bushnell, both of whom had preceded me on the IREX program by a year but stayed on to work as translators. Though helpful, the workshop could not overcome the disadvantages my students faced when it came to competition for jobs. Placing those who earned their PhD degrees under my supervision in tenure-stream positions became well-nigh impossible after the great recession of 2007–2008. Truly excellent students with published articles (yes, in the plural) and lots of appropriate experience teaching wound up outside the university system or clinging to part-time and makeshift positions and even then, only thanks to the fact that the institutions had hired their spouses. Because their degree came from a middling Big Ten school without a renowned Russian/Slavic studies center as opposed to an Ivy League school or Berkeley or Chicago, they had the deck stacked against them.

To return to a happier subject, the presentations on car rallies culminated in an article in *Slavic Review* that situated them in the effort to advance along the metaphorical road to socialism.[21] The metaphorical and the actual coincided in the case of rallies, for they promoted the building and improvement of roads, themselves symbols of modernity and connectivity. Roadlessness (*bezdorozh'e*) necessitated campaigning for roads. As Ossinskii wrote in his account of a 2,000 km rally through the Central Russian provinces in 1929: "our attitude towards roads is one of the clearest manifestations of the survival of barbarism, Asiaticness [*aziatchina*], indolence, and idleness," the very antithesis of socialist modernity. Ossinskii's message was "the road to socialism lay in road building."[22]

I thereby yoked the story of car rallies in the 1920s and '30s to the larger tale I had been telling for several decades about the building of socialism in the USSR—its tragedies, its triumphs, and now, its comedies. I relied on contemporary press reports and the archives, but emboldened by the Seventeen Moments experience, I inserted into the mix film (Mikhail Kalatozov's 1930 documentary *Salt for Svanetiia* about the isolation and poverty of the Svan people of mountainous northwest Georgia and the building of a road to connect them to the outside world) and comedic literature (Il'ia Ilf and Evgenii Petrov's *The Golden Calf* from 1931, also adapted to the screen in 1968). I adapted observations by Emma Widdis, Diane Koenker, Jim von Geldern, Yuri Slezkine, Karen Petrone, Doug Northrop, and others about travel, tourism, Soviet spatiality, time transcendence, the functions of staged events and the fragility of the organizations staging them. I even found room for Eisenstein's aborted film on the Fergana canal, cited the literature I was reading at the time on cars and "autopias," and included four very evocative photographs from RGAKFD, the film and photographic archive.

I now can see the article was bursting with ideas that *Cars for Comrades* would develop. Those ideas came from soaking up everything I could find on the history of the automobile in the USSR—and, because that history needed to be placed in a global context, elsewhere as well. Two related things stand out about writing this book: its entire structure came to me all at once and quite early in the process of researching and writing, and the fun doing it far surpassed that of any other book I wrote. I decided the book would move from production to consumption with a spinal chapter on roads. The three production chapters would be anchored to the principal sites of production—Moscow (AMO/ZIS/ZIL); Nizhnii Novgorod/ Gorky (GAZ); and Togliatti (VAZ/AVTOVAZ).[23] Each would begin with the enterprise's foundation and work forward toward the present. The chapter on roads would encompass the entire Soviet period and incorporate much of the discussion about Avtodor from the article on rallies. The two succeeding chapters would be chronologically organized—the first from the 1917 Revolution up to the Great Patriotic War; the second from the war to the end of the Soviet Union.

The fun is hard to convey except to say that I ate, slept, and dreamed about the Soviet automobile a good deal during the five years or so I actively researched and wrote the book. For two years, however, it had to share time with my editing of a collection of essays on private spheres in Soviet Russia. That came about when, on the drive home from that conference in Toronto in 2003, I told Leslie I had heard quite a few papers that spoke to issues of consumption and private life. She thereupon suggested I edit a volume of essays and begin by asking some of the presenters to work up their papers. Even before we had reached the Blue Water Bridge connecting Ontario with Michigan, the book took shape. Notes Leslie took give *Borders of Socialism* as a tentative title. Under that heading I issued a call for papers on H-Russia—part of the same H-Net that would cut Seventeen Moments adrift years later. "The principal aim," I wrote, "would be neither to celebrate nor lament the emergence/resilience of a private sphere within Soviet socialism, but rather to offer the field a new and challenging lens through which to understand what Soviet socialism was."[24] The call received a robust response. Of the initial group of eleven, only one subsequently withdrew and someone emerged to replace her.

In the meantime, I had immersed myself in the relevant literature. I had two objectives: to better inform myself about conceptualizations of the public/private distinction, and to construct a list of common readings for contributors. The most rewarding reading included a forum on "Rethinking Public and Private" from a 2003 issue of the *Journal of Women's History*; two essays in a social scientific collection on meanings of public and private; Svetlana Boym's idiosyncratic book about commonplace objects and domestic spaces; and the first of what would become three collections of essays edited by Susan Reid and David Crowley.[25] What I learned is that notions of private and public are historically and culturally specific, but that in the case of the Soviet Union and by extension, other state socialist societies, certain ideologically inspired notions and valences overlaid whatever cultural specificities had been inherited from earlier times. I considered this formulation enormously helpful when conceiving of my own contribution to the book, an essay in which I treated cars as a "Faustian bargain" in the era of Leonid Brezhnev.

The introduction to the volume, "Mapping Private Spheres in the Soviet Context," turned into one of the most conceptually ambitious pieces of writing I ever did. It began with a section on "The Private as a Universal Category of Historical Analysis," which drew on medievalists, Middle Eastern studies, feminists, and others, among them Vladimir Shlapentokh, my old nemesis at Michigan State. Shlapentokh had pioneered historical inquiries into "privatization" in the USSR with a book from 1989 that, as I wrote, "was both pathbreaking and prescient," if different from my own orientation and that of other contributors to the volume.[26] We did not assume that private spheres were exclusively sites of resistance to the state. Nor did we argue for the inevitability of their expansion at the expense of the state. Rather, the contributions provided "evidence of symbiosis and hybridity, as well as antimony."[27]

Of the twelve contributors themselves, women made up six, and we achieved a nice mix of historians who had recently received their PhD degrees, mid-career scholars, and those late in their careers. Relations with everyone proved non-conflictual, and even pleasant. That went for Palgrave Macmillan too until one editor after another left the firm and the cover illustration never made the final cut allegedly because "our art director felt that the image did not represent clearly enough the themes of the book." Not for the first time, then, the arrival of the book itself produced mixed emotions. Palgrave virtually did nothing to promote or advertise it, and correspondingly sales have been small. Only *The Slavonic and East European Review* and *The Journal of Contemporary History*, both British-based, carried reviews. I felt badly for the contributors and frankly for myself. But lo and behold in May 2017, more than a decade after the book appeared, I received an invitation to give the keynote address at a conference in Germany on "Privacy Outside Its 'Comfort Zone.'" The organizers wrote that "your expertise in the field is familiar to us through your edited volume *Borders of Socialism* . . . which influenced our own research on privacy in the contexts of Late Socialist GDR and USSR."[28]

While editing the volume, I completed my five-year term as chairperson of the History Department at MSU. Just as in the spring of 2004 when I anticipated research leave for the following academic year, so now in retrospect, my project on the history of the Soviet automobile is a source of pleasure. The application

I submitted pointed to a key dimension of the proposed research, namely that the introduction of mass car production in the Soviet Union represented a real departure from the previous organization of Soviet society. "What accounts for that departure," my application continued, "is the core of my research agenda, but the larger point is, surely, that Cold War obsessions long obscured the internal dynamics of Soviet societies and their cultural matrices." By the same token, by inquiring into the very different history of the Soviet automobile, "we may learn more about how the use of the automobile in our own society reflects our own culturally specific dispositions."[29]

If only. In using the first-person plural in that sentence, I had hoped to elicit from the university administration some identification with my research. The university did provide me with funding in the following year, but that is where the institutional commitment ended. My friend and colleague, Lisa Fine, who had written a book on the history of a local Lansing automobile plant and its workers, joined me in trying to initiate a university-wide Center for Automobile Research (with the irresistible acronym of CAR).[30] We succeeded in bringing together a bunch of professors from the engineering college and the School of Labor and Industrial Relations, but either we were lousy salespeople, or they lacked the necessary imaginativeness to engage in a cross-disciplinary initiative, for the scheme went nowhere. How paradoxical and sad that this major university in a state whose economy and identity for so long depended on the automobile could not sustain its support for research on this "most richly symbolic artefact of the twentieth century."[31]

Being in Michigan did afford me the opportunity to interact with students whose lives automobile production had shaped for better or for worse. In a course I taught for advanced undergraduates on "A Global History of the Automobile," I encountered a student who explained his motivation for enrolling and the paper he hoped to write as follows:

> My father worked his entire life making car brakes for Bendix, which was bought out by Allied Signal, which was bought out by Bosch Corp. He started in the pattern shop, and when Bosch finally bought the company, . . . [it] sent him to finish a degree in business and engineering. . . . As an honor to my father (who passed away this last Thanksgiving to pancreatic cancer), I would like to write a paper not just on what the auto industry meant to my father, but the changes that his job and the company encountered as jobs were outsourced overseas. You see, for the past few years, my dad's job was to go overseas to instruct workers in Mexico and China how to do the Michigan plant's

job in making car brakes. This was done to close down the plant he worked at. So, I will also research why exactly Bosch did this, and the trend of shipping these U.S. jobs out of the state, and what conditions are like overseas for this to happen.[32]

How could I say no? The fate of this student's father—training people overseas so that the company could relocate, thereby depriving his workmates and friends of their jobs—encapsulated the heartlessness of corporate America, and the pathetic condition in which all too many workers in the "rust belt" found themselves. Is it any wonder that a decade later, so many white working-class voters in Michigan and elsewhere in the Midwest voted for the presidential candidate who cynically promised to restore their jobs?

During 2004–2005, my sabbatical year, Leslie and I lived in a house outside Ann Arbor we rented from the anthropologist Katherine Verdery. We needed somewhere away from East Lansing but not too far away because Leslie had to teach at MSU. The Ann Arbor area seemed ideal as a break from the cares of departmental administration. We knew Katherine from the MSG, and when she told us she would be spending that year in New York, we jumped at the chance to live in her house with its wide-open rooms, lofty two-story ceiling, and wrap-around deck. It is the house in which we got married in May 2005 on a day that started out blustery and cloudy but by the time everyone had assembled, turned sunny and pleasantly warm. Catered by an old friend from East Lansing and attended by some forty friends and family (including our aged parents whom we assumed would not have another chance to meet), the event could not have been more joyous.

Most of that year I spent editing the papers for *Borders of Socialism* and drafting chapters of my book on cars. While Leslie worked downstairs in her study or commuted to East Lansing, I sat in an upstairs room in splendid isolation from the world except for the internet connection to my computer. Every other day, usually in the morning, I would go for a run through the Loch Alpine subdivision along hilly and lightly trafficked roads past the golf course and tracts of lake and forest. In the afternoon, I would take a break by shopping, usually stopping for coffee in Dexter, the nearest town. Sasu, a freshman at the University of Michigan, occasionally came by for dinner and to do his laundry. "And you got paid to do this?" I can hear incredulous voices asking. Guilty as charged!

I interrupted this idyll a few times. I spent September–October 2004 in Moscow working in GARF, the Russian State Archive of the Economy (RGAE), and Leninka. But I also felt the urge to visit one of the provincial auto-towns to better visualize the operations, where and in what kind of dwellings people lived, and how they got to work. One day, I walked into a travel agency off a courtyard near the Kremlin to book a flight to the Volga River town of Togliatti. The travel agent furrowed her brow as if unaware of the existence of Togliatti. "I can't find the airport on the map," she told me. "It's a big place," I replied, "there must be an airport." Together, we surmised that Togliatti must share an airport with Samara, a larger city around the bend of the river to the south about 100 km away. In the end, I decided on the safer, albeit slower, option of the railroad. The train deposited me in Syzran, a full 90 km from Togliatti. Fortunately, my hosts from the History Department at Togliatti State University had arranged for a taxi to pick me up. Did Togliatti also lack a train station, I wondered?

Honored to have an American visitor, the department's youthful staff treated me warmly, but they had a surprise in store. When someone asked me to address a group of students, I of course agreed, thinking I would have at least a few hours to prepare my remarks. Instead, no sooner had I given my assent than I was ushered into a hall where a substantial audience awaited me. Startled, I didn't have time to worry about what to say or how to say it. Through my hosts, I met AVTOVAZ's public relations director Leonid Pakhuta, a fast-talking, no-nonsense kind of guy. Pakhuta gave me a tour of the assembly line, sat with me at lunch in the executive dining room, and then accompanied me to the lounge perched atop the sleek, blue-tinted, corporate headquarters with a spectacular view of the mighty river. I also obtained permission to work in the local city archive where the archivist accommodated all my requests for photocopies and refused to charge anything, the most generous service I ever received anywhere. I thereby obtained some good data on absenteeism and thefts at VAZ, but more valuable still was a thick file from 1972 of a case of marital deceit that came before the district commission on socialist legality and the maintenance of public order. I devoted four pages of *Cars for Comrades* to the case.[33] Thanks to that trip, I completed drafts of two chapters— one on Togliatti and other on roads—during my sabbatical leave.

In March 2005 Leslie and I gave lectures at the École des Hautes Études en Sciences Sociales in Paris. We lived in a tiny mansard apartment on Rue Cler in the seventh arrondissement above an aromatic bakery, frequently dined out with friends, visited museums free of charge thanks to our academic affiliation, and in general had a grand time. To the Centre d'Études du Monde Russe, Soviétique et Post-Soviétique, I talked about "Mapping the Private in the Soviet Union." I began the talk by referring to the abortive attempt by George Bush to privatize the Social Security system. This was a calculated risk, for I could not be sure how much the French knew of American domestic politics, to say nothing of my

American-accented English. More generally, I found it hard to read yet another country's academic culture. Would humorous asides work? Judging from the guffaws in the room, this talk went over well. The other two proved less successful. The critical commentary on the literature devoted to the Soviet "self" that I gave to the seminar led by my host, Yves Cohen, impressed neither him nor the rest of the audience. Perhaps they had become invested in this literature and expected me to endorse it. Finally, I presented an overview of my book project on the Soviet car to a research center called GERPISA (Groupe d'études et de recherche permanent sur l'industrie et les salaires de l'automobile). Here, the audience's technical expertise, as evidenced during the Q and A session, far exceeded mine.

Although it now seems irresponsible and a bit crazy, I went back to Togliatti scarcely two months after the fall 2005 semester began. AVTOVAZ had invited me to participate in its second academic conference on the history of the firm, and I could not refuse. I thus found myself one-third of the "foreign delegation," joining Manfred Grieger, the director of Volkswagen's history department, and Jukka Gronow, a sociologist at Uppsala University. AVTOVAZ also had invited my old friends Andrei Sokolov and Sergei Zhuravlev as well as Rudolf Pikhoia, a luminary among historians in Moscow. The company duly published our contributions to its conference and issued other publications commemorating the event.[34] I remember little of the conference sessions, mainly because, as my diary attests, jet lag made it difficult for me to stay awake.[35] By contrast, the night Manfred, Jukka, and I sat in the hotel bar drinking beer remains vivid, demonstrating how three properly lubricated foreign males who had never met each other could establish instantaneous camaraderie.

Returning home, I once again plunged into research and writing on the car book. I dwelled increasingly in the company of those who concerned themselves with the vast impact that automobiles had made on the economies, cultures, and environments of countries throughout the world. In the Soviet Union, communist ideology and state priorities had vitiated that impact, but, so I began to argue, cars loomed large in people's imaginations despite—or maybe because of—official prohibitions. To track the growth of car consciousness and the desire for cars in a country where commerce did not play a role in shaping desire, I started to pay attention to Soviet feature films, especially of the 1950s–70s, and thanks to Leonid ("Leonia") Weintraub, I acquired many of them. During a visit to Moscow in 2004, Leonia took me to the "Gorbushka," a vast market of stalls selling audiovisual products close to the Bagratsionovskaia metro station. We approached vendors and explained that we needed videos featuring cars. Thus, among others, I acquired, watched, and transcribed relevant dialog from Eldar Riazanov's classic comedies *Beregis' Avtomobilia* (Beware of the car, 1966) and *Garazh* (Garage, 1979); *Tri plius dva* (Three plus two, 1963), a silly movie about three guys who have driven down to the Black Sea coast where they meet two girls, also motorists, at a "wild" (unofficial) camping site; *Shofer ponevole* (A chauffeur against his will, 1958), a case of mistaken identity involving a real chauffeur and an archetypal bureaucrat; and *Gonshchiki* (Racers, 1982), a film about two rally driving friends who become rivals and the only one not a comedy.

Novels, short stories, and other belles lettres also contributed to the book's source base. *The Life of the Automobile* (1929), described by its author Il'ia Ehrenburg as "not a novel," but rather "a chronicle of our time,"[36] underscored the horror with which some intellectuals held those mechanical beasts in the first few decades of the automobile's existence and also provided the subtitle to *Cars for Comrades*. Vladimir Mayakovsky, the erstwhile Futurist poet who purchased a "Renoshka" (Renault) in France for his mistress and had it transported (by rail?) to Moscow, tended to worship automobiles as did his Italian Futurist counterparts. Other, lesser known, writers had more intimate knowledge of cars. Anatolii Rybakov worked as a driver at the front during the war and drove an Opel Kapitan all the way back to Moscow after his discharge. *Drivers*, his novel from 1950, earned its author a Stalin Prize. For Vasilii Shukshin, who tended to write about loners, truck drivers provided natural subjects, figuring as heroes in several stories I read. Some of the literature seemed contrived and pretty dreadful, but useful all the same.

Aside from movies and works by Soviet authors, I consulted reports by Western correspondents and more occasional visitors including emissaries of American and Italian car companies; analyses by Western Sovietologists and intelligence service personnel; the local, regional, and central Soviet press; as well as ministerial, municipal, factory-based, and civic organizations' archives. I worked with the papers of the Austin Company of Cleveland, Ohio in the Western Reserve Historical Society and the Reuther Archive at Wayne State University. I read books in German and Italian to the limited extent I could to familiarize myself with both comparative and entangling details unavailable in languages I knew better. My knowledge of Russian nomenclature for auto mechanics increased exponentially.

Nothing could match spending time in Soviet archives and reading in the Leninka till my eyeballs would nearly drop out from fatigue. I did just that during a three-week trip to Moscow in May–June 2006. According to my travel diary, when I announced to the driver who picked me up at the airport that I came to continue my research on the history of the Soviet automobile, he exclaimed, "There was no such history. What they made were excuses for vehicles, all except the GAZ-51. That was a truck and a mighty fine one too."[37] The diary also testifies to another serious bout of jet lag, occasional pleasures ("The *kliukva* [cranberries] and 21°[C] vodka hit the spot"), but also occasional self-doubt ("I'm finding it difficult to articulate what my book is about, or even more to the point, what is its thesis") and irritations (my suitcase failing to be delivered to my apartment after not showing up at the airport; the policeman at the entrance to the archives' reading room contesting my right to bring in my computer; and the archivists repeatedly rejecting requests for files).

The academy prioritizes research over teaching by offering inducements in the form of fellowships and grants to expand opportunities to engage in the former while reducing time spent on the latter. This may be justified, but rather than assume an antagonistic relationship between the two, we should highlight the synergies. The course I taught on the global history of the automobile grew out of but also provided new insights into my research agenda. Similarly, presenting work-in-progress should not only advertise forthcoming publications, but ideally improve them. I found this to be the case with successive versions of the "Faustian Bargain of the Brezhnev Era"—at the University of California's Irvine and San Diego campuses, and the University of Michigan at Dearborn's Center for the Study of Automotive Heritage. And sometimes, conferences generate not only interest but future collaboration. A conference on the automobile "revolution" after 1945, organized by the Moscow-based German Historical Institute (GHI) in February 2007, enabled me to renew my acquaintance with several of the participants in AVTOVAZ's conference and to meet other scholars for the first time.[38] Corinna Kuhr-Korolev, GHI's very able assistant director and the conference's organizer, made the Institute a convivial place to wind down at the end of the working day. That it shared the same building with the Institute for Scientific Research in the Social Sciences (INION) whose library only the Leninka surpassed for my purposes made it all the more attractive.[39]

When possible, Leslie and I traveled together. Social Science History Association conferences both in Europe and North America afforded us the chance to present our work in our respective networks, hers in migration and mine either in labor or technology. In March 2007 we arranged for our classes to be covered at MSU for a few weeks (plus spring break) so that we could accept an invitation from the University of Toulouse-Mirail to give lectures. We took advantage of the opportunity to do some sightseeing in the city and its glorious surrounding region—Carcassonne, Albi, Narbonne. I spoke to the university's Slavic languages department on the 1933 Moscow-Kara Kum car rally and to another seminar on . . . what else? . . . the Faustian bargain. As if a sixth time didn't suffice, what about a seventh? Flying from Toulouse via Paris to Trondheim, I rolled out Faust yet again to a Norwegian audience that seemed as cold as the weather.[40] But the restaurant dinner with my host, the transplanted Hungarian György Péteri, surpassed expectations—a different wine with every course and each course outstanding. What was it Toshi Hasegawa said in reply to my question about "where is the struggle?"

Sadly, during these years—2006–2008—Alzheimer's claimed my father. I am haunted still by a phone call he made to me one day in July 2006. He talked about this other person who was trying to gain control of him, someone he didn't know and feared. His voice trembled with fright. I felt helpless. I already suspected by that time that he had the dreaded disease, but this call brutally confirmed my suspicions. Calls to my parents that usually left me melancholic punctuated the otherwise perfect year, 2007–2008, that Leslie and I spent as fellows at the Netherlands Institute for Advanced Study (NIAS). Each conversation repeated what the previous conversation already had covered, and the one before that. Many elderly people descend into senility; Dad descended into idiocy and then into nothingness. He recognized me when I visited in November 2007 en route to the AAASS conference in New Orleans and even after we returned from the Netherlands in June 2008. By then he resided in the absurdly named "memory unit" of an assisted living facility in Ardsley, New York, where my parents had moved a year earlier. Mom lived in an apartment down the corridor. She never forgot the day she came into his room and he asked her, "Do you work here?" He died in November 2008 two days after the election of Barack Obama as president.

By the time we arrived at NIAS, I had finished the manuscript for *Cars for Comrades* and submitted it to Cornell University Press, then still directed by John Ackerman. I had known John for a long time; he had offered to publish *Stakhanovism*, and although I went with Cambridge instead, evinced no hesitation when I approached him about the car book. On the contrary, he decided to adopt it as his personal project. A resident of Ithaca, New York—erstwhile home of that car-loving Russian expatriate Vladimir Nabokov—John seemed taken with the quirkiness of the car-USSR pairing. His careful and critical reading of the manuscript complemented those of the two external readers. Neither before nor since have I worked so closely and beneficially with an editor.

John helped me recognize and emphasize the three axes that structured the manuscript: foreign/domestic, public/private, and continuity/change. Of course, the Soviet automobile did not have to reinvent the wheel, but it also did not merely imitate others; it adapted to prevailing conditions, political, environmental, and otherwise. Legally speaking, the Soviet automobile fell into one of two categories: either state or personal property, not private, a category that meant income generating. In practice, many bigwigs with access to state cars used them for personal purposes, and many car owners employed them for monetary gain. Even trucks, although quintessentially state property, wound up performing heterodox services as fuel suppliers, taxis, and conveyors of stolen property. As for the third axis, significant change did not come until late in the Soviet period when the VAZ plant in Togliatti began mass-producing the 2101, the car derived from the FIAT 124 that was known as the Zhiguli (or Lada in its exported version).

The book argued that the automobiles born in the USSR were Soviet not only because of where and how they were produced and who got to use them but how they were used. Appreciating their particularity could "defamiliarize an object long associated with twentieth-century industrial capitalism" at the same time as "it should defamiliarize certain narratives based on the paramountcy of centralized political power and the centralized system of resource extraction and redistribution."[41] In other words, "if the particularities of Soviet socialism can better inform us about the history of cars and trucks, then the Soviet automobile can help teach us about Soviet socialism."[42]

This double defamiliarization stemmed from my desire to reengage with Soviet history in a way that would connect with other fields. Why "reengage"? Because I wearied of repeating the same point via social history about the resilience of ordinary people in the Stalin era, because I yearned for a broader temporal and geographic canvas on which to paint my picture of Soviet history, and because material culture fascinated me. I wanted to learn new things about being Soviet and cars counterintuitively fulfilled that desire. At least one reviewer, a Russian literature professor at Georgetown, got the point. She wrote that this "alternative history, or rather, . . . alternative angle on [the] history . . . of an everyday object, close in its orientation toward the new historicism, opens perspectives that the traditional macro-history is lacking; it allows us to see the history of everyday life, and thus helps to defamiliarize existing stereotypes."[43] Just so.

At NIAS, all the fellows had to present five-minute summaries of their projects, an exercise well worth wider adoption. Only a few had the opportunity to discuss their work at greater length, I among them. Most days Leslie and I cycled on those big Dutch bikes that provided our only mode of transportation in Wassenaar along a tiny canal through polder and then leafy suburban streets to the main building at NIAS, a refurbished 1920s mansion. We sat in our adjacent offices with their gabled ceilings, rooms large enough to accommodate a couch for leisurely reading and afternoon naps. The staff—from Joe the American expatriate handyman to Dindy van Maanen, the librarian; Joos Hooghuis, the chief of staff; and

Wim Blockmans, the rector himself—not only responded to our every need, but often anticipated them. The institute's chef and his assistant, a husband and wife team, prepared lunch, the sole obligation, and an enjoyable one at that, in our diurnal regimen.

Leslie and I soon realized that in the absence of any cause for complaint, we could devote our time with the fellows to discussing each other's work and substantive issues of mutual interest. This usually happened over lunch, though we also met each other socially in the evenings. An Israeli couple from Haifa University lived a few floors below us in a building located in what we jokingly referred to as the "proletarian district" of the exceedingly affluent town of Wassenaar. They were among our closest friends, who also included a Dutch professor of literature who lived in Leiden with her journalist husband; an Irish-born legal scholar who worked on the executive power of the European Union; and a medical sociologist from Rutgers. I also found a tennis partner, a young Mozambican who worked on restorative justice in his native country. With the Israelis we rented a car to do some sightseeing through Zeeland, and a bunch of us traveled by ferry to the westernmost Frisian island of Texel where we rented bikes. Midway through the excursion, we discovered a cemetery containing the remains of Soviet Georgians who went over to the German side during the war, sought to escape from their clutches as the tide of war turned, and met their deaths—presumably by firing squad—in April 1945. In June toward the end of our stay, several of us luxuriated at an Umbrian villa owned by the Irish legal scholar and her Dutch husband.

How did NIAS contribute to my research, an end-of-the-year form asked. I interpreted the question to mean how it had helped expand my intellectual horizons. Two lunchtime conversations came to mind. One began when my Mozambican tennis partner recommended a book by the French historian Annette Wieviorka on how to assess and employ witnesses' testimonies. He found it a reliable guide in his study of peace and reconciliation; I found it helpful in formulating my criticism of *The Witnesses*, a controversial book I reviewed for *The London Review of Books*.[44] In the second conversation, a South African woman off-handedly remarked on the parallels between her country's post-apartheid history and Russia in the post-communist era. Wow, I thought, that would be an interesting course to co-teach.

NIAS also gave its fellows the precious gift of time—time to pursue what they wished, chase up leads, indulge their curiosity, go down new paths. In my case, having invoked the Faustian bargain so often, I decided to acquaint myself with Johann Wolfgang von Goethe's classic two-part play based on a German legend from the sixteenth century. I already knew (thanks to Lenin!) that "all theory is gray, my friend. But forever green is the tree of life."[45] But Goethe's version of the romantic hero who would do anything to transcend human limitations surprised and excited me. I associated such yearnings with bourgeois man and the growing sense of his potential power at the dawn of the Industrial Revolution. "To seize the highest and the lowest," Faust muses, to "expand my single self titanically."[46] No wonder Goethe worshipped Napoleon Bonaparte, I mused. Letting my mind wander, I pondered the outsized role that transcendence seemed to play for those German philosophers Johann Gottlieb Fichte, Friedrich Schelling, and Heinrich von Treitschke. All sought to break the bonds of German political impotence in the late eighteenth and early nineteenth centuries. Marx, abandoning Georg Wilhelm Friedrich Hegel's idealism, found the key to transcendence in overcoming capital's contradictions, while Nietzsche's Übermensch was perhaps closest to Goethe in his nihilistic flouting of ordinary morals and mortals. This urge had a darker side, too: Carl Schmitt saw in the Nazis the means to transcend the limitations of bureaucratic norms; and Martin Heidegger notoriously associated them with "inner truth"—but all could be linked to Goethe.

Well, maybe. But with the last remaining tasks on *Cars for Comrades* out of the way, I turned my attention while at NIAS to a new project. It happened that the fiftieth anniversary of Expo '58, otherwise known as the Brussels World's Fair, coincided with my relative proximity to the Belgian capital. A chance encounter put me in touch with a Belgian architectural historian, Rika Devos, from whom I learned that the Royal Archives in Brussels contained considerable material on the Soviet pavilion. Opportunity is one thing, but why would I care? It might have reminded me of exhibitions of peasant crafts in late Imperial Russia. Or, perhaps, its revival of a theme I had addressed in the book on Stakhanovism intrigued me—the use of *tekhnika*, or as I termed it, a "technological wonder," to enhance the Soviet Union's prestige, both domestically and internationally. That wonder took the shape of a silver ball with mustachioed antennae, a replica of Sputnik, launched in October 1957. Year after year in my Soviet history class, I stressed that the late 1950s and early 1960s corresponded to the peak of that country's international prestige, when real fear existed in the United States and more generally the West that the Soviet Union would win the Cold War. To a large degree, Sputnik made it so.

I took the train from The Hague to Brussels to read French-language correspondence among Belgian administrators and between them and Soviet officials. In March 2008, I spent two weeks at GARF in Moscow reading internal Soviet correspondence relating to plans for its pavilion and popular reception to its exhibits. I also read more broadly—on the Soviet space program, on previous Soviet participation in world's fairs, on soft power during the Cold War, and in cultural studies literature on how museums and exhibitions shape meanings. From this thick stew came a couple of conference papers and an article I contributed to a special issue of the *Journal of Contemporary History*, an earlier version of which I contributed to a collection on Soviet space culture.[47]

From cultural studies, I employed a 1980 essay by the Marxist cultural theorist Stuart Hall called "Encoding/decoding." I modified Hall's terminology by inserting "reproduction" between what I called production and consumption. Each of the three components had its own source base: for production, the discussions behind closed doors among members of the Soviet pavilion's organizing committee, advice from its board of consultants, and correspondence with party officials; for reproduction, published reports on reactions to Sputnik among visitors to the Soviet pavilion; and on consumption, comments in visitors' books deposited by the Soviet Chamber of Commerce in RGAE, as well as commentary in foreign newspapers and journals. These different kinds of material clearly related to and in a sense produced each other. An essay about how the Soviet Union represented itself to both a foreign audience and its own citizens back in the USSR, "Sputnik Goes to Brussels" concluded diffidently that "there is little to suggest that foreign visitors who were not already favorably disposed changed their attitudes . . . based on what they saw." It also asserted the impossibility of determining much at all about how Soviet citizens consumed the propaganda, although in one instance a few apartment dwellers in Leningrad invoked the launching of the two artificial satellites in their efforts to get their apartments fixed—in other words, if it was possible to perform the complicated task of . . . , then surely . . .[48]

I learned while resident in Wassenaar that NIAS would host conferences organized by fellows. I immediately thought of one comparing car cultures and practices throughout the Soviet-bloc countries. Because many whose work I already knew about or had heard of lived in Europe, travel costs would be reasonable. On the basis of a healthy response to a preliminary call for papers, I approached the appropriate staff at NIAS. "Where is your funding coming from?" the good Rink van den Bos, who controlled NIAS's purse strings, asked me. Oops. I mumbled something about misunderstanding and slunk out of his office. Corinna Kuhr-Korolev and Luminita (Luma) Gatejel came to the rescue. Together, they concocted a plan to hold the conference at the Collegium for Comparative European History at the Free University of Berlin where Luma was a graduate student. Thanks to Luma's persuasiveness, funding came from the Hertie Stiftung and thanks to Corinna, from GHI. I had met Luma at the conference in Moscow in February 2007. A native of Romania, she had decided to write her thesis on a comparison of Romanian, Soviet, and East German car production and distribution systems, and she struck me as both brilliant and fearless. Corinna became my co-organizer and confidante. The three of us made a good team.

I wrote to John Ackerman shortly before departing for Berlin, attaching the program of the conference:

> I now have the papers in hand and can in all honesty say that they are fabulous. Really. Auto history, as you may have had a glimpse based on my own book, is a rapidly expanding field with hitherto unimagined possibilities for casting new light on social/cultural and political history. That the Socialist Countries could be revisited in this light I only had a glimmer of when it occurred to me to organize this conference. The freshness, the depth—in a word, the brilliance—of the papers I can now attest to.[49]

I laid it on pretty thick. But the papers genuinely impressed me, and they only got better as a result of the conference. Over that weekend of June 12–13, 2008, twelve scholars from nine different countries sat around a big table swapping tales about cars in the distressed circumstances of the Eastern Bloc. The papers fell inevitably into three categories that later comprised the book's structure: systems of production and distribution; mobility and urban planning and housing; and car cultures.[50] "Inevitably," because as a colleague at Michigan State once observed, I thought in triads. That third part consisted of chapters by Luma on common elements among Romanian, East German, and Soviet practices; Kurt Möser on do-it-yourself repairing of Trabants in East Germany; me on the popular associations with Soviet truck drivers (heroes, professionals, loners, wheeler-dealers); and Corinna on women drivers in post-Soviet Russia. My chapter ("Little Tsars of the Road") is one of my favorite pieces of writing, probably because nobody had ventured into this territory before, at least not from a cultural historical perspective. The entire project, in fact, pleased me from beginning to end.

It coincided with the translation into Russian of *Cars for Comrades*. The idea to translate it might have germinated when *Car & Driver* included the book on its list of gift suggestions for Christmas 2009. If, I surmised, the book had such crossover appeal among car buffs in the United States, what about Russians? I also began noticing more and more translations of historical monographs and began to wonder, "If so-and-so's book could be published in Russian translation, why not mine?" I discussed the matter with Corinna whose colleague at the institute knew Andrei Sorokin, the managing director at ROSSPEN, the publisher of many books in Russian translation. I called Sorokin in Moscow. Notes of my conversation indicate I told him "my university will give me $5000 toward the translation of the book but only on condition that I present a contract from the publisher." For his part, Sorokin expressed interest but in a subsequent letter noted that "Rosspen would require a subvention amounting to $5,000 US . . . to hire a translator, reproduce illustrations, and defray other expenses." Which was the cart and which the horse here? The suspense ended on January 11, 2010, when MSU's Office of the Vice President for Research and Graduate Studies informed me that it would fund my proposal in the amount of $5,000. This information satisfied Sorokin who issued the contract.

ROSSPEN hired a translator who initiated an intensive e-mail exchange with me that would continue, chapter by chapter, until the end of the year. The stickiest problem stemmed from my note-taking technique, which had not always recorded the original Russian she required. With published material and online sources, I could retrieve the original Russian, but what about archival citations? At first, I tried to pass off as originals my translations back into Russian, but she quite soon detected my ruse, and forced me to confess that I simply could not confirm the original Russian. She managed nevertheless and by spring 2011, just as Leslie and I were about to arrive in Moscow to begin yet another project, ROSSPEN informed me that I could pick up my two free copies.

That warm sunny day in late May when I emerged from ROSSPEN's office at Profsoiuznaia 82 in Moscow's Cherëmushki district carrying the two copies is etched into my memory as among my happiest. I beamed with unadulterated pride and bonhomie. As I was about to enter the Kaluga metro station, a woman of about forty years old approached me to ask how to get to Rechnoi vokzal (the river station). The rest of the encounter, told a few years later in the third person, is as follows:

> "Oh," he replied, "that's quite far but it's not that difficult," and as he pointed to the small metro map she was carrying, he suggested she get off at the Tret'iakovskaia station, change to Novokuznetskaia, and then take the train to the last stop. But she didn't seem to understand these directions. He thereupon offered to accompany her at least until he had reached his destination. As they entered the metro, it became clear that she had no idea what to do. After he ushered her through the turnstile, they approached the escalator and, as fear gripped her, she gripped his arm.

"We can conclude," Leslie and I wrote, "that some things do not change; provincial people continue to be bowled over by the urban features of Moscow or

Petersburg."[51] At the time, I didn't quite know what to make of the woman's agitation. It altered my mood.

These years spent online and on the road coincided with my transition from mid- to late-career. The process developed as ineluctably as it happened without my notice. At some point, late in the process, I had that conversation with Sheila Fitzpatrick that here serves not just as a fitting coda to this chapter but as one of the central themes of the memoir—my ambivalence about academic life and my unwillingness to abandon identification with the embattled, the subaltern, and the outsiders. Provoked, I think, by some scurrilous attack on "revisionists" that may even have mentioned us by name, I fulminated and maybe even tried to recruit Sheila for some kind of counterattack. Her response disappointed me, but now I can see her point that we had become "the establishment." Sitting on editorial and institutional boards, chairing prize committees, and giving keynote speeches at conferences suggests being the recipient of a certain degree of deference. Yet, I resist being associated with the establishment. I still have those feelings of inadequacy, of having failed to make a significant difference.

I think the end of the Cold War has a lot to do with these feelings. I confess to a certain nostalgia about the Cold War—the clarity of identifying friends and enemies, the importance (or apparent importance) of the stakes—even though at the time I wanted it to end. The problem is that while I did not expect or desire an outright Soviet victory, the country's unmitigated defeat and dissolution irrevocably changed the reception to the kind of history I and others wrote. A quarter century on, the alignments have changed. They are more blurred. To be sure, there still is a market for Cold War–type anti-communist history. I already have noted the centennial retrospectives on the 1917 Revolution with their nonsense about the accidental nature of the Bolsheviks' rise to power.[52] Despite all our efforts to introduce other themes and demonstrate their salience, what the reading public best knows about Soviet history is still the Gulag, Stalin's brutality, the absence of freedom within the country, and variations on the Soviet Union as a totalitarian empire. Putin's crackdown on democratic practices at home and the flexing of Russian military power abroad have only helped to maintain if not strengthen these emphases.[53]

Still, the push toward the history of late socialism, that is, the post-Stalin decades, has led to a shift from an earlier emphasis on state coercion, resistance, and strategies of survival ("Soviet history with tears," I once called it)[54] to less doleful subjects: private life, consumption and material culture, gender and sexuality, nationality and transnationality within the USSR, and nongovernmental contacts with the world beyond Soviet borders. Unlike Cold War–era historiography, much of this literature eschews the East-West binary in favor of interrogating similarity, interactivity, and mutual shaping. Sports, nuclear power, industrial agriculture, and the cinema are some of the topics illustrating this approach. And then, there is migration, a subject whose attractiveness caused me to reinvent my professional persona one more time.

CHAPTER 8

THE MIGRATION CHURCH

"A real, if far-flung community without the dubious benefit of e-mail," I wrote in an earlier chapter, describing the cohort of budding labor historians at the outset of the 1980s. That community eventually broke up, as many do, when new interests replaced old ones, the old ones having become prison-like or just stale. The MSG, a community closer to home, had more staying power not only because of Ron Suny's geniality, but also because it satisfied the need among us to keep abreast of historical literature that spoke to our interests and inclinations—books like Dipesh Chakrabarty's *Provincializing Europe* (2000), Timothy Mitchell's *Rule of Experts* (2002), Mark Mazower's *Salonica, City of Ghosts* (2004), David Harvey's *A Brief History of Neoliberalism* (2005), Todd Shepard's *The Invention of Decolonization* (2006), and Peter Linebaugh's *The Magna Carta Manifesto* (2008). For me, many fulfilled another need—what to assign beginning graduate students in a course on "Theory and Methods of Historical Analysis" that I taught roughly every other year.

I didn't find another far-flung community until I switched the focus of my research from production to consumption and material culture. The new field appealed to me on several levels. It took me beyond the Stalin era where I had been stuck for some time, introduced a new comparative dimension to Soviet history, and presented fresh, sometimes counterintuitive, arguments. Conceptualizations of how people related to things and the mediations between them excited me, particularly when their authors situated their work in one or another Eastern Bloc country.[1] I derived real intellectual satisfaction from my encounters with art, architectural, and urban historians all the more in that the terrain we traversed together seemed, if not virgin, then at least lightly trod.

Nevertheless, the joint endeavors—panels and conferences organized, books edited, contributed to, and reviewed—did not entail much if any political commitment, and I frankly missed the rough and tumble of the Cold War era. Sometime during the early years of the new millennium, I made the acquaintance of historians of migration, mostly through Leslie, whose *Moving Europeans* had become central to the long-term study of migration tendencies and patterns.[2] They usually participated in the European Social Science History Conferences that the Institute of Social History in Amsterdam organized semiannually. Among them, I probably saw Leo Lucassen most often. He occasionally came to the United States from the Netherlands to give lectures, including at Michigan State. So too did Dirk Herder, a German historian of migration to North America whose *Cultures in Contact* (2002) laid out systems of migration on a global scale. Donna Gabaccia, the historian of European (originally, Italian) migration to the United States, Jose Moya of Columbia University, and Nancy Green at the École des Hautes Études in Paris rounded out Leslie's circle of close friends in the field.

While these migration historians regarded me as Leslie's new partner who did Russian history, I envied their easy informality, the liveliness of their discussions, and the contemporary resonance of their work. I also came to realize through listening to them and reading what they wrote that the history of migration opened an important window onto labor history. It occurred to me that via this route I could return to labor history. If I did, though, it would have to be on a broader scale, not the revolution and civil war, not the interwar period, nor the Stalin era, but the whole kit and caboodle.

Credit should go where credit is due. Leslie, not I, came up with the idea of combining our areas of expertise to write a book together, a book on migration in Russian political space across the Imperial, Soviet and post-Soviet periods. She assumed that it would be on the order of *Moving Europeans*, covering several centuries of migration. She would provide the conceptual framework and offer comparative perspectives, and I would do the legwork of tracking down the data and, it went without saying, taking notes from and translating Russian-language sources. Not everything worked out that way. First, we both conceptualized. For example, almost from the beginning I came up with the distinction between regimes and repertoires of migration—between "the politics and practices of the state" and "those of migrants themselves," to cite an early draft from an unsuccessful grant application. This just may have constituted the signal contribution of the book to migration studies, suggesting that sometimes newbies can provide fresh perspectives. Second, although we did pursue migrants across the Imperial/Soviet/ post-Soviet Russian divides, the original notion of starting sometime in the eighteenth century did not survive. After listening to me whine once too often about how much ground we had to cover—this during our first research trip to Moscow in 2011—Leslie calmly asked, "what if we limited ourselves to the twentieth century?" before pointing out "that would still give us the three political frameworks."

Indeed, it would. At an early stage in thinking and reading about migration in Russian political space, one or the other of us announced to Leo what we had decided to do. He responded with a hearty "welcome to the migration church," which caused much mirth among everyone present. But how to proceed? We started our research abroad with a trip to the Helsinki National Library's Slaavilainen Kirjasto (Slavonic Library), brought back to its original location in the building off Senate Square. In 2011, we spent weekdays during May and into June in the library, where thickly bound volumes of the Imperial Russian Geographic Society's *Zapiski* (Notes), *Vestnik Evropy* (News of Europe), *Otechestvennye zapiski* (Fatherland notes), and *Sibirskie voprosy* (Siberian questions), to name the ones I consulted, stood on open shelves. If I needed monographs or other sources in the stacks, the library's staff, headed by the upbeat and solicitous Irina Lukka, would retrieve them. For lunch, we trouped off with Dan Orlovsky to the cafeteria attached to the Finnish archives, a short walk from the library. Dan, a Helsinki perennial at that time of year, provided good company in the evenings as well. We also saw a lot of Kaarina Timonen, a retired journalist and an old friend whom I had met back in 1973. Only Richard Stites, whose seat in the library bears a plaque testifying to the universal love he inspired up to his death in 2010, was missing.

I began with *khodoki* (scouts), a peasant institution of obscure—at least to non-peasants—origin that facilitated decisions among those who depended on their information about whether and where to resettle. *Khodoki* interested us because once state authorities began encouraging peasants from the European Russian provinces to resettle east of the Urals, they sought to coopt scouts, offering them incentives (such as reduced rates on railroads) to play by official rules. Yet, for a variety of reasons, many and in some years the majority of scouts traveled irregularly (*samovol'no*, literally, "self-willfully"). Once again, I felt among my own people, "ordinary" people contending with authorities who sought to control their behavior but could not tame them. Scouts could not be mistaken for political revolutionaries or for being political at all. Only a few seem to have left behind anything in writing. Still, they gave off an unmistakable whiff of rambunctiousness that I couldn't avoid inhaling.[3]

"When I began researching scouts in earnest," I wrote, "I assumed that their dependence on the Resettlement Administration . . . made their survival much beyond the October Revolution unlikely. I was wrong." And then, I suggested impishly that "my error is symptomatic . . . of how little attention scholars have paid to voluntary long-distance migration in the Soviet era . . . as if the Gulag, the special settlements, and the deportations of nationalities precluded this possibility."[4]

FIGURE 8.1   Leslie Page Moch in front of the Winter Palace, St. Petersburg, 2012.

Scouts served me as an entrée into voluntary migration in the Soviet era. Except for occasional comparative investigations and a good deal of reading about migration in post-Soviet Russia, I stuck to the Soviet period. This left Leslie responsible for rural-to-urban migration in the late nineteenth and early twentieth centuries, conscription and military mobilization during World War I, the Siberian exile system as represented by George Kennan and other curious contemporaries, and reindeer herding in the Far North, which pleased her the most.

We went back and forth about how to structure the book before deciding by fait accompli to organize it according to categories of migrants. We began with the least coercive (resettlers) and move toward the most (deportees), except for a final chapter on those who escaped or defied regimes of migration altogether—a motley lot of itinerants ranging from those reindeer herders to Kazakh mobile pastoralists, the Roma, and tramps, orphans, and beggars on the move. For each, we needed to explain the range of migration regimes and repertoires and the ways they interacted. We tracked regimes largely through official documents—archival, published, and online—as well as newspapers and secondary sources. In such a vast and varied country, regimes rarely functioned smoothly or without contradictions, so our story could get complicated. And, in the case of itinerants, the regimes flipped from those of migration to anti-migration, that is, ways to control, capture, or otherwise confine people on the move.

More complicated still were migrants' repertoires. Just as with settlers' reliance on *khodoki*, other kinds of migrants had repertoires that included practices peculiar to their needs. Seasonal migrants, the subjects of our second chapter, relied in the prewar decades on the artel, a self-governing work gang often from the same village. Sometime in the 1950s, references began to appear in the press to *shabashniki*—part-time or seasonal workers who typically left cities in the summer to work in agriculture and construction in rural areas to compensate for the growing shortage or low productivity of labor on collective farms. Risking arrest, they worked and were paid under the table, earning enough in one or two months to "walk around like kings."[5] Migrants to the city often drew on the "strength of weak ties," that is, connections with distant relatives or people from the same region (*zemliaki*);[6] young specialists and other career migrants engaged in informal negotiation to go where they wanted to go or at least avoid being sent to less desirable parts of the country; demobilized soldiers whose homes had been destroyed during the Great Patriotic War or who wanted to start anew received assistance from friends they had made in the service, sometimes joining them in settling in the Baltic republics; refugees and evacuees poured out their hearts in letters to authorities to obtain better supplies, or rejoin loved ones; deportees resorted to guile and bribes to escape from their places of exile. We had to tease out these and other repertoires from the sources, often reading official documents against the grain.

We interspersed the general argument about the mutual shaping of regimes and repertoires with individual stories culled from memoirs, diaries, and other sources. We could not help identifying with some of the individuals, although our list of favorites differed. Mine included M. V. Sumkin, a peasant from Kaluga province whose memoir tells of his desire to build "a good peasant life without eternal need, without frequent harvest failures, and without cruel bondage to rural kulaks"; the *shabashnik* Viktor Gal'chenko (possibly a pseudonym) who recounted his picaresque travels to an economic journalist in the late 1980s; and Genia Batasheva, an eighteen-year-old Jewish girl who after escaping from the Nazis' genocidal massacres at Babi Yar embarked on an odyssey that took her to Tashkent, a collective farm on the Kazakh steppe, Omsk, and finally the Altai in Siberia where she reunited with her father in 1944. Only slightly less memorable were the stories that many former soldiers told in interviews published on Ia pomniu/I remember, a remarkable and constantly expanding website founded in 2000 by Artem

Drabkin.[7] I fell under the spell of the sources, identifying with these individuals as I had with those workers who defied labor discipline and explained why. Such empathy, I would argue, is valuable, even if the closeness one can develop with historical subjects is illusory. I loved the illusion nonetheless.

Working together in the same household differed from previous collaborative experiences. Conversations about domestic chores—what to cook for dinner, or whether we should call the plumber about the leak in the bathtub—suddenly could be interrupted by some thought about how to conceptualize the Northern Increment, the post-Gulag Soviet system for encouraging people to settle in remote parts of the country. Although we had dissimilar work habits, the division of labor accommodated our differences. We exchanged drafts periodically, sometimes on a daily basis, inevitably quarreling over the appropriateness of a particular phrase. But at some point, we found ourselves sitting side by side at the dining room table and actually composing together. This method proved amazingly efficient. As soon as one of us would lag, the other would pick up the slack and go with the thought until mental exhaustion would set in at which point the one who had had time to recover would take it from there. We could only sustain these sessions for about three hours until we both needed a break, but even so, we finished several chapters in this fashion far more quickly than those for which we exchanged portions.

Looking back, some things fell into place weirdly as if on their own. How, for instance, did I happen to come across the article by the aeronautical engineer Stephan Prociuk from 1967 that opens the book? The Isaak Levitan painting we chose for the cover, *A Train on Its Journey*, popped up online. As for the book's title, we started off with some rather pedestrian versions that John Ackerman eventually informed us would not do. That news reached me during a visit to my mother. I must have told her about our difficulty because, as we sat at lunch in a restaurant next door to the assisted living facility where she spent her last decade, she startled me by saying "let's see if we can come up with a title for your book." She even suggested one, which for someone in her ninety-fifth year was impressive. I wish I could remember her suggestion because it provoked me to recall a lyric ("Shiroka moia strana rodnaia") from "Song of the Motherland," the best-known song from the 1936 musical comedy film *Circus*. That lyric—broad is my native land—became our title.

We presented parts of the book locally before hitting the road. We traveled abroad to conferences both individually and together to deliver papers on refugees and evacuees in twentieth-century Russia and the applicability of the concept of transnationalism to cross-border internal migration within the Soviet Union.[8]

These talks provoked both respectful criticism and praise. At the 2014 Social Science History Association conference in Toronto, we confronted four "critics" in what proved to be an enjoyable and rewarding series of exchanges. Reviews of the book pleased us too. Even one in a Russian journal that took issue with our emphasis on the agency of migrants engaged seriously with the argument. For satisfaction, it is hard to beat coming across in the introduction to a dissertation on seasonal migrants in the last decades of the Soviet Union that the approach relies "on the conceptual framework of intertwined state-supported regimes and autonomously pursued repertoires of migration."[9]

And yet, aside from four graduate students earning their doctorates under my supervision at the moment, I haven't persuaded any Russianists to convert to the migration church. It turns out that the influence one has in shaping graduate students' perspectives, work habits, and even goals is not as straightforward as I once thought. Sometimes, things about which I am quite passionate seem to leave students cold. But students generally have a pretty good idea what to expect of their major professors and the relationship is mutually beneficial. Indeed, supervision of graduate students may be among the last vestiges of the medieval origins of universities, akin to apprenticeship training in crafts. When, as happened in two cases, students failed to complete their degree, I felt I let them down. By the same token, I have delighted in the successes of students who after earning their degree under my supervision secured academic or other kinds of employment in education.

To refer to some but not others by name would be invidious, but two deserve special mention even if here they remain nameless. One is a South Korean who struggled in the program partly because of a shaky command of English and partly because of reluctance to construct original arguments. He persevered though, spent a year in the field (Cheliabinsk, Magnitogorsk, Moscow) and defended a decent dissertation. After receiving his degree, he returned with his wife and infant son to South Korea. Appointed to a research position at Hankuk University in Seoul, he recruited me as one of two editors-in-chief of a journal sponsored by his employer. The journal, now in its eighth year, publishes biannually.[10] Evaluating submissions, making judgments about the journal's policy and standards, and recruiting book review editors (two of my former students, as it happens!) have engaged my intellect and ingenuity, though sometimes also tried my patience. The other former student has managed to combine African American and Soviet histories in a way that has significantly contributed to both. She has taught me a lot about race in its Soviet and immediate post-Soviet contexts and sensitized me to how African Americans on the Left viewed the Soviet Union during the 1920s–1930s.

But I have saved for last the description of one of my most gratifying experiences, one that helped to close the circle between work and family, intellectual and paternal pleasures. Sometime in 2010, Bob Edelman, a preeminent historian of Soviet sport, approached me with the suggestion that Sasu and I contribute an essay on "Class and Sport" to *The Oxford Handbook of Sports History*, which Bob was coediting. Sasu, then enrolled in an MA program in journalism at the University of Missouri, was no less keen to try than I. We discussed what to read, with Sasu, a passionate follower of soccer, providing suggestions for some excellent monographs, and took advantage of his two-week visit to draft something together. Our penalty for finishing the draft in short order was that we had to wait a long time for other contributors to catch up, but eventually, in 2017, the handbook appeared.[11] Both father and son were pleased. Somehow, it all worked out.

UNFINISHED THOUGHTS

"You're always traveling," my friend Carroll, who lives in Sidney, British Columbia and who herself has done a bit of traveling herself, says when we speak by phone every few months. Much of my traveling in recent years has been of a familial nature and limited to the United States. But a great deal is work-related and has taken me abroad. That is a privilege of academia, especially if one's institution covers the bulk of the costs. In Soviet times, traveling to Moscow or another Soviet city entailed entering not just a different country, but a different world—the Second World. No matter how many times I made the journey, no matter how familiar I became with the taxi ride into the city from Sheremetevo Airport, I immediately felt swallowed up, and—this was the great thing about the experience—assumed an alternative persona. Who did I become? A more determined, but also more tentative Lewis. My research trips always had finite, self-defined, purposes that, notwithstanding occasionally excessive alcoholic consumption and the dalliances mentioned earlier, required my full attention. Despite all the fuss and bother of obtaining a visa, the arbitrariness of Soviet officialdom, and other irritations, I treasured these visits. For the first few years after 1991, the magnitude of changes to quotidian life made the experience of going no less fascinating. But as Russia increasingly opened itself up to foreign investment and tourists, it shed its Sovietness and other-worldness. Opportunities for experiencing the other Lewis correspondingly diminished. He became more like the one in East Lansing.

Conference travel is another perk. One gets to see old friends and make new ones, dine in some great restaurants, visit museums, attend concerts, and even lie on beaches, as Leslie and I did a few years ago in Valencia before we took a bus straight to the conference venue. All the same, I don't enjoy the experience as much as in the past. I don't know whether it is because of ever-more intrusive security regimes at airports, more crowded seating on planes, or that as I get older, my level of anxiety at arriving on time, making connections, and navigating in strange surroundings has increased. Probably all of the above. Like Richard, the protagonist of Jenny Erpenbeck's brilliant novel about a retired professor's encounters with African refugees in Berlin, I find the routines of home—raking leaves, mowing the lawn, fixing myself some tea, watching Alex Trebek preside over

Jeopardy!—comforting.[1] This is why, now in retirement, I am far more selective about which conferences to attend and what sort of research to undertake. Scholars who feel it necessary to tell me how far they have advanced in their projects, how many conferences they have attended, how busy they are, and other indices of academic worth evoke indifference, maybe even pity. This too is a privilege.

I am privileged in many other ways: as a white male, as someone who grew up in the United States during its economically expansionary decades, as the son of middle-class parents who so highly valued education, as the father of two wonderful sons, and as Leslie's partner. There is something else too that, considering current conditions in academia, gives me the sense of privilege: I swam in the tenure-stream and kept my head above water. I actually did more than that. I advanced from step to step adding honors along the way. I state this not to be boastful but in sorrow. Particularly in the humanities, the tenure stream is drying up like an arroyo in the desert. Positions of retirees including Leslie's and, since May 2018, mine are not being retained. At most, they revert to some other unit considered by administrators more deserving or they convert to administrative positions. Indeed, the difficulty of my students obtaining academic positions, which I lamented above, can be related directly to the exponential expansion of administrative positions as universities pivot toward the corporate model of income generation rather than education. Data from 2014 indicate an increase of over 500,000 administrators and professional employees added to universities and colleges between 1987 and 2012. Full-time non-faculty professional employees increased by 369 percent, part-time faculty by 286 percent, and full-time non-tenure-track faculty by 259 percent between 1976 and 2011. That compares to an increase of 23 percent for full-time tenured and tenure-track faculty.[2]

What am I doing with my privilege? That is a painful question to address because the answer that screams in my head is "not enough!" I began this memoir with my teenaged existence defined by tennis and communism. I still play tennis after a fashion, but what about communism? I still see it, much as Rosa Luxemburg did in 1915, as the only real alternative to the barbarism of capitalism.[3] Barbarism, I hear my colleagues say, really? Yes, really. The relentless drive for profit is now endangering the world as never before, pitting humans against every other species on the planet more starkly than at any time since the rise of capitalism. As for class against class, the old animus of Marxism, the pharaohs would blush at the inequality of wealth and power in contemporary capitalist societies, not least in the United States. In terms of shortened and immiserated lives, this too is barbaric.

Ah, but you say, the record of "actually existing" communist states hardly recommends itself. True enough. But it has taken me nearly a lifetime's work as a historian to fully appreciate two things about the Soviet Union as an object of study. First, the communism that Lenin and then Stalin sought to build represented an impoverished version, one overdetermined by war, civil war, and state collapse, as well as their own and their comrades' impatience, congenital intolerance of opposition, and suspiciousness of the outside world. This is another way of saying that although ripe for communist revolution in 1917, Russia was a terrible place for building communism. Many of the same factors applied to East Asia, Eastern Europe, and Cuba.

Second, Soviet leaders from Lenin to Brezhnev and maybe even Gorbachev shared with their counterparts in the "capitalist world" the belief that the application of advanced fossil-fueled technologies held the key to solving the problems that held their respective countries back, all the while regarding global resources as infinite or at least not paying sufficient attention to their limits. This characteristically twentieth-century attitude cannot be sustained without jeopardizing life on earth. We all know this now, but only a different kind of postcapitalist order governed by the cardinal principle of living within the means of the planet can effectively apply that knowledge. Otherwise, the children of our grandchildren are not going to make it.

It's easy for me to make these judgments from my ivory tower. It is part of my privilege. It is why all these years later I can be satisfied with having fulfilled my youthful ambition to find out what made the first state run by Communists tick. But—and, as readers of this memoir can testify, there always is a "but" whenever I have registered an achievement—satisfaction does not last long, lest it give way to complacency. I am, for better or for worse, still the same person, still my father's son, still hopeful, and as Dad would say, "full of piss and vinegar."

NOTES

NOTES TO CHAPTER 1

1. Tarik Cyril Amar, *The Paradox of Ukrainian Lviv: A Borderland City between Stalinists, Nazis, and Nationalists* (Ithaca, NY: Cornell University Press, 2015), 84, notes the redistribution of residential space was "an essential practice of Soviet social transformation," and adds that "forced redistribution of residential space was the topic of the first Soviet feature film," which premiered in 1918. For the film itself, unfortunately without any intertitles, see "Uplotnenie@Lenfil'm, 1918 god," Kinostudiia Lenfil'm, YouTube, published May 18, 2016, https://www.youtube.com/watch?v=5kpA9RNCKS8.

2. Ronald Grigor Suny, "Living in the Soviet Century: Moshe Lewin, 1921–2010," *History Workshop Journal* 74, no. 1 (Autumn 2012): 194.

3. Lewis H. Siegelbaum and Leslie Page Moch, *Broad Is My Native Land: Repertoires and Regimes of Migration in Russia's Twentieth Century* (Ithaca, NY: Cornell University Press, 2014), 244.

4. For a day-by-day summary of events at Columbia during the spring '68 semester, see "The Occupation of Columbia University," *Minerva* 6, no. 4 (1968): 788–93.

5. When my father started his teaching career, "Communists held important leadership positions in the [Teachers U]nion. . . . By December 18, 1937, fifteen of the twenty-four members on the [executive] board were in the Party." Such unusual representation stemmed from the walkout in 1935 by seven hundred "social democrats" who proceeded to form a rival union, the Teachers Guild. Clarence Taylor, *Reds at the Blackboard: Communism, Civil Rights, and the New York City Teachers Union* (New York: Columbia University Press, 2011), 33, 42, 45.

6. Ibid., 60. Or, "the union's adherence to the CP line did not prevent it from wholeheartedly advocating for teachers, parents, and children." Marjorie Heins, *Priests of Our Democracy: The Supreme Court, Academic Freedom, and the Anti-Communist Purge* (New York: New York University Press, 2013), 96.

7. Taylor, *Reds at the Blackboard*, 89.

8. Ethel Rosenberg, *The Death House Letters of Ethel and Julius Rosenberg* (New York: Jero, 1953).

9. Dad's boss at Digitronics and then Redactron was Evelyn Berezin, "a computer pioneer" who built and marketed "the first computerized word processor." See Robert D. McFadden, "Evelyn Berezin, 93, Dies; Built the First True Word Processor," *New York Times*,

December 10, 2018, A25. See also Leonard Sloane, "Woman in Business," *New York Times*, February 20, 1972, 7. My father always referred to her in laudatory terms.

10. The tourist agency had included the last of these cities as a substitute for Kiev because the nuclear explosion at Chernobyl two weeks earlier had put the Ukrainian capital off limits.

11. Honoré Daumier, *The Third-Class Carriage*, H. O. Havemeyer Collection, The Metropolitan Museum of Art, accessed September 14, 2018, https://www.metmuseum.org/art/collection/search/436095.

12. Bernard A. Drew, *Gibson's Grove & Turner's Landing: Lake Buel's Century as a Summer Resort* (Great Barrington, MA: Attic Revivals, 2009), 129–30.

13. "Are you by any chance the son of the late Morton Siegelbaum?" So began an e-mail message I received on August 24, 2017, from Gabi Lewton-Leopold, who is "working on a book about my late grandmother, Rose Leopold (née Kagan)." It turns out that just before my father and mother got together, Rose Kagan's boyfriend, "a teacher in NYC, and a counselor at a socialist summer camp in Great Barrington, MA," was Morty Siegelbaum. They both were party members. I had no wind of this before.

14. George Kleinsinger and Paul Tripp, *Tommy Pitcher: A Folk Opera* (New York: Chappell, 1954).

15. OCLC credits Kleinsinger with "242 works in 409 publications." "Kleinsinger, George 1914–1982," OCLC WorldCat Identities, accessed September 15, 2018, http://worldcat.org/identities/lccn-n85367851/. The Wikipedia entry for Kleinsinger (in Dutch) lists inter alia a symphony, a concerto and fantasy for violin and orchestra, and three cantatas including "The Brooklyn Baseball Cantata," with text by Michael Stratton, the pseudonym of Michael Siegelbaum (no known relation). "George Kleinsinger," Wikipedia, The Wikimedia Foundation, last modified May 18, 2018, https://nl.wikipedia.org/wiki/George_Kleinsinger.

16. Personal communication, September 16, 2018. Since Alan Arkin is fifteen years my senior, he would have performed this role before I was born. It is entirely possible that either I saw a much later performance or merely imagined seeing it on the basis of family descriptions.

17. Tom Waddell, *Gay Olympian: The Life and Death of Dr. Thomas Waddell*, with Dick Schaap (New York: Alfred A. Knopf, 1996).

18. "Camp Half Moon," Wikipedia, The Wikimedia Foundation, last modified December 2, 2018, https://en.wikipedia.org/wiki/Camp_Half_Moon. In this respect, To-Ho-Ne resembled Camp Kinderland, which attracted many "Red diaper babies."

19. I had heard Pete was the namesake of the anarchist philosopher and scientist Petr Kropotkin (1842–1921); Daniel Menaker, Pete's nephew, cites Pete's middle name as Lavrov. Petr Lavrov (1823–1900), the revolutionary socialist, lived a great deal of his adult life abroad and, like Kropotkin, ardently supported the Paris Commune. See Daniel Menaker, *My Mistake, a Memoir* (Boston: Houghton Mifflin Harcourt, 2013), 76.

20. Harvey Klehr and John Earl Haynes, *Venona: Decoding Soviet Espionage in America* (New Haven, CT: Yale University Press, 1999), 266. Two members of the Arenal family,

Leopolo and Luís, participated in the unsuccessful assassination attempt against Leon Trotsky organized by the painter David Siqueiros in May 1940. For a recent lecture by Klehr "on McCarthy and American Communism," see http://polisci.emory.edu/home/neh_2016 /about/klehr.html (accessed March 22, 2017).

21. Daniel Menaker, *The Old Left* (New York: Knopf, 1987).

22. John Jeremiah Sullivan, introduction to *String Theory: David Foster Wallace on Tennis*, by David Foster Wallace (New York: Library of America, 2016), 5.

23. Quoted from "Dr. Alexander Meiklejohn Dead; Champion of Academic Freedom; Ex-President of Amherst Was 92—Philosopher Received Medal of Freedom in '63," *New York Times*, December 17, 1964, 41. The exchange appeared as Sidney Hook, "Should Communists Be Permitted to Teach?" *New York Times*, February 27, 1949, SM7, and Alexander Meiklejohn, "Should Communists Be Allowed to Teach?" *New York Times*, March 27, 1949, SM 10. Marjorie Heins refers to this debate as "a much-discussed exchange." Heins, *Priests of Our Democracy*, 73.

NOTES TO CHAPTER 2

1. "Tuition Will Increase by $200; Rise in Room Rates is Unlikely," *Columbia Daily Spectator*, December 19, 1967, at http://spectatorarchive.library.columbia.edu/?a=d&d= cs19671219-01.2.7&srpos=1&dliv.

2. See inter alia Jerry Avorn, *Up against the Ivy Wall: A History of the Columbia Crisis* (New York: Atheneum Press, 1969); James S. Kunen, *The Strawberry Statement: Notes of a College Revolutionary* (New York: Random House, 1969); Paul Cronin, ed., *A Time to Stir: Columbia '68* (New York: Columbia University Press, 2018).

3. See Michael Stern, "Walkout Disrupts Memorial to King," *Columbia Spectator*, April 10, 1968, 1; and for SDS's version, Bob Feldman, "The King Memorial—Why We Disrupted," *Up against the Wall* 3, no. 1 (April 22, 1968): 3, both available online at "1968: Columbia in Crisis," Columbia University Libraries, accessed October 29, 2017, https:// exhibitions.cul.columbia.edu/exhibits/show/1968/causes/mlk.

4. *Columbia Spectator*, April 30, 1968, 1–2, available at "1968: Columbia in Crisis," Columbia University Libraries, accessed October 29, 2017, https://exhibitions.cul.columbia .edu/exhibits/show/1968/bust. Over 700 students were arrested that night including 268 at Fayerweather Hall.

5. For an announcement of one such ("open-ended") teach-in held on May 2 with the English professor Eric Bentley, Margaret Mead, Murray Kempton, and other speakers, see "1968: Columbia in Crisis," Columbia University Libraries, accessed October 29, 2017, https://exhibitions.cul.columbia.edu/exhibits/show/1968/campus.

6. These events, including the burning by J. J. Jacobs (whom I knew) of ten years' worth of research collected by Professor Orest Ranum of the History Department, are recalled in a National Public Radio (NPR) interview with Mark Rudd and Ranum. For the transcript, see "Around the Nation: Ex-Student Recalls '68 Columbia University Protests," *All Things Considered*, National Public Radio, February 21, 2010, http://www.npr.org/templates/story/story

.php?storyId=123950416. Rudd describes the night as follows: "The police had attacked the students. There were barricades built at the entrances of campus. It felt like war."

7. Jennifer Schuessler, "Columbia's Uprising: A 50-Year-Old Legacy," *New York Times*, March 22, 2018, C1. See also Jamie Katz, "A Tinderbox, Poised to Ignite," *Columbia College Today* 45, no. 3 (Spring 2018), accessed January 23, 2019, https://www.college.columbia.edu /cct/issue/spring18/article/tinderbox-poised-ignite.

8. As Raymond Brown, a leader of SAAS, put it fifty years later, "We knew that we [the black students] occupied a key strategic place, that the university administration didn't want to move on us, and this would keep the whole thing going." Clara Bingham, "'The Whole World Is Watching': An Oral History of the 1968 Columbia Uprising," *Vanity Fair*, March 26, 2018, https://www.vanityfair.com/news/2018/03/the-students-behind-the-1968 -columbia-uprising/amp.

9. For an extraordinary apology for the police's brutality, issued by Benjamin Ward, then head of the New York Police Department (NYPD)'s Civilian Complaint Review Board, see John Kantor, "An Overdue Apology," *Columbia College Today* 45, no. 4 (Summer 2018): 4.

10. Apropos of France, I distinctly remember a rally at Columbia at which someone with a very strong French accent shouted out, "If we can overthrow De Gaulle, you surely can oust Grayson Kirk!"

11. "Josephine Drexel Duke Is Engaged to John Marshall Geste Brown Jr.," *New York Times*, August 31, 1969, 49.

12. The manifesto, "You Don't Need a Weatherman to Know Which Way the Wind Blows," was taken from the Bob Dylan song, "Subterranean Homesick Blues." For the text of the manifesto, see *New Left Notes* 4, no. 22 (June 16, 1969): 3–4.

13. In reading over old issues of *The Spectator* to reacquaint myself with the events of '68 at Columbia, I came across a column by Robert Ast who, in 2008, wondered "whether or not the students' demand for amnesty were [sic] an attempt to legitimize their right to protest or an attempt to cover their asses." See "Still More 1968: Discipline and Rubbish," *Columbia Daily Spectator* 132, no. 55, April 17, 2008.

14. In a letter to Ginna of October 6, 1968, I wrote "my hearing was postponed (again) until November 20 and I still have not responded to the Dean's letter requesting me to respond or face suspension." I seem to have let matters take their course, a position with some, but not much, risk.

15. Juan Gonzalez, a charismatic member of SDS's coordinating committee, later a reporter and columnist for New York's *Daily News* and a cofounder and cohost with Amy Goodman of "Democracy Now!" recently noted in reference to the protests in '68, "Ultimately, we won everything that we set out to do. We stopped the gym. We got the university to cut its ties with I.D.A. We got amnesty for most of the strikers, and Grayson Kirk resigned in August." Bingham, "The Whole World Is Watching."

16. Stephen F. Cohen, *Bukharin and the Bolshevik Revolution: A Political Biography, 1888–1938* (New York: Knopf, 1973). In 1965 Cohen and his mentor Robert C. Tucker had

published *The Great Purge Trial* (New York: Grosset & Dunlap), the English-language version of the Bukharin trial in March 1938 based on the official Russian transcript.

17. Lewis H. Siegelbaum, "Modernity Unbound: The New Soviet City of the Sixties," in *The Socialist Sixties: Crossing Borders in the Second World*, ed. Anne E. Gorsuch and Diane P. Koenker (Bloomington: Indiana University Press, 2013), 66–83.

18. Rothschild had published *Pilsudski's Coup d'État* (New York: Columbia University Press) in 1966. He would go on to publish *East Central Europe between the Two World Wars* (Seattle: University of Washington Press) in 1974 and *Return to Diversity: A Political History of East Central Europe since World War II* (New York: Oxford University Press) in 1989. The course thus served to adumbrate his scholarly career.

19. Roger Hilsman, *To Move a Nation: The Politics of Foreign Policy in the Administration of John F. Kennedy* (Garden City, NY: Doubleday, 1967).

20. The reference here is to Crane Brinton, *The Anatomy of Revolution* (New York: Vintage, 1965).

21. See Oksenberg's obituary: Paul Lewis, "Michael Oksenberg, China Expert in Washington," *New York Times*, February 24, 2001, http://www.nytimes.com/2001/02/24/world/michael-oksenberg-62-china-expert-in-washington.html.

22. Isaac Deutscher, *The Non-Jewish Jew and Other Essays* (London: Oxford University Press, 1968). A new edition of the book was published by Verso in 2017.

23. Many years later, I published an article in the newsletter of the Association for Slavic, East European, and Eurasian Studies in which I returned to this subject, this time addressing its presence in the historiography of the Soviet Union and former communist Eastern Europe. See "The Fetishism of Commodities Revisited," *ASEEES NewsNet* 53, no. 1 (2013): 2–5. I had completely forgotten—or had I?—my earlier venture into this territory.

24. The French sociologist Didier Eribon refers in his memoir to Goldmann as "a sociologist who is mostly—and perhaps unjustly- forgotten these days, but who was extremely important at the time." Along with Karl Korsch and "a number of other authors," Eribon considers Goldmann to have "supported an open, non-dogmatic form of Marxism." See *Returning to Reims*, trans. Michael Lucey (South Pasadena: Semiotext(e), 2013), 181.

25. Zinn, best known for his *A People's History of the United States* (New York: Longman, 1980), had published *Vietnam: The Logic of Withdrawal* (Boston: Beacon) in 1967.

26. "Ferment in the Universities," *Newsweek*, June 15, 1970, 66.

NOTES TO CHAPTER 3

1. Richard Polton recently recalled an incident from that trip: ". . . in the south of France . . . we decided to stop at a large parking lot where there wasn't a tree in sight. Not a stick rising above ground level. . . . It was a hot and very sunny day. As we pulled up to the store, Melaine called out from the back seat—'Richard, make sure you park in the shade.' Shade? What Shade? There wasn't any shade for miles. We all laughed hysterically. As I recall, you nearly lost your mind. That night, Bobbie and I turned to each other and

said—this relationship is not going to last. We got that right." (E-mail communication from October 17, 2018).

2. Maria Filomena Mónica, *Bilhete de Identidade, Memórias 1943–1976* (Lisbon: Alêtheia Editores, 2005).

3. Roger Brew (1947–1979) earned his DPhil in 1974 and then entered the British civil service, working in the Ministry of Overseas Development. He died tragically young in Colombia. The Latin American History Seminar at Oxford is named in his honor. See St. Antony's College, What's On: Roger Brew Memorial Seminar, modified May 4, 2017, http://www.sant.ox.ac.uk/events/roger-brew-memorial-seminar-regional-disparities-pre-industrial-economy-gdp-capita-colombian.

4. Sheila Fitzpatrick, *A Spy in the Archives: A Memoir of Cold War Russia* (London: I. B. Tauris, 2014).

5. Ibid., 12–15, 267–69, 338–39.

6. Class is a funny thing. Some of my leftist English friends affected working-class accents, presumably to hide their class origins.

7. Harold Shukman, *War or Revolution: Russian Jews and Conscription in Britain 1917* (London: Vallentine Mitchell, 2006).

8. Mónica, *Bilhete de Identidade*, 268. Mena attributed my Marxism to my father's persecution at the hands of McCarthyites.

9. See, for example, Timothy Mason, *Arbeiterklasse und Volksgemeinschaft: Dokumente und Materialien zur deutschen Arbeiterpolitik, 1936–1939* (Opladen: Westdeutscher Verlag, 1975); Lutz Niethammer, *Angepasster Faschismus: Politische Praxis der NPD* (Frankfurt: S. Fischer, 1969); and Detlev Peukert, *Ruhrarbeiter gegen den Faschismus: Dokumentation über den Widerstand im Ruhrgebiet 1933–1945* (Frankfurt: Röderberg-Verlag, 1976).

10. It should be pointed out that both the English-based *Social History* and *History Workshop Journal* did not start publishing until 1976. Only much later did I read—and assign to a class on global communism—Samuel's masterful posthumously published *Lost World of British Communism* (London: Verso, 2006). For three "Tributes to Raphael Samuel," see *New Left Review* 1/221 (1997): 119–38.

11. See G. N. Kitching, *Development and Underdevelopment in Historical Perspective: Populism, Nationalism, and Industrialization* (London: Routledge, 1989).

12. For her biography of Münzenberg, see Babette Gross, *Willi Münzenberg: A Political Biography* (East Lansing: Michigan State University Press, 1974).

13. For a fascinating and deeply moving biography of Abramsky by his grandson, see Sasha Abramsky, *The House of Twenty Thousand Books* (New York: New York Review of Books, 2015).

14. This, upon reflection, is an ungenerous view that probably owed more to Western academics' biases than to the reality of Soviet academic practices. For an example of an excellent Soviet-era study of the Russian economy during the First World War, published during the year I was an exchange student in the USSR, see A. L. Sidorov, *Ekonomicheskoe polozhenie Rossii v gody pervoi mirovoi voiny* (Moscow: Nauka, 1973).

15. Moshe Lewin, *Political Undercurrents in Soviet Economic Debates: From Bukharin to the Modern Reformers* (Princeton, NJ: Princeton University Press, 1974).

16. For another memoir of a Western scholar suspected of spying—in Romania—see Katherine Verdery, *My Life as a Spy: Investigations in a Secret Police File* (Durham: Duke University Press, 2018).

17. John Bushnell, "The New Soviet Man Turns Pessimist," in *The Soviet Union since Stalin*, ed. Stephen F. Cohen, Alexander Rabinowitch, and Robert Sharlet (Bloomington: Indiana University Press, 1980), 179–99. So perceptive did I find this article that I was still assigning it to my Soviet history classes thirty-five years later.

18. Fitzpatrick, *A Spy in the Archives*, 114–20, 169–70. Fitzpatrick, who matriculated at St. Antony's College six years before I did, published a revised version of her thesis as *The Commissariat of Enlightenment: Soviet Organization of Education and the Arts under Lunacharsky, October 1917–1921* (Cambridge: Cambridge University Press, 1970).

19. I am grateful to one of the anonymous readers of the manuscript for this insight.

20. V. Ia. Laverychev, *Po tu storonu barrikad: Iz istorii bor'by moskovskoi burzhuazii s revoliutsiei* (Moscow: Mysl', 1967).

21. S. V. Voronkova, "Shkola Valeriia Ivanovicha Bovykina (K voprosu o traditsiiakh i novatorstve v razvitii sovetskoi istoricheskoi nauke)," in *Rossiia na rubezhe XIX–XX vekov: Materialy nauchnykh chtenii pamiati professora V. I. Bovykina* (Moscow: ROSSPEN, 1999), 31–49.

22. The book was John McKay, *Pioneers for Profit: Foreign Entrepreneurship and Russian Industrialization, 1885–1913* (Chicago: University of Chicago Press, 1970).

23. The reference here is to Joan Scott, "Gender: A Useful Category of Historical Analysis," *American Historical Review* 91, no. 5 (1986): 1053–1075. This is not to overlook some fine works on women such as Barbara Alpern Engel, *Mothers and Daughters: Women of the Intelligentsia in Nineteenth-Century Russia* (Cambridge: Cambridge University Press, 1983).

24. The same year I defended my dissertation, Norman Stone, a lecturer at Gonville and Caius College, Cambridge, published his book, *The Eastern Front, 1914–1917* (London: Penguin, 1975), which characterized the WICs as follows: "Where they succeeded they were unnecessary, where they did not they were a nuisance" (10).

25. See Project 17, https://project1917.com/. For the Russian version see https://project1917.ru (both accessed January 24, 2019). More recently, Zygar and his team have created the "map of history" (*karta istorii*), "a documentary game about the main events of Russia in the twentieth century" in which one is presented with choices to make for real individuals confronted by the actual dilemmas they faced. See Karta istorii, accessed January 24, 2019, https://kartaistorii.ru/.

26. Victor Sebestyen, *Lenin: The Man, the Dictator, and the Master of Terror* (New York: Pantheon Books, 2017).

27. Andy Willimott, *Living the Revolution: Urban Communes & Soviet Socialism, 1917–1932* (Oxford: Oxford University Press, 2017).

28. Diane Koenker, "Talkin' about Class Formation," *Kritika* 18, no. 2 (2017): 377–88. The editors had asked Diane and two other historians to respond to Boris Mironov, "Cannon Fodder for the Revolution: The Russian Proletariat in 1917," *Kritika* 18, no. 2 (2017): 351–70.

29. Here, the key texts are Yanni Kotsonis and David L. Hoffmann, eds., *Russian Modernity: Politics, Knowledge, Practices* (New York: St. Martin's Press, 2000); Peter Holquist, *Making War, Forging Revolution: Russia's Continuum of Crisis, 1914–1921* (Cambridge, MA: Harvard University Press, 2002); Daniel Beer, *Renovating Russia: The Human Sciences and the Fate of Liberal Modernity, 1880–1930* (Ithaca, NY: Cornell University Press, 2008).

30. See also Joshua Sanborn, *Drafting the Russian Nation: Military Conscription, Total War, and Mass Politics, 1905–1925* (DeKalb: Northern Illinois University Press, 2003).

31. Lewis H. Siegelbaum, "The War-Industries Committees and the Politics of Industrial Mobilization in Russia, 1915–17" (DPhil thesis, University of Oxford, 1975), 223, 159, 162.

32. Ibid., 263.

33. Ibid., 241, 262.

34. V. S. Diakin, *Russkaia burzhuaziia i tsarizm v gody pervoi mirovoi voiny, 1914–1917* (Leningrad: Nauka, 1967). In the published version of my dissertation, I praised it as "judicious and closely argued." See Lewis H. Siegelbaum, *The Politics of Industrial Mobilization in Russia, 1914–17: A Study of the War-Industries Committees* (London: Macmillan, 1983), xiii.

35. Leopold Haimson, "The Problem of Social Stability in Urban Russia, 1905–1917," *Slavic Review* 23, no. 4 (1964): 619–42; 24, no. 1 (1965): 1–22.

36. Alec Nove, *An Economic History of the U.S.S.R.* (London: Allen Lane, 1969); Nove, *Was Stalin Really Necessary? Some Problems of Soviet Political Economy* (London: Allen & Unwin, 1964).

NOTES TO CHAPTER 4

1. Robert B. Townsend, "Precedents: The Job Crisis of the 1970s," *Perspectives on History* 35, no. 4 (April 1997): 16–18. See also Townsend, "History in Those Hard Times: Looking for Jobs in the 1970s," *Perspectives on History* 47, no. 6 (September 2009): 33–35.

2. Herbert J. Ellison, "Eastern Europe and USSR" (appendix H), in *Beyond Growth: The Next Stage in Language and Area Studies*, ed. Richard D. Lambert et al. (Washington, DC: Association of American Universities, 1984), 403. The Kennan Institute, founded countercyclically in 1974, continues to provide long- and short-term fellowships to scholars using Washington, DC's vast library and other resources. I received several short-term fellowships in the early 1980s while still based in Australia and again in 2014.

3. Geoffrey Blainey, *The Tyranny of Distance: How Distance Shaped Australia's History* (Melbourne: Macmillan, 1966).

4. Dening (1931–2008), who taught at La Trobe before becoming the Max Crawford Professor of History at the University of Melbourne, was something of a cult figure among "the Melbourne Group," as Geertz referred to them. For an appreciative reminiscence, see Bronwen Douglas, "Greg Dening: Wayfinder in the Presents of the Past," *Journal of Pacific History* 43, no. 3 (2008): 359–66.

5. Inga interrupted her sterling career as a historian of New World contact between the Spanish and indigenous peoples by addressing the no less painful subject of the Holocaust. See Inga Clendinnen, *Reading the Holocaust* (Cambridge: Cambridge University Press, 1999).

6. Nikita Khrushchev, *Khrushchev Remembers: The Last Testament*, ed. and trans. Strobe Talbott (Boston: Little, Brown, 1974), 283–85, 330–32.

7. Lewis H. Siegelbaum, "Another Yellow Peril: Chinese Migrants in the Russian Far East and the Russian Reaction before 1917," *Modern Asian Studies* 12, no. 2 (1978): 307–30.

8. Lewis H. Siegelbaum, "Peasant Disorders and the Myth of the Tsar: Russian Variations on a Millenarian Theme," *Journal of Religious History* 10, no. 3 (1979): 225–35.

9. Lewis H. Siegelbaum, "The Odessa Grain Trade: A Case Study in Urban Growth and Development in Tsarist Russia," *Journal of European Economic History* 9, no. 1 (1980): 113–51. I remember receiving a check for tens of thousands of lire, which when converted to Aussie dollars barely covered the cost of a nice dinner in Melbourne.

10. Ibid., 118–19.

11. Siegelbaum, *The Politics of Industrial Mobilization*, 212.

12. Jonathan Haslam, *The Vices of Integrity: E. H. Carr, 1892–1982* (London: Verso, 1999), 52, 55.

13. E. P. Thompson, *The Making of the English Working Class* (Harmondsworth: Penguin, 1980), 12.

14. Ibid., 431.

15. Joshua Clover, *Riot, Strike, Riot: The New Era of Uprisings* (London: Verso, 2016).

16. Lewis H. Siegelbaum and Ronald G. Suny, "Class Backwards? In Search of the Soviet Working Class," in *Making Workers Soviet: Power, Class and Identity*, ed. Lewis H. Siegelbaum and Ronald G. Suny (Ithaca, NY: Cornell University Press, 1994), 4. This paragraph paraphrases one that appeared in my survey of Soviet labor history: Lewis H. Siegelbaum, "The Late Romance of the Soviet Worker in Western Historiography," *International Review of Social History* 51, no. 3 (2006): 468–69.

17. Siegelbaum, "The Late Romance."

18. Robert C. Tucker, ed., *Stalinism: Essays in Historical Interpretation* (New York: Norton, 1977).

19. Ibid., 111.

20. Moshe Lewin, *La paysannerie et le pouvoir soviétique, 1928–1930* (Paris: Mouton, 1966); Lewin, *Russian Peasants and Soviet Power: A Study of Collectivization* (New York: Norton, 1975); Lewin, *Lenin's Last Struggle* (New York: Pantheon, 1968); and Lewin, *Political Undercurrents*.

21. Moshe Lewin, "Society, State, and Ideology during the First Five-Year Plan," in *Cultural Revolution in Russia, 1928–1931*, ed. Sheila Fitzpatrick (Bloomington: Indiana University Press, 1978), 41–77.

22. See also Kendall Bailes, "The American Connection: Ideology and the Transfer of American Technology to the Soviet Union, 1917–1941," *Comparative Studies in Society and*

History 23, no. 3 (1981): 421–48. I also cited Nicholas Lampert, *The Technical Intelligentsia and the Soviet State: A Study of Soviet Managers and Technicians, 1928–1935* (London: Macmillan, 1979). Ken, a meticulous scholar who got his doctorate at Columbia in 1971 (and therefore overlapped with my undergraduate years there), also spent 1973–1974 in Moscow on the IREX program. In 1981 we shared a room—or rather, a cabin—at the annual convention of the American Association for the Advancement of Slavic Studies (AAASS) in Asilomar, CA, a beautiful stretch of the Pacific coast. I saw him briefly thereafter at subsequent AAASS conferences until in 1987 he told me over the phone that he had contracted AIDS. He died the next year at forty-seven.

23. Samuel Lieberstein, "Technology, Work and Sociology in the USSR: The NOT Movement," *Technology and Culture* 16, no. 1 (1975): 48–67.

24. For an unsurpassed analysis of the initial impact of Taylorism in Europe, see Charles S. Maier, "Between Taylorism and Technocracy: European Ideologies and the Vision of Industrial Productivity in the 1920s," *Journal of Contemporary History* 5, no. 2 (1970): 27–61.

25. Harry Braverman, *Labor and Monopoly Capital: The Degradation of Work in the Twentieth Century* (New York: Monthly Review Press, 1974). See also Richard Edwards, *Contested Terrain: The Transformation of the Workplace in the Twentieth Century* (New York: Basic Books, 1979).

26. Miklós Haraszti, *A Worker in a Worker's State: Piece-Rates in Hungary* (Harmondsworth: Penguin, 1977).

27. Lewis Siegelbaum, "Production Collectives and Communes and the 'Imperatives' of Soviet Industrialization, 1929–1931," *Slavic Review* 45, no. 1 (Spring 1986): 65–84.

28. Lewis Siegelbaum, "Socialist Competition and Socialist Construction in the USSR: The Experience of the First Five-Year Plan (1928–1932)," *Thesis Eleven*, no. 4 (1982): 48–67.

29. Clover, *Riot, Strike, Riot*, 145.

30. Lewis H. Siegelbaum, "Soviet Norm Determination in Theory and Practice, 1917–1941," *Soviet Studies* 36, no. 1 (1984): 45–68. Most of the sources for this article I obtained as photocopies via interlibrary loan, my lifeline while at La Trobe. I forever will be grateful to John Horacek and others on the staff of La Trobe's Borchardt Library for invariably and efficiently fulfilling my numerous requests.

31. Siegelbaum, "Soviet Norm Determination," 64.

32. Lewis H. Siegelbaum, "Masters of the Shop Floor: Foremen and Soviet Industrialization," in *Stalinism: Its Nature and Aftermath*, ed. Nicholas Lampert and Gabor Rittersporn (London: Macmillan, 1992), 127–56; and in William G. Rosenberg and Lewis H. Siegelbaum, eds., *Social Dimensions of Soviet Industrialization* (Bloomington: Indiana University Press, 1993), 166–92.

33. As recently as January 2018 in response to a forlorn New Year's message I sent to him, Roger wrote, "Hang in there! No need to apologise. Sad to say, you are one of the few people in our field with whom I can really communicate."

34. Lewis H. Siegelbaum and Michael Morgan, "'State' vs. 'Society' in Tsarist and Soviet History," *Radical History Review*, nos. 28–30 (1984): 90–112.

35. Richard Pipes, *Russia under the Old Regime* (London: Weidenfeld and Nicolson, 1974); Richard Hellie, "The Structure of Modern Russian History: Towards a Dynamic Model," *Russian History* 4, no. 1 (1977): 1–22.

36. Orientalism, of course, is associated with Edward Said's book by that name. Although it had been published in 1978, we failed to cite it, probably because we had not read it.

37. Richard Hellie, *Slavery in Russia, 1450–1725* (Chicago: University of Chicago Press, 1982), 505–6; Hellie, *Economy and Material Culture of Russia, 1600–1725* (Chicago: University of Chicago Press, 1999), 258. For a thoughtful essay on Pipes and other foundational figures in Russian historical studies in the United States, see Jonathan Daly, "The *Pleiade*: Five Scholars Who Founded Russian Historical Studies in the United States," *Kritika* 18, no. 4 (2017): 785–826.

NOTES TO CHAPTER 5

1. For a decade or so, Volodia and I sparred whenever we encountered each other, much to Bill McCagg's distress. Sometime in the early 1990s, however, we discovered a mutual antipathy toward Boris Yeltsin and otherwise decided to bury the hatchet. Aside from temperamental and political differences, I suspect that our initial dislike for each other reflected mutual suspicion between an emigré scholar who previously monopolized local expertise on the USSR and a native-born American upstart.

2. As Gail Sheehy noted already in 1970, "Home is the place to measure the growth potential of women's lib. Because what has grown spectacularly, even beyond the movement, is the movement's offspring. A little bundle … for every doorstep—personal acrimony." Gail Sheehy, "The Men of Women's Liberation Have Learned Not to Laugh," *New York Magazine*, May 18, 1970, 32 accessed January 24, 2019, https://books.google.com/books?id=8OICAAAAMBAJ&pg=PA28&lpg=PA28&dq=little+bundle+of+acrimony+on+every+doorstep&source=bl&ots=vvoEkEmMAe&sig=ACfU3U3IuethVsl1Wwxd9j8API2Z7YShEQ&hl=en&sa=X&ved=2ahUKEwjYoIr5qIngAhUKQK0KHZtsAqQQ6AEwEnoECAoQAQ#v=onepage&q=little%20bundle%20of%20acrimony%20on%20every%20doorstep&f=false. I thank Leslie Moch—and Google—for retrieving this quotation.

3. For my brief obituary of him, see "William O. McCagg (1930–1993)," Michigan State University, Department of History, http://history.msu.edu/william-o-mccagg-1930-1993/ (accessed September 7, 2018).

4. As the obituary mentions, Bill found funds to finance a feature film on the subject of his own deafness. The film *Ben's Bridge* (1992) was a German-Hungarian-US coproduction. Bill wrote the screenplay and also appeared in the role of a deaf professor alongside the well-known Polish actors Jerzy Stuhr and Dorota Segda. The film had its world premiere at the Odeon Theater in Lansing's Frandor Shopping Center.

5. For one such testimonial, see Michael Rasell and Elena Iarskaia-Smirnova, *Disability in Eastern Europe and the Former Soviet Union: History, Policy, and Everyday Life* (New York: Routledge, 2013), 9.

6. Lewis Siegelbaum, "Industrial Accidents and Their Prevention in the Interwar Period," in *The Disabled in the Soviet Union: Past and Present, Theory and Practice*, ed. William O. McCagg and Lewis Siegelbaum (Pittsburgh, PA: University of Pittsburgh Press, 1989), 85–118.

7. For example, "The Making of Stakhanovites, 1935–36," presented at the American Historical Association's ninety-eighth annual meeting in San Francisco, December 27, 1983, and published in *Russian History/Histoire Russe* 13, nos. 2–3 (1986): 259–92.

8. Siegelbaum, "Production Collectives and Communes," 65, 72. The article anticipated the principal argument in Willimott, *Living the Revolution*.

9. For a sample review, see *The Russian Review* 46, no. 1 (1987): 100–101. The encyclopedias were *The Modern Encyclopedia of Russian and Soviet History (MERSH)*, ed. Joseph L. Wieczynski et al. (Gulf Breeze, FL: Academic International Press, 1976–1994); *The Blackwell Encyclopedia of the Russian Revolution*, ed. Harold Shukman (London: Blackwell, 1988); and *The Dictionary of the Russian Revolution*, ed. George D. Jackson and Robert James Devlin (New York: Greenwood, 1989).

10. Allan Kassof, the director, corrected me by pointing out I had not been denied a visa but simply not placed with a collaborating Soviet institution. I did travel to the Soviet Union twice to research the subject in libraries. As early as June 1980, Dan Orlovsky wondered in a letter to me, "Will the soviets give you Sheila Fitzpatrick-type access?"

11. The quotation is from "The Immediate Tasks of the Soviet Government" (1918). See V. I. Lenin, *Polnoe sobranie sochinenii*, 5th ed., 55 vols. (Moscow: Partizdat, 1958–65), 34:187.

12. Lewis H. Siegelbaum, *Stakhanovism and the Politics of Productivity in the USSR, 1935–1941* (Cambridge: Cambridge University Press, 1988), 308.

13. Hiroaki Kuromiya, *Stalin's Industrial Revolution: Politics and Workers, 1928–1932* (Cambridge: Cambridge University Press, 1988); Vladimir Andrle, *Workers in Stalin's Russia: Industrialization and Social Change in a Planned Economy* (New York: St. Martin's Press, 1988); Francesco Benvenuti, *Fuoco sui sabotatori! Stachanovismo e organizzazione industriale in Urss, 1934–38* (Rome: V. Levi, 1988).

14. Robert Maier, *Die Stachanov-Bewegung, 1935–1938* (Stuttgart: Franz Steiner Verlag, 1990).

15. For a recent critical assessment of the impact of the cultural turn, see Ronald Grigor Suny, *Red Flag Unfurled: History, Historians, and the Russian Revolution* (London: Verso, 2017), 17–52, 102–5.

16. William Husband, *"Godless Communists": Atheism and Society in Soviet Russia, 1917–1932* (DeKalb: Northern Illinois University Press, 2000).

17. Joan Neuberger, *Hooliganism: Crime, Culture, and Power in St. Petersburg, 1900–1914* (Berkeley: University of California Press, 1993); Brian LaPierre, *Hooligans in*

Khrushchev's Russia: Defining, Policing, and Producing Deviance during the Thaw (Madison: University of Wisconsin Press, 2012).

18. For Campbell's own desultory account of his consultancy, see Thomas D. Campbell, *Russia: Market or Menace?* (London: Longmans, Green and Co., 1932). The Montana Historical Society in Helena contains the Campbell Farming Corporation Records from 1918 to 1975. For an overview, see "Campbell Farming Corporation Records, 1918–1975," Archives West, accessed March 13, 2018, http://archiveswest.orbiscascade.org/ark:/80444 /xv96804.

19. William Chase and Lewis Siegelbaum, "Work Time and Industrialization in the USSR, 1917–1941," in *Worktime and Industrialization: An International History*, ed. Gary Cross (Philadelphia: Temple University Press, 1988), 183–216.

20. William Chase, *Workers, Society, and the Soviet State: Labor and Life in Moscow, 1918–1929* (Urbana: University of Illinois Press, 1987).

21. I am thinking in particular of Sheila Fitzpatrick, *Education and Social Mobility in the Soviet Union, 1921–1934* (Cambridge: Cambridge University Press, 1979) and Moshe Lewin, *The Making of the Soviet System: Essays in the Social History of Interwar Russia* (New York: Pantheon, 1985).

22. Rosenberg and Siegelbaum, *Social Dimensions of Soviet Industrialization*.

23. Lewis H. Siegelbaum and Ronald G. Suny, "Conceptualizing the Command Economy: Western Historians on Soviet Industrialization," in Rosenberg and Siegelbaum, *Social Dimensions of Soviet Industrialization*, 12. We recycled this essay and published it as "Making the Command Economy: Western Historians on Soviet Industrialization," *International Labor and Working-Class History* 43 (1993): 65–76.

24. Siegelbaum and Suny, "Class Backwards?," 11.

25. Ibid., 26.

26. Stephen Kotkin, "Workers' Lives in Stalin's Showcase City," in Siegelbaum and Suny, *Making Workers Soviet*, 310.

27. Natalie Zemon Davis, *Fiction in the Archives: Pardon Tales and Their Tellers in Sixteenth Century France* (Stanford, CA: Stanford University Press, 1987), 4.

28. Lewis H. Siegelbaum, "Defining and Ignoring Labor Discipline in the Early Soviet Period: The Comrades-Disciplinary Courts, 1918–1922," *Slavic Review* 51, no. 4 (1992): 705–30.

29. Ibid., 707.

30. I am referring here to William H. Sewell Jr., *The Logics of History: Social Theory and Social Transformations* (Chicago: University of Chicago Press, 2005), especially chapter 3—namely, "during the very period when historians have gleefully cast aside the notion of structural determination, the shape of our own social world has been fundamentally transformed by changes in the structures of world capitalism" (49).

31. Alkhimova "misnames" or rather appropriates the Council of Labor and Defense (Sovet truda i oborony) as an institution that should be defending labor, which is to say, her.

32. Siegelbaum, "Defining and Ignoring Labor Discipline," 717–18, 728.

33. "Narratives of Appeal and the Appeal of Narratives: Labor Discipline and Its Con-testation in the Early Soviet Period," *Russian History/Histoire Russe*, special issue on "Peti-tions and Denunciations in Russia from Muscovy to the Stalin Era," ed. Sheila Fitzpatrick, 24, nos. 1–2 (1997): 65–88.

34. In 1992 TsGAOR became GARF (State Archive of the Russian Federation).

35. See, respectively, William H. Sewell Jr., "Toward a Post-Materialist Rhetoric for Labor History," in *Rethinking Labor History*, ed. Lenard R. Berlanstein (Urbana: Univer-sity of Illinois Press, 1993), 15–38, quotation from 34; and Margaret R. Somers, "Narrativ-ity, Narrative Identity, and Social Action: Rethinking English Working-Class Formation," *Social Science History* 16, no. 4 (1992): 591–630.

36. Siegelbaum, "Narratives of Appeal," 87, drawing on Diane Koenker, "Factory Tales: Narratives of Industrial Relations in the Transition to NEP," Paper presented at the Fifth World Congress for Central and East European Studies, Warsaw, August 1995, 2.

37. Ilmari Susiluoto, *The Origins and Development of Systems Thinking in the Soviet Union: Political and Philosophical Controversies from Bogdanov and Bukharin to Present-Day Re-evaluations* (Helsinki: Suomalainen tiedeakatemia, 1982). For Ilmari's obituary in Finland's leading newspaper, see Arto Luukkanen, Pekka Kauppala, "Monipuolinen Venäjä-tutkija," *Helsingin Sanomat*, April 6, 2016, 18.

38. Lewis H. Siegelbaum, "Exhibiting *Kustar'* Industry in Late Imperial Russia/Exhib-iting Late Imperial Russia in *Kustar'* Industry," in *Transforming Peasants: Society, State and the Peasantry, 1861–1930, Selected Papers from the Fifth World Congress of Central and Eastern European Studies, Warsaw, 1995*, ed. Judith Pallot (Basingstoke: Macmillan, 1998), 37–63.

39. Lewis H. Siegelbaum, "'Dear Comrade, You Ask What We Need': Socialist Pater-nalism and Rural 'Notables' in the Mid-1930s," *Slavic Review* 57, no. 1 (1998): 107–32. I subsequently published a slightly revised version in Sheila Fitzpatrick, ed., *Stalinism: New Directions* (London: Routledge, 2000), 231–56.

40. Lewis H. Siegelbaum, "State and Society in the 1920s," in *Reform in Russia and the Soviet Union, Past and Prospects*, ed. Robert Crummey (Urbana: University of Illinois Press, 1989), 240–62.

41. See Andrei Nuiukin, "Idealy ili interesy?" *Novyi mir*, no. 1 (1988): 190–211; Vasilii Seliunin, "Istoki," *Novyi mir*, no. 5 (1988): 162–89; "Kruglyi stol': Sovetskii Soiuz v 20-e gody," *Voprosy istorii*, no. 9 (1988): 3–58.

42. The book was Mary McAuley, *Labour Disputes in Soviet Russia, 1957–1965* (Oxford: Clarendon Press, 1969).

43. Lewis H. Siegelbaum, *Soviet State and Society between Revolutions, 1918–1929* (Cambridge: Cambridge University Press, 1992), 3–4. See John Keane, ed., *Civil Society and the State: New European Perspectives* (London: Verso, 1988), 20.

44. Lewis H. Siegelbaum, "The Shaping of Soviet Workers' Leisure: Workers' Clubs and Palaces of Culture in the 1930s," *International Labor and Working-Class History* 56 (1999): 78–92.

45. See, for example, J. Arch Getty and V. P. Kozlov, eds., *Kratkii putevoditel': fondy i kollektsii, sobrannye Tsentral'nym partiinym arkhivom* (Moscow: Blagovest, 1993). For additional volumes in the series, see The Russian Archive Project, accessed January 25, 2019, http://www.sscnet.ucla.edu/history/getty/RAS.html.

46. For a brief account, see Jonathan Brent, "The Order from Lenin: 'Find Some Truly Hard People,'" *New York Times*, May 22, 2017, https://www.nytimes.com/2017/05/22 /opinion/lenin-stalin-bolshevism-soviet-russia.html?_r=0.

47. For a complete listing of the twenty-nine volumes in the series, see "Books from the 'Annals of Communism' Series," Yale University Press, accessed January 25, 2019, http:// yalebooks.yale.edu/series/annals-of-communism-series.

48. For an obituary that Arch Getty and I wrote of Andrei Sokolov (1941–2015) see *Slavic Review* 75, no. 1 (2016): 241–43.

49. Andrei Sokolov, ed., *Obshchestvo i vlast' 1930-e gody: Povestvovanie v dokumentakh* (Moscow: ROSSPEN, 1998).

50. Lewis H. Siegelbaum and Andrei Sokolov, *Stalinism as a Way of Life: A Narrative in Documents* (New Haven, CT: Yale University Press, 2000), 6.

51. Elena Krevsky, "Stalinism in Its Own Words," review of *Stalinism as a Way of Life: A Narrative in Documents*, by Lewis Siegelbaum and Andrei Sokolov, April 2002, H-Russia, http://www.h-net.org/reviews/showrev.php?id=6166.

52. Penson, a Belarusian Jew whose family had fled to Kokand during World War I, became one of the premier photojournalists of the 1920s and '30s. His work remained unknown outside the Soviet Union until the 1990s when his descendants who still lived in Tashkent began releasing it. See Stephen Kinzer, "Chronicle of an Upheaval the World Couldn't See," *New York Times*, January 25, 1998. Between 2004 and 2015 the Nailya Alexander Gallery in New York held four exhibitions in which Penson's work figured prominently. See "Max Penson," Nailya Alexander Gallery, accessed January 25, 2019, http://www .nailyaalexandergallery.com/russian-photography/max-penson.

53. I later would use this term in the brief essay I wrote to accompany documents associated with the entry for 1939 on the Great Fergana Canal in Seventeen Moments in Soviet History at http://soviethistory.msu.edu/1939-2/great-fergana-canal/.

54. Eisenstein's papers are in *fond* 1923 in RGALI (Russian State Archive of Literature and Art). At the film and photographic archive (RGAKFD), I saw newsreel (from *Soiuzkinozhurnal*), two documentary films (*The People's Initiative*, dir. M. Kaiumov, and *A Powerful Flow*, dir. L. Varlamov and B. Nebylitskii), raw footage, and hundreds of photographs.

55. I wrote a brief obituary about her which was published as "Rakhima Khodievna Aminova: Otsenka istorika," *Uzbekiston Tarihi* [Uzbekistan history] (May 2004): 86–88.

56. Krista A. Goff and Lewis H. Siegelbaum, eds. *Empire and Belonging in the Eurasian Borderlands* (Ithaca: Cornell University Press, 2019).

57. For the most articulate rejection of this framework, see Adeeb Khalid, "Backwardness and the Quest for Civilization: Early Soviet Central Asia in Comparative Perspective,"

Slavic Review 65, no. 2 (2006): 231–51. See also Khalid, *Making Uzbekistan: Nation, Empire, and Revolution in the Early USSR* (Ithaca, NY: Cornell University Press, 2015).

NOTES TO CHAPTER 6

1. For a brief account by Larry of his stewardship of *The Mill Hunk Herald* (1979–1989), see Larry Evans, "The Next Page: How We Punched It Out; From Mill Hunk Herald to Northside Chronicle," *Pittsburgh Post-Gazette*, November 28, 2010, http://www.post-gazette .com/opinion/Op-Ed/2010/11/28/The-Next-Page-How-we-punched-it-out-From-Mill -Hunk-Herald-to-Northside-Chronicle/stories/201011280190/. Larry passed away in 2014 at age fifty-four.

2. Ted had just completed a two-volume history of Iuzovka, the original name for Donetsk. See Theodore Friedgut, *Iuzovka and Revolution: Life and Work in Russia's Donbass, 1869–1924* (Princeton, NJ: Princeton University Press, 1989). Our collaborative effort appeared as Theodore H. Friedgut and Lewis H. Siegelbaum, "The Soviet Miners' Strike, July 1989, Perestroika from Below," *The Carl Back Papers in Russian and East European Studies*, no. 804 (1990).

3. In 1980 Walkowitz made *The Molders of Troy*, a film version of his own *Worker City, Company Town: Iron and Cotton-Worker Protest in Troy and Cohoes, New York, 1855–84* (Urbana: University of Illinois Press, 1978).

4. *Perestroika from Below*, produced by Daniel Walkowitz and Barbara Abrash (New York: Past Time Productions, 1990).

5. For a partial transcript of this conference, see Lewis H. Siegelbaum and Daniel J. Walkowitz, *Workers of the Donbass Speak: Survival and Identity in the New Ukraine, 1989–1992* (Albany: State University of New York Press, 1995), 99–105.

6. Lewis H. Siegelbaum, "Behind the Soviet Miners' Strike," *The Nation*, October 23, 1989, 451–54.

7. Siegelbaum and Walkowitz, *Workers of the Donbass Speak*, 108.

8. Lewis H. Siegelbaum, "Labor Pains in the Soviet Union; Miners' Hopes Deferred," *The Nation*, May 27, 1991, 693.

9. See Stephen Crowley, *Hot Coal, Cold Steel: Russian and Ukrainian Workers from the End of the Soviet Union to the Post-Communist Transformations* (Ann Arbor: University of Michigan Press, 1997).

10. Siegelbaum and Walkowitz, *Workers of the Donbass Speak*, 71–72, 143, 172.

11. Ibid., 197.

12. Lewis H. Siegelbaum and Daniel Walkowitz, "The A.F.L.-C.I.O. Goes to Ukraine," *The Nation*, November 2, 1992, 502–5.

13. See "Adrian Karatnycky: Nonresident Senior Fellow, Eurasia Center," Atlantic Council, accessed August 21, 2018, http://www.atlanticcouncil.org/about/experts/list /adrian-karatnycky#fullbio.

14. For these insurgencies and their sad aftermath, see Jefferson Cowie, *Stayin' Alive: The 1970s and the Last Days of the Working Class* (New York: The New Press, 2010): "What other

recourse did working-class Americans have in the face of lost wars, rusting factories, wilting union strength, and embattled hometowns? One answer was to accept the New Right's retooled discourse of what it meant to be born in the U.S.A.: populist nationalism, protection of family, and traditional morality" (364). The AFL-CIO's website characterizes Kirkland's "greatest legacy" as "global," namely, his "early and passionate support for the Polish labor movement, Solidarity," which "proved pivotal in ensuring the ultimate collapse of Soviet-dominated regimes throughout Eastern Europe." See "Lane Kirkland," AFL-CIO: America's Unions, accessed August 21, 2018, https://aflcio.org/about/history/labor-history-people/lane-kirkland.

15. Siegelbaum and Walkowitz, *Workers of the Donbass Speak*, 120.

16. Lewis H. Siegelbaum, "Freedom of Prices and the Price of Freedom: The Miners' Dilemma in the Soviet Union and Its Successor States," *Journal of Communist Studies and Transition Politics* 13, no. 4 (1997): 5.

17. Or, as Valerii Samofalov put it in May 1991, "The mines, all mines, should not be asking the Union or republic government to raise the price for coal, but set it themselves instead." Siegelbaum and Walkowitz, *Workers of the Donbass Speak*, 114–15.

18. Crowley, *Hot Coal, Cold Steel*, 136. See also the interview with Mikhail Krylov in Siegelbaum and Walkowitz, *Workers of the Donbass Speak*, 149: "We want every person to be the master of the fruits of his labor."

19. Siegelbaum, "Freedom of Prices," 22; *New York Times*, February 29, 1996, A5. The Iron Lady was Margaret Thatcher. The epithet derives from her confrontation with the miners' strike in Britain in 1984–1985. The term "bloated" comes from the *New York Times*, February 29, 1996, A5.

20. Lewis H. Siegelbaum, "The Condition of Labor in Post-Soviet Russia: A Ten-Year Retrospective," *Social Science History Journal* 28, no. 4 (2004): 637–65.

21. Lewis H. Siegelbaum, "Does Donetsk Have a Future in the New Ukraine?," *The Nation*, August 1, 2014, http://www.thenation.com/article/180851/does-donetsk-have-future-new-ukraine.

22. My judgment was accurate. Two months after I had sent it, the letter was returned to me "not deliverable as addressed—unable to forward."

23. "Guidelines for January 1990 Survey of Soviet Archives." Undated memorandum from Brewster Chamberlin to Judith Davidson, Raul Hilberg, Edward Keenan, Louis [*sic*] Siegelbaum.

24. See Raul Hilberg, *The Destruction of the European Jews* (Chicago: Quadrangle, 1961). Hilberg was the only expert to appear in Claude Lanzmann's film *Shoah* (New Yorker Films, 1985).

25. Kate Brown, *Dispatches from Dystopia: Histories of Places Not Yet Forgotten* (Chicago: University of Chicago Press, 2015), 5.

26. See Helen Segall's introduction to Ilya Ehrenburg and Vasily Grossman, eds., *The Complete Black Book of Russian Jewry* (New Brunswick, NJ: Transaction, 2002).

27. For details of these holdings, now on microfilm at the United States Holocaust Memorial Museum, see the finding aid to RG-31.010M at United States Holocaust

Museum Finding Aid RG-31 Ukraine, accessed August 6, 2018, https://www.ushmm.org
/online/archival-guide/finding_aids/RG31010M.html. For a general overview of what we
found in Soviet archives on this survey trip, see Josh Friedman, "A New Light on a Dark
Era," *Newsday*, February 18, 1990, 4–5. *Einsatzgruppen* (German: deployment groups)
were Nazi paramilitary death squads. *Einsatzgruppe* C was attached to the Wehrmacht's
Army Group South.

28. United States Holocaust Memorial Museum, RG-22.027M: GARF, f. A-327 (Main
Resettlement Administration under RSFSR Council of People's Commissars); RG-22.033:
Tsentral'nyi Gosudarstvennyi Arkhiv Sankt-Peterburga (TsGA SPb), f. 330 (City Evacuation
Commission of Leningrad City Soviet); RG-22.020 Gosudarstvennyi Istoricheskii Arkhiv
Chuvashskoi Respubliki (GIAChR), f. 1263 (Office of Evacuation of Chuvash Republic
Council of People's Commissars).

29. Kim Palchikoff, "Magician Flies into Moscow," *The Moscow Times*, September 10,
1997, 12.

30. Arkady Ostrovsky, *The Invention of Russia: The Journey from Gorbachev's Freedom
to Putin's War* (London: Atlantic Books, 2015).

31. Svetlana Alexievich, *Secondhand Time: The Last of the Soviets*, trans. Bela Shayev-
ich (New York: Random House, 2016).

32. Ibid., 72. For my review of this and two other books reconstructing the impact of
the collapse of the USSR on formerly Soviet citizens, see Lewis H. Siegelbaum, "Both Sides
Now," *Kritika* 18, no. 2 (2017): 444–49.

33. Francis Fukuyama, "The End of History?" *The National Interest*, no. 16 (Sum-
mer1989): 3–18. Fukuyama later expanded the essay into *The End of History and the Last
Man* (New York: The Free Press, 1992).

34. Or, as he put it to me in an e-mail message from March 30, 2018, "In the spring of
1991 a day came that I woke up and thought to myself: communism is over, let it go into
history, and I turned in my party card." Mark has written eloquently about his communist past on his blog: "Capitalism and Communism: A Few Things I Changed My Mind
About," August 19, 2009, https://blogs.warwick.ac.uk/markharrison/entry/capitalism_and
_communism/ and "Marxism: My Part in Its Downfall," March 24, 2014, https://blogs
.warwick.ac.uk/markharrison/entry/marxism_my_part/.

35. Taibbi and Ames recount their experiences editing the hilarious English-language
newspaper in Mark Ames and Matt Taibbi, *The Exile: Sex, Drugs, and Libel in the New Russia* (New York: Grove Press, 2000).

NOTES TO CHAPTER 7

1. See James von Geldern and Richard Stites, eds., *Mass Culture in Soviet Russia: Tales,
Poems, Songs, Movies, Plays, and Folklore, 1917–1953* (Bloomington: Indiana University
Press, 1995); and James von Geldern and Louise McReynolds, eds., *Entertaining Tsarist Rus-
sia: Tales, Songs, Plays, Movies, Jokes, Ads, and Images from Russian Urban Life, 1779–1917*
(Bloomington: Indiana University Press, 1998).

2. Initially, Mark Steinberg of the University of Illinois, Urbana-Champaign was also part of the project, but he dropped out sometime in 1999.

3. Lewis Siegelbaum, "The Gift of Crimea," Seventeen Moments in Soviet History, accessed November 17, 2017, http://soviethistory.msu.edu/1954–2/the-gift-of-crimea/.

4. National Public Radio, for one, drew heavily on the entry and interviewed me for its story on the annexation, then impending, on February 27, 2014. See Krishnadev Calamur, "Crimea: A Gift to Ukraine Becomes a Political Flashpoint," Parallels, NPR, February 27, 2014, http://www.npr.org/sections/parallels/2014/02/27/283481587/crimea-a-gift-to-ukraine-becomes-a-political-flash-point. Trending data showed that the entry on Crimea had 50,000 visitors in March 2014.

5. Draft of NEH proposal, attachment to e-mail message from Jim von Geldern, September 28, 1999.

6. Russian Archives Online accessed January 26, 2019, http://www.pbs.org/redfiles/rao/about/manag.html.

7. Amy Nelson, "Saving Seventeen Moments in Soviet History, an Interview with Lewis Siegelbaum and James von Geldern," *ASEEES NewsNet* 56, no. 1 (2016): 20.

8. Laura Pappano, "The Year of the MOOC," *New York Times*, November 2, 2012, ED26.

9. Lewis Siegelbaum, "The Khrushchev Slums," Seventeen Moments in Soviet History, accessed October 23, 2017, http://soviethistory.msu.edu/1961–2/the-khrushchev-slums/.

10. Amy Nelson, "A Hearth for a Dog: The Paradoxes of Soviet Pet Keeping," in *Borders of Socialism: Private Spheres of Soviet Russia*, ed. Lewis H. Siegelbaum (New York: Palgrave Macmillan, 2006), 123–44.

11. The URL of Seventeen Moments changed in 2009 from soviethistory.org to soviethistory.macalester.edu and in August 2015 to soviethistory.msu.edu.

12. I found, for example, the following: "Pri vzryve v Bagdade ispol'zovali vzryvchatku sovetskogo proizvodstva," *Utro.ru*, August 21, 2003, accessed September 18, 2003, http://www.utro.ru/news/2003/08/21/224994.shtml; *Vesti*, accessed September 18, 2003, http://www.vesti.ru/news.html?id=38935&date=20-08-2003. Neither is available any longer via the web.

13. "Bomb at UN's Base Seen as Inside Job," *Guardian Weekly*, August 28, 2003, 4.

14. Despite the passage of an additional fourteen years, this tendency has not abated as anyone who has witnessed the hammer and sickle on banners critical of Putin (and Trump!) can testify.

15. Joe Vialls, "Decoding Media Lies about the Bomb at Baghdad UN HQ," IndyMedia UK, August 21, 2003, www.indymedia.org.uk/en/2003/08/275949.html.

16. Lewis H. Siegelbaum, "The Case of the Phantom Soviet Truck," *Radical History Review* 90 (Fall 2004): 142–49; Roy Rosenzweig, "Scarcity or Abundance? Preserving the Past in a Digital Era," *American Historical Review* 108, no. 3 (2003): 739.

17. The *New York Times* subsequently reported that "the vehicle used in the bombing was among a number of trucks purchased by the Iraqi government in 2002 for use by

ministries responsible for activities like agriculture, mining, and irrigation." Thus, in all likelihood, the truck was not "Soviet." See David Johnston, "The Struggle for Iraq: Evidence; Plenty of Clues in Iraqi Crimes but Few Trails," *New York Times*, September 23, 2003, A13.

18. El-Registan and Lazar Brontman, *Moskva, Kara-Kum, Moskva* (Moscow: Sovets-kaia literatura, 1934). The Kara-Kum desert lies east of the Caspian Sea, occupying most of Turkmenistan.

19. El-Registan coauthored with Sergei Mikhalkov the words to the new Soviet national anthem, which was adopted during the Great Patriotic War. His papers can be found in RGALI, f. 1126.

20. Kevin Hardy, "McPherson: Cool under Pressure," *The State News*, July 3, 2003. My letter appeared in the July 10 issue. On MSU's Vietnam Advisory Group (MSUG), see "Vietnam Project Archives," University Archives and Historical Collections, Michigan State University, accessed July 11, 2017, http://archives.msu.edu/collections/vietnam_msug.php.

21. Lewis H. Siegelbaum, "Soviet Car Rallies of the 1920s and 1930s and the Road to Socialism," *Slavic Review* 64, no. 2 (Summer 2005): 247–73.

22. Ibid., 254–55.

23. AMO/ZIS/ZIL = Moscow Automobile Society/Stalin Factory/Likhachev Factory; GAZ = Gorkii Automobile Factory; VAZ/AVTOVAZ = Volga Automobile Factory.

24. H-Russia Discussion Logs, December 2003, sent Monday, December 08, 2003, accessed January 26, 2019, https://lists.h-net.org/cgi-bin/logbrowse.pl?trx=vx&list=H -Russia&month=0312&week=b&msg=XUKE4u1D2zgrDPhuMJHJBA&user=&pw=.

25. *Journal of Women's History* 15, no. 1 (Spring 2003); Marc Garcelon, "The Shadow of the Leviathan: Public and Private in Communist and Post-Communist Society," in *Public and Private in Thought and Practice*, ed. Jeff Weintraub and Krishan Kumar (Chicago: University of Chicago Press, 1997), 303–32; Oleg Kharkhordin, "Reveal and Dissimulate: A Genealogy of Private Life in Soviet Russia," in Weintraub and Kumar, *Public and Private*, 333–63; Svetlana Boym, *Common Places: Mythologies of Everyday Life in Russia* (Cambridge, MA: Harvard University Press, 1994); and Susan E. Reid and David Crowley, eds., *Style and Socialism: Modernity and Material Culture in Post-War Eastern Europe* (Berg: New York, 2000).

26. Lewis H. Siegelbaum, *Borders of Socialism: Private Spheres of Soviet Russia* (New York: Palgrave Macmillan, 2006), 18. See Vladimir Shlapentokh, *Public and Private Life of the Soviet People: Changing Values in Post-Stalin Russia* (New York: Oxford University Press, 1989). See also his earlier book, *Love, Marriage, and Friendship in the Soviet Union: Ideals and Practices* (New York: Praeger, 1984).

27. Siegelbaum, *Borders of Socialism*, 5.

28. Tatiana Klepikova, e-mail message to author, May 4, 2017.

29. I quote from my application for an All-University Research Initiation Grant (AURIG), April 7, 2004.

30. Lisa M. Fine, *The Story of Reo Joe: Work, Kin, and Community in Autotown, U.S.A.* (Philadelphia: Temple University Press, 2004).

31. Tim Edensor, *National Identity, Popular Culture and Everyday Life* (London: Bloomsbury, 2002), 118.

32. E-mail message [from name withheld] to author, January 9, 2007.

33. Lewis H. Siegelbaum, *Cars for Comrades: The Life of the Soviet Automobile* (Ithaca, NY: Cornell University Press, 2008), 109–12.

34. See A. E. Stepanov, ed., *Itogovye rekomendatsii II Vserossiiskoi nauchnoi konferentsii istorii OAO 'AVTOVAZ': Uroki, problem, sovremennost'* (Togliatti: OAO AVTOVAZ, 2005); Lewis H. Siegelbaum, "Fragmenty istorii sovetskogo avtomobilia," in *Shagi derznovenii* [Audacious steps], A. E. Stepanov (Togliatti: OAO AVTOVAZ, 2006), 145–65.

35. Another diary entry refers to a presentation by the Russian historian Maria Zezina about gender and driving during which Leonid Pakhuta interjected that "women are a danger on the roads, a danger everywhere."

36. Cited in Siegelbaum, *Cars for Comrades*, 175.

37. This might have been the same "citizen of Moscow" whom I quote in the preface as opining, "That will be a very small book." See Siegelbaum, *Cars for Comrades*, ix.

38. See Manfred Grieger, Ulrike Gutzmann and Dirk Schlinkert, eds., *Towards Mobility: Varieties of Automobilism in East and West* (Wolfsburg: Volkswagen AG, 2009). My contribution appears as "The Impact of Motorization on Soviet Society," 21–30.

39. A fire on January 30, 2015, consumed more than five million items from INION's library and resulted in the relocation of the German Historical Institute and its French equivalent.

40. Lewis H. Siegelbaum, "The Faustian Bargain of the Soviet Automobile," *Trondheim Studies on East European Cultures & Societies*, no. 24 (January 2008): 1–32.

41. Siegelbaum, *Cars for Comrades*, 8.

42. This is from my grant application to several foundations.

43. Milla Fedorova, review of Lewis H. Siegelbaum, *Cars for Comrades: The Life of the Soviet Automobile*, *Slavic and East European Journal* 54, no. 1 (2010): 205–6.

44. Annette Wieviorka, *The Era of the Witness*, translated from the French by Jared Stark (Ithaca, NY: Cornell University Press, 2006). My review appeared in *London Review of Books* 30, no. 7 (April 10, 2008): 13–14.

45. Lenin quotes this line from *Faust*, part 1, scene 4 shortly after citing Engels's statement from 1886 that "our theory is not a dogma, but a guide to action." Lenin was writing, shortly after his return to Russia in early April 1917, in response to the groundswell of support for the soviets among soldiers and workers. See V. I. Lenin, *Polnoe sobranie sochinenii*, 5th ed. 55 vols. (Moscow: Izdpollit, 1967–81), 31:134.

46. Johann Wolfgang von Goethe, *Faust*, trans. and ed. W. Daniel Wilson and Martin Greenberg (New Haven, CT: Yale University Press, 2014), 1765–68.

47. Lewis H. Siegelbaum, "Sputnik Goes to Brussels: The Exhibition of a Soviet Technological Wonder," *Journal of Contemporary History* 47, no. 1 (2012): 120–36; and Eva Maurer, Julia Richers, Monica Rüthers, and Carmen Scheide, eds., *Soviet Space Culture: Cosmic Enthusiasm in Socialist Societies* (London: Palgrave Macmillan, 2011), 170–88.

48. Siegelbaum, "Sputnik Goes to Brussels," 135–36.

49. I quote from my e-mail message of June 8, 2008.

50. Lewis H. Siegelbaum, ed., *The Socialist Car: Automobility in the Eastern Bloc* (Ithaca, NY: Cornell University Press, 2011).

51. Siegelbaum and Moch, *Broad Is My Native Land*, 147–48.

52. See, for example, Sean McMeekin, *The Russian Revolution: A New History* (New York: Basic Books, 2017); Mironov, "Cannon Fodder for the Revolution," 351–70; and a judiciously unimpressed review of four recent books, including McMeekin's, by Daniel Orlovsky, "The Russian Revolution at 100: Four Voices," *Slavic Review* 76, no. 3 (2017): 763–71.

53. See works by Anne Applebaum, the most recent of which is *The Red Famine: Stalin's War on Ukraine* (New York: Doubleday, 2017), and Tim Snyder, particularly *Bloodlands: Europe between Hitler and Stalin* (New York: Basic Books, 2010) and *The Road to Unfreedom: Russia, Europe, America* (New York: Tim Duggan, 2018).

54. Lewis H. Siegelbaum, "Whither Soviet History? Some Recent Reflections on Anglophone Historiography," *REGION: Regional Studies of Russia, Eastern Europe, and Central Asia* 1, no. 2 (2012): 29.

NOTES TO CHAPTER 8

1. These, among many, had formative influence on my thinking: Kate Brown, "Gridded Lives: Why Kazakhstan and Montana Are Nearly the Same Place," *American Historical Review* 106, no. 1 (2001): 17–47; Susan E. Reid, "The Khrushchev Kitchen: Domesticating the Scientific-Technological Revolution," *Journal of Contemporary History* 40, no. 2 (2005): 289–316; Krisztina Fehérváry, "Goods and States: The Political Logic of State-Socialist Material Culture," *Comparative Studies in Society and History* 51, no. 2 (2009): 426–59.

2. Leslie Page Moch, *Moving Europeans: Migration in Western Europe since 1650* (Bloomington: Indiana University Press, 1992; 2nd ed., 2003).

3. Lewis H. Siegelbaum, "Those Elusive Scouts: Pioneering Peasants and the Russian State, 1870s–1950s," *Kritika* 14, no. 1 (2013): 31–58.

4. Ibid., 52–53.

5. Siegelbaum and Moch, *Broad Is My Native Land*, 89.

6. Mark S. Granovetter, "The Strength of Weak Ties," *American Journal of Sociology* 78, no. 6 (1973): 1360–80.

7. "Vospominaniia veteranov Velikoi Otechestvennoi Voiny," Ia pomniu, accessed January 18, 2019, www.iremember.ru.

8. For the St. Petersburg talk presented on March 9, 2016, at the European University, see Lewis H. Siegelbaum, "Transnationalism in One Country?: Seeing Migration in Soviet History, March 9, 2016," EUSP Channel, YouTube, April 15, 2016, https://www.youtube.com/watch?v=XwEg_Q38vFo. For an article stemming from the project, see Lewis H. Siegelbaum and Leslie Page Moch, "Transnationalism in One Country?: Seeing and Not Seeing Cross-Border Migration within the Soviet Union," *Slavic Review* 75, no. 4 (Winter 2016): 970–86.

9. Kateryna Burkush, "Inglorious Heroes of Labor: Transcarpathian Seasonal Workers during Late Socialism," PhD thesis submitted for assessment at the Department of History and Civilization, European University Institute, Florence, Italy, 2018, 5.

10. *REGION: Regional Studies of Russia, Eastern Europe, and Central Asia.*

11. Lewis H. Siegelbaum and Sasu Siegelbaum, "Class and Sport," in *The Oxford Handbook of Sports History*, ed. Robert Edelman and Wayne Wilson (Oxford: Oxford University Press, 2017), 429–44.

NOTES TO UNFINISHED THOUGHTS

1. Jenny Erpenbeck, *Go, Went, Gone*, trans. Susan Bernofsky (New York: New Directions, 2017).

2. "New Analysis Shows Problematic Boom in Higher Ed Administrators," *Huffington Post*, February 6, 2014, www.huffingtonpost.com/2014/02/06/higher-ed-administrators -growth_n_4738584.html; Trevor Griffey, "The Decline of Faculty Tenure: Less from an Oversupply of PhDs and More from the Systematic De-Valuation of the PhD as a Credential for College Teaching," LAWCHA: The Labor and Working Class History Association, January 9, 2017, accessed January 27, 2019, https://www.lawcha.org/2017/01/09/decline -faculty-tenure-less-oversupply-phds-systematic-de-valuation-phd-credential-college -teaching/. See also Marc Bousquet, *How the University Works: Higher Education and the Low-Wage Nation* (New York: New York University Press, 2008).

3. Rosa Luxemburg, "The Junius Pamphlet," Marxists.org, https://www.marxists.org /archive/luxemburg/1915/junius/ch01.htm.

INDEX